M000249380

APR 1999

FINE GUNMAKING

DOUBLE SHOTGUNS

STEVEN DODD HUGHES

Published by

 **krause
publications**

700 E. State Street • Iola, WI 54990-0001
Telephone: 715/445-2214

Please call or write for our free catalog.
Our toll-free number to place an order or obtain a free catalog is 800-258-0929
or please use our regular business telephone 715-445-2214
for editorial comment and further information.

Library of Congress Catalog Number: 98-84095
ISBN: 0-87341-601-5

Printed in the United States of America

Dedication

Although he didn't live to read a single word of this material, my father, Douglas William Hughes Jr., was with me every day as I sat at his roll-top desk writing it. He gave me my first camera when I was 7, a plastic-model kit, and helped me build it. Dad was always making something special and would have loved to have earned his living that way. Although he would have preferred I'd gone to Yale as he did, he encouraged me to attend gunsmithing school. My father edited all of my early writing and offered good advice, even if I didn't heed it. He would have been delighted to see this book, and would have criticized it unmercifully.

Acknowledgments

I want to express my appreciation to the publishers of *Shooting Sportsman* magazine for permission to reprint much of this material.

So many folks to thank: Bill Buckley, former *Shooting Sportsman* editor, who kept asking me for double gun stories and convinced me to write the Fine Gunmaking column in the first place. My current editors at *Shooting Sportsman* Ralph Stuart, Silvio Calabi and Vic Venters for an education and for improving my writing. John Barsness for friendship, guidance and the Foreword. James Tucker who read the columns throughout and let me know when I looked weak in print and when other's criticism was unfounded. Kevin Michalowski, editor at Krause. My editor and now friend Ned Schwing, who kept encouraging me, "It's your book. Put your thoughts, feelings and opinions into it!"

For photography: Engravers Winston Churchill and Geoffrey Gournet, Charles Semmer, Jon Blumb, Mustafa Bilal, barrelsmith Kirk Merrington and my good friend Tim Crawford (who helped me return to Montana).

For illustration: Willing and talented artist Thomas L. Eversman and engraver Eric Gold.

And, alphabetically, the many gunmakers, gunsmiths and engravers who assisted with the stories and advanced my knowledge along the way: Dietrich Apel, Larry Brace, John Bivins, Abe Chaber, Daniel Cullity, Dennis Detloff, Michael Dubber, Bud Duncan, D'Arcy Echols, Jerry Fisher, Cathy Forester, Jim Greenwood, Bill Heckman, Paul Hodgins, Nick Makinson, Pete Mazur, Steve Moeller, Stephen Nelson, Hugh O'Kelly, Maurice Ottmar, Les Paul, Dennis Potter, Bill Prator, Jack Rowe, Bruce Russell, Ed Schulin, Herb Stratemeyer, David Trevallion, Doug Turnbull, Sam Welch and generous Ed Webber.

Suppliers who have provided books, products and tools: Larry and Carol Barnes, Bruce Bowen, the late Bob Brownell, Frank Brownell, Rene and Jon Doiron, Tony Galazan and Dick Perrett, Stan McFarland, Ed and Jim Preslik and Stan Wasserfall.

For Fox inspiration and information: Michael McIntosh, Tom Kidd and Daniel Cote'.

Patrons, clients and customers who made the guns possible: J.C. Flack, Ian Shein, Terry Buffum, Dart Warth, Mike Altman, Dennis Crocker, Randy Hart and others who wish to remain nameless.

Good friends: Penny McAvoy, David and K.C. Joyce, my pals with MensCo., Dave Orchard, Herb and Diane Hazen, Bruce Jaffa, Robert F. Jones, Molly Brooks, Nick Kenney, Mike Catlin, Shawn Olesen, Eileen Clarke, Tom Turpin, my workshop sidekick Thomas Harms and Janie Camp.

And family: Doug and Cathy, Rob, Diane and Alyssa, Chris and Jacki Hughes.

You each played a part in making this dream come true. Thanks.

Table of Contents

Forward 6

Introduction 7

Section One - Stock Wood and Shotgun Stocks

Chapter 1   Good Wood..9

Chapter 2   Blueprinting The Gunstock 17

Chapter 3   Get a Grip - The Wrist..22

Chapter 4   A The Balancing Act of Dynamic Handling 27

Chapter 5   Lead-Hand Handle - Forends 30

Chapter 6   Closest To Your Heart - The Butt 35

Chapter 7   Checkering 40

Chapter 8   Fanatic Finishes - Stock Finishes 46

Section Two - Gun Metal

Chapter 1   Mikes, Pulls and Gauges - Metal Measuring.......................52

Chapter 2   Blueprinting The Shotgun Barrel 58

Chapter 3   Barrels, Bores and Resurrection 63

Chapter 4   Proper Repair V. The Bloody Bodgers - Actions.................87

Chapter 5   Double-Triggers and Trigger Guards 93

Chapter 6   Single-Triggers 99

Section Three - Engraving and Metal Finishes

Chapter 1   Why Engrave? 104

Chapter 2   Stylishly Scrolled..110

Chapter 3   More Than Meets The Eye 114

                     The Rest of the Parker Story..121

Chapter 4   Black, Brown and Blue - Metal Finishes..............................123

Chapter 5   Only Skin Deep - Color Case Hardening 128

Section Four - A Hughes/Fox Custom Shotgun In The Making

Full Circle Fox 134

Glossary of Terms 159

Selected Books..166

Foreword

There is a certain indefinable something about shotguns, a combination of easy grace and the omnipotent ability to strike birds from the sky above us. Sometimes, admittedly, these are only clay birds, but often enough they are tasty game birds that satisfy the whole circle of humanity's needs, from basic sustenance to the highest of culinary craft. Add some understanding of wild nature, a partnership with dogs that goes back to fireside rests inside early man's most primitive shelters, the mastery of tools and even fine art, and you begin to understand the odd smile that appears on some humans when a quality shotgun is lifted in appreciation.

So there is a lot more to a shotgun than mere weaponry. Yes, we can hunt birds with basic shotguns such as pumps and autoloaders. They work fine, and on a purely functional level might even work best for certain kinds of shooting. But there is another level here, of owning and using a shotgun that not only works very well for you - and perhaps only you - but with full appreciation of both the craft and, sometimes, art that make it a fine shotgun.

The finest shotguns have always been double-barreled, and the very finest hunter's shotguns have been side-by-sides. Lately there's been a renewed interest in fine doubles, especially the classic English-European gun perfected in the last half of the 19th century. Consequently we have a lot of writers trying to explain the double gun to a wondering public. Many of these are very good writers, and some know a lot about shotguns. Some can even shoot. But there is a depth of understanding missing from much of the new writing - and a lot of the old. Yes, these authors can write and shoot, and even partially explain some of the mechanical details that make a truly great shotgun. But they cannot make such a shotgun themselves.

And that is where Steven Dodd Hughes differs from virtually everyone else writing about shotguns. Steve is a fine gunmaker, who knows not just the history and mechanics of shotguns, but can construct a period flintlock fowler or create a new custom gun from an old double.

But as with shotguns themselves, there is more to the man than gunmaking. Steve never loses sight of the

fact that shotguns are made to shoot, and especially hunt. If humans never hunted birds, the fine shotgun would not exist. By choice Steve lives in the open West where he can hunt birds, with his own Fox shotgun and bird dog. He likes to eat wild birds, too. On top of all that he can write clearly and even gracefully about the most graceful sporting guns humanity has ever produced.

In *Fine Gunmaking: Double Shotguns* Steve doesn't simply tell us how all those wondrous functional and artistic facets of a fine double come together. Instead, he brings us into his own shop, in both words and photos (he is also a fine photographer), and almost puts the gun into our hands as he describes how and why each part of a double gun should work, from buttstock and triggers to forends and chokes. The last chapter of the book puts it all together, describing the transformation of a plain Fox Sterlingworth into one of the finest shotguns I have ever handled and shot, the Hughes/Fox. (It does, by the way, kill both clay and live birds very well, almost as if it helps direct the shooter, and that is the highest compliment that can be paid any shotgun.)

I have been in Steve's shop and seen bare steel and wood blocks transformed into something that almost comes alive in the hands. A book cannot provide the slightly acrid smell of walnut dust, the transformation of metal from rough filing to smooth polish, the changing balance of a double in the making, or the give and take of conversation. But, it does compress the knowledge of years, and that is what the best books do.

In the end Steve provides all of us who love fine double guns with an additional layer of understanding that, like the reach of human history that a shotgun objectifies, completes the circle of our days under open skies. When we know more about the craft and art of the tools we use, then we cannot help but know more about ourselves. I can think of no other writer who can share the complete world of the fine shotgun like Steven Dodd Hughes.

John Barsness
Townsend, Montana
February 1998

Introduction

Fine Gunmaking: Double Shotguns began back in 1993 with my first *Shooting Sportsman* column also called *Fine Gunmaking*. In it I wrote, "I want to take you into the workshop, show you the art, and explain the mystery." The second column - titled "One Good Gun" - told about the principles of creating a custom shotgun, ordering an imported double or restoring an older classic. Every shooter ought to have one *good* gun, but what is a good gun and what makes a gun good? That is what this book is about.

I've been creating custom guns and rifles for more than 20 years. As my work improves and as I grow with experience, some of my ideas, opinions and techniques will change. (I'll be rewriting part of the stock-finishing chapter before this goes to press. I've just tried a new technique and achieved the finest stock finish ever. It's not perfect, but...).

This book is not, in any way, meant to be a how-to-do-it. On many occasions professionals in the trade have said I've given a good explanation of how it was done. Recently two gunsmiths told me they where doing custom Fox guns based on the material outlined in the final section of this book. This tells me that my goals are coming to fruition.

I want to strongly emphasize, this material is not meant to encourage the reader to try these processes. Inexperienced experimenters are more likely to damage themselves, or their double guns, than accomplish any good. Simply put, the details aren't here. I quit writing how-to's years ago because of the liability; I could never relate *all* of the nuances, and my conscience can't bear the weight of mistakes or accidents that may result from reading this book and trying to do the work yourself. *Don't try these processes at home, in the basement, workshop, on the kitchen table or anywhere else.* Locate and patronize competent professional gunsmiths and talk to them about *their* processes.

My number one goal for writing about custom guns and gunmaking is to educate the reader. I've tried to give you something to take home, something worth remembering. Education is the surest way to stimulate the trade and assure its continuation. When I started gunsmithing school I had no idea that someone could begin with a Mauser action and build a rifle. During my early years in the trade I realized few folks knew anything about the making of guns. Those who could recognize quality either came to it by some intuitive connection or they learned to identify certain obvious indicators. Few knew how it came about or what it looked like *inside* a gun. Thankfully, many want to know.

As Robert Pirsig wrote in *Zen and the Art of Motorcycle Maintenance* the pursuit of quality can bankrupt you, run your lover off and drive you crazy. I've had a fair share of each during my career. And while I have regrets about my personal life, I can't imagine changing much of my professional life. I've made a lot of mistakes and have learned from them. There is only one thing I'm certain of when it comes to guns; the the topic is so vast, I'll spend my lifetime learning. And I'll do my best to keep passing it on.

I started shooting firearms photos because once the guns left my hands no one ever saw them again. Unless otherwise noted, all of the photos are mine. They were shot in large, medium and 35mm formats. In-progress and at-the-bench views were inspired by people saying they'd love to see my shop or watch me work. But accomplishments happen so slowly, photo documentation was the only way for anyone to see any progress. Fine guns don't magically appear, they evolve with foresight, planning, creativity, drudgery and the single-minded goal of seeing them finished.

I imagine that many people dream they might have been born in another time or place. I've certainly had those visions. Right now I don't, and am thankful to be where I am doing what I do. There has never been a better time or place to be a custom gunmaker. We are experiencing a rebirth of interest in fine guns and the political correctness of firearms is coming full circle. Many who shot or hunted as children, who gave it up because of economics, politics, their location or the pursuit of their career, are returning to field sports.

We who enjoy quality sporting firearms are increasing in number. As we instill this pleasure in our children and legitimize recreational shooting and simple blood sports as natural inclinations, we will continue to grow. As our world turns toward technology some folks are starting to realize the importance of arcane craftsmanship and the joy of holding a handmade gun in their hands. It is more than nostalgia, it is the sure realization that certain objects of functional art don't need to technologically advance. Our lives don't need to be more complicated. Enjoying days afield, with a fine gun in hand and your dog at your side, is more than enough.

Steven Dodd Hughes
Livingston, Montana

Section 1

Stock Wood
and
Shotgun Stocks

Chapter 1

Good Wood

Don't think I'm being condescending when I remind the reader that a gunstock starts out as a tree. In this age of rifle stocks that begin life as man-made spun fibers, or a petroleum by-product, it is good to remember our roots, so to speak.

In order to produce gunstock wood, the tree must be at least 30 inches in diameter at the butt and it's wood is so valuable that the woodcutter will dig out the root wad (the best part which is used for veneer) in addition to cutting the tree into sections. The stump and the trunk are debarked and sawn into slabs. Templates approximating the layout of a stock blank are traced on to the slabs - avoiding knots, cracks and bark inclusions - and the stock blanks band-sawn to shape.

The fellow that determines the initial layout of the planks is the one who makes or breaks the character and strength of the finished gunstock. If the blanks survive the drying process without checking, splitting or horribly warping, the stockmaker has the beginnings of the gunstock.

I categorically reject all other trees, except walnut, as suitable gunstock wood. The mass manufacturers can fool with beech and birch, the long-rifle builders can have all of the fiddleback maple and, as far as I'm concerned, the exotics (ebony, rosewood, cocobolo and so on) are only good for rifle tips and knife handles. Don't think this is the viewpoint of a wood snob or someone lacking imagination. You can brand me a traditionalist and should understand that I've personal experience with three species of maple, madrone, cherry and even curly ash as gunstock material.

There's the written word to back me up as well. Listen to what three gunmaking brothers had to say in their *Espengarda Perfeyta, (The Perfect Gun)* originally published in Portugal in 1717.

There are various woods of which Stockmakers make Stocks, but all must choose Walnut, for it is the best, and possesses those qualities which make it more proper for being worked, and also for its security, this being what makes it more durable. It is light to handle, attractive by nature, and lastly it keeps straight, a singular quality for our purpose...

(They are saying the wood works well, is relatively hard for its weight and is dimensionally stable.)

These three pieces of English walnut display the variety of the "cut" of the wood. The stick in the foreground shows the end grain and wavy black streaks of slab sawing. The center block is quarter-sawn and has thinner black lines on the side. The stock blank's end grain is halfway between showing broader black lines that are nearly identical side to side.

After explaining why cherry, maple and Brazil wood (rosewood) are not so great, The authors go on to state: *"Thus only Walnut should be chosen, and from the heart of the timber, where are to be found the good qualities we have described."*

The walnut used in Portugal at that time was most assuredly *Juglans regia*. We know this tree as the English walnut and it produces the thin-shelled nuts so popular during the holiday season. *Regia* is Latin for royal which certainly describes the nut and the wood, if not the tree itself.

The trees are typically short, gnarly and slow growing. It is the last tree to leaf out in the spring and the first to drop its leaves in the fall. The fruit, or nut, is sheathed in a spongy green case that will stain any driveway, porch or car hood it lands on. The fruit and bark have been used as a pigment dye for centuries. Whenever I work with English walnut for a few hours, my hands take on a purplish cast that takes days to wear off. ("Stockmaker's stains" easily recognized at the Custom Gun Show as an indication of last-minute work.)

Different sources show English walnut native to the Middle East, India and Circassia - the legendary name for the finest gunstock wood, Circassian walnut. And history points out that the easily transportable nuts were likely brought to Italy, Spain, France and England by the Moors and the so-called Crusaders.

In the older gun texts are reference to each of these countries as the source for gunstock wood with different working qualities. I prefer to continue the tradition of naming the wood by its point of origin. Today *J. regia* is cut for gunstocks and imported to the U.S. from Morocco, Turkey, France, New Zealand, and California. Hence the term "California English walnut". For the sake of convenience, I'll refer to the wood by the common name for the nut, English walnut.

As for the "royal" qualities of the wood, I've already pointed out that for at least 300 years English walnut has been the pick of the professional stockmaker. The wood has moderately long fibers that give it good shear strength, yet small enough pores for a smooth and uniform finished surface. Maple has short fibers and is more likely to break through a thin-wristed stock. (Oak and hickory have long, flexible fibers that make excellent hammer handles but the pores are so open that it is difficult to achieve a perfect surface finish.)

English walnut is hard enough that it works extremely well with edge tools (chisels, gouges, knives) yet soft enough that it doesn't immediately wear the edge off the tool as sugar, or rock, maple will. When an edge tool catches the long grain, walnut is not so prone to splitting with the grain as the more fibrous wood.

Walnut cuts very cleanly which allows precise inletting without crushing, chipping or breaking away at a hard corner. Compared with other woods it is average for hardness, shear strength, shock-resistance, dimensional stability and weight. The important fact is that the wood is average in *all* aspects, without extremes in *any* category.

To my eye, the one quality that sets English walnut apart from all other woods is its unsurpassed beauty. Again, I'm not alone in my thinking that it is the most beautiful wood in the world. Jaguar dashboards, book-match veneer on the classiest furniture and the finest gunstocks; that's where you'll find English walnut. Show me another wood that regularly commands $250 a board foot.

The base color of English walnut varies from a golden-yellow to nearly chocolate-brown, with a whole range of reddish tones in between. It's most distinctive color characteristic is black streaking that has been described as swirling, smoke lines and marbling. Certain cuts from certain trees will yield fiddleback or feather-crotch figure. When high-graded for gunstock blanks, it is *all* beautiful and *all* different - explaining why it is extremely difficult to find a matched pair of English walnut blanks anytime, anywhere.

Gunmaker Maurice Ottmar, of Coulee City Washington, has been using English walnut of various origins for more years that he cares to admit, so I asked him to describe his experiences with the different woods. Each of these is *Juglans regia* as it has been planted for nuts and then harvested for gunstock wood the world over.

New Zealand: Wood from the North Island is generally lighter in weight and less dense than wood from the South Island. It all cuts, carves and checkers well. Some will be so darkly marbled that the streaking almost blacks out the background color.

Australia: The wood is hard, heavy, and dense. It works and checkers well. The colors are more subdued and running to gray tones requiring staining. Fiddleback and figure are fairly common.

Morocco: Flatter in color and not as pretty as others - especially when kiln-dried. Air-dried wood works well, although it all seems more brittle than others.

Turkey: This one is multi-colored, with a great variety running from honey to chocolate with red tones as well. Ottmar calls this the Queen Mother of wood. It works extremely well and is the closest to true Circassian. Ottmar had the opportunity to build several gunstocks from Circassian walnut many years ago but hasn't seen any since. That wood came from southern Russia and I expect more will be imported before long.

France: Works extremely well. Generally a reddish background color not as marbled or contrasty as the others. The black streaking is not generally as pronounced, but the blanks are often quarter-sawn. (I must inject that one of my California suppliers swears that he sells several hundred green blanks for export to France each year and that he is sure that some come back into this country labeled "French walnut".)

California: This wood has a honey to very yellow background color with tones from a light reddish-brown to almost gray-green. It has high contrast, often with pitch-black marbling. Working qualities vary considerably, partially depending on the method of drying. Good wood.

In my opinion, regardless of where it was grown or what color or figure the wood has, high-grade English walnut will work better, finish finer and look prettier than any of the other walnut species used for gunstocks.

There are three other walnut trees that are regularly cut for stock blanks in this country; Black Walnut (*Juglans nigra*), Claro walnut (*Juglans hindsii*) and Bastogne walnut which is an English/Claro hybrid.

If English walnut is the "Queen Mother" then black walnut is the "working man" of gunstock wood. The trees are found throughout the Eastern US. Although they are quite hearty, black walnut trees won't be found north of the Great Lakes or along the Gulf Coast. Missouri has been the center of the black walnut gunstock trade for decades. The trees are large and leafy and I find them quite beautiful. The nuts are small and hard to crack and I don't know of anyone that eats them.

Black walnut is used for more gunstocks than all of the other species combined. Of course the vast majority of these stock are on factory guns. The wood is a dark reddish brown with some pieces running towards pink and some to almost maroon. Occasionally, dark mineral streaking will be found in the wood, but radical figure is much more common. Black walnut is highly prized for its crotch grain blanks. Although fiddleback black walnut is less common than curly maple, many choice blanks can be had if one prefers this figure.

The term "figure" as used to describe wood refers to the luminescent cross-grain most commonly seen as fiddleback or feather-crotch grain. One look at the back of a violin is all that is necessary to recognize the cross-grain stripes of fiddleback. If you look at the stripes of fiddleback in good light, then tilt the blank, one stripe will disappear and two stripes adjacent will appear, much like a hologram.

"Tiger stripe" and "curly" are popular terms for fiddleback maple. Although this figure is found in many types of wood, I've never seen a satisfactory explanation of why one tree will have it and the one growing next to it won't. I do know that a good fiddleback tree may have this grain all the way out to the tiniest branches.

Crotch, or feather-crotch, grain appears in the tree at the joint of a large limb or root. With a similar luminesces as fiddleback, the "feather" radiates through the wood like a large plume. If the root or limb is large enough to span three blanks, the middle blank will show the feather on both sides while the other two will be "one-sided".

Without English walnut as a comparison, black walnut could be the top-rated stock wood. An exceptional blank will be as hard, but probably more brittle, brash and open-pored than English. Black walnut is more likely to chip, splinter or crush when inletting and the open pores make it much more of a chore to finish properly. Black walnut is heavier per cubic unit and not quite as seasonally stable as its European counterpart.

Claro walnut is native solely to California and much is cut for gunstocks. About half of the Parker Reproduction stocks are Claro (the other half English) and many Weatherby stocks are made from Claro walnut. This wood is very attractive, running the gamut of colors from honey-yellow to reds and browns - often showing all of these colors in the same blank. But it is generally softer, more open pored and lighter in weight than English walnut. (Translate that to read: More difficult to work, takes more time to finish and won't hold checkering as well.)

The notion of "checkering well" is one of the stockmaker's best judgements of wood quality. The harder, denser and more closely pored the wood, the finer line checkering it will take. I was asked to remove the factory checkering from a Browning stock and recut it with a fancier pattern. The wood was clearly Claro and, as a test, I put my thumbnail up against one of the rather course diamonds. It popped right off into outer space which was a pretty good indication of soft and brittle wood. I wound up recutting the existing 20 lines per inch (lpi) pattern, which fuzzed and chipped continually as I worked on it. Cutting 26 lpi checkering was futile as the diamonds would have broken off readily.

In contrast, I just finished checkering a semi-pistol grip and semi-beavertail forend for a Fox project. The wood was an extremely high-quality piece of California English. Checkering around the edge of the round knob grip is always a challenge because the wood pores change from edge-grain to end-grain. Around the apex of the curve the tool-to-wood surface angle changes dramatically as well. Because this stock was very dense, the checkering cutter could be controlled so that it didn't dig into the wood.

This particular checkering pattern had extensive coverage with borders and ribbons separating different panels of diamonds. With any lesser quality wood the checkering job would have been an exercise in frustration. As it was an exceptional stick of walnut, the process was time-consuming but enjoyable to accomplish. The finished results offer a good 24 lpi gripping surface, enhancement of the gun's overall lines as well as applied decoration to visually please the eye. And the diamonds are not likely to break off or wear excessively as the gun is used.

Claro makes a beautiful gunstock and if one is not fanatical about filling the pores and doesn't expect ultra-fine checkering it has its own particular beauty. Bastogne walnut on the other hand, often provides the glitz of stockdom.

Popular gun mythos has the Bastogne name coming from the bastardization, or hybridization, of the English and Hinds walnut trees. Bastogne trees do not bear

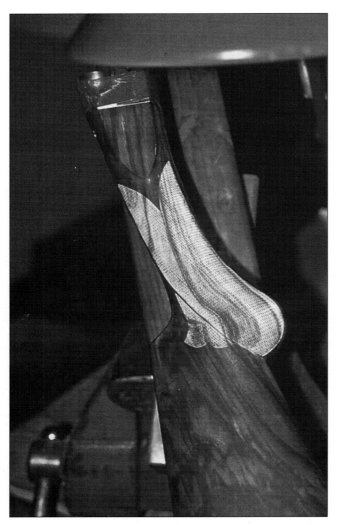

Checkering around the edge of a round-knob pistol grip requires quality wood. This California English stock is hard, dense, has gorgeous marbling and perfect layout for a pistol-grip stock.

GOOD TREES, GOOD WOOD

To continue our saga of gunstock wood we must return to the beginning, the tree. How and where it is grown, and how it is cut and dried will have a profound effect on the quality of the finished product; the gunstock.

As one might imagine, an arid climate will make for a slow-growing tree. The annular rings will be closer together and therefore the wood will be close-celled and dense.

Similarly, the fertility of the soil affects its growth rate and mineral content will increase or decrease the amount of streaking in the wood's coloration.

It is good to remember that English walnut trees are grown for the nuts and the trees are only harvested for wood when their production of nuts drops below an acceptable level. I've heard that as with all orchard crops, hybrid trees are replacing the older varieties. The new strains have been developed for shorter trees with a greater yield of nuts. These easy-to-pick, nut-machines will never grow large enough to harvest for gunstock wood. Who knows what the future will bring for California English walnut?

Much of the walnut coming out of Turkey is reported to be cut from 300-year-old trees. The wood has exceptional working qualities, is extremely dense and gorgeous to ogle. Other questions arise. How numerous are these ancient trees? Are the groves being replanted? What is the future for Turkish walnut?

Commercial growers learned long ago English trees do best in the US when grafted to black walnut root-stock. There are many English walnut orchards in Oregon's Willamette Valley, my old stomping grounds. In the mature orchard down the road from my home one could see the dark-brown furrowed bark at the base of the tree (black walnut) becoming smoother gray bark (English walnut) with a lump at the graft.

I've built two gunstocks cut from this grafted section of the tree. In each, it was clear to see the dark reddish-brown wood of the black walnut become the golden-honey color with the black mineral streaking of the English. When the grafted section is in the butt end of the stock it can offer a beautiful contrast as well as a great topic for conversation. Many purists don't care for the grafted look, preferring their stock to be all of one specie.

So-called "seedling" English trees have actually grown from English walnuts. They are scarce and usually big trees discovered growing in someone's backyard. They are most often cut when the tree becomes a problem. Though the wood isn't necessarily better, the lack of irrigation has made it somewhat denser. In blank form it often looks different with broader black streaking and an orange background color.

(In one of the minor tragedies of my life I had an English walnut naturally sprout and take root in my backyard in Oregon. Months later I clumsily ran it down with the lawn mower. Although I'm years away

fruit and are only planted a few to an orchard for pollination purposes. If you see a blank of West Coast wood that has so much fiddleback that you'd have to push one stripe off of the front to add another on the butt, chances are it is Bastogne walnut. (The same description for Eastern wood means black walnut.)

Bastogne is generally heavier, denser and harder than Claro walnut and is preferred by stockmakers in the know. Because of the multi-colors (Bastogne has the same variety as Claro but is darker brown) and the magnificent fiddleback, both Claro and Bastogne are attractive to the uninitiated. (You get much fancier wood per dollar than you do with English.) But almost anyone who has made a half-dozen stocks from either wood will pick a plainer English blank over all but the very best of the others.

from that home in Oregon, I still mourn the loss of that seedling English tree.)

As with any orchard tree there are several varieties of English walnut. In California, the Mayette variety will often yield darker wood and the Francette is known to have the most contrast between a light background color and deep, black streaking, or marbling. According to Ed Preslik, of Preslik's Gunstock Blanks in Chico, California, telling one variety from another when looking at blanks is mostly guesswork. Preslik has been cutting, drying and selling California English, Claro and Bastogne walnut for more than 20 years and I've bought a great deal of my English from him (and his son Jim).

When the Presliks buy the wood it is "dripping wet" and most often in slab form right from the saw mill. They layout the slabs with templates approximating the shape of sporting rifle blanks and "two-piece" blanks for shotguns stocks. Patterns are then drawn on the slabs to provide the best grain flow for gunstocks. The color, figure and marbling of the wood is secondary as we will discuss a bit later. After the slab is sawn into blanks, the scrap pile is bigger than the gunstock pile.

All English walnut trees have a generous layer of sap wood next to the bark. In a large tree, the sap is 6 to 8 inches thick, quite yellow in color and devoid of any of the black coloration that makes English so beautiful. This wood must all be cut away and scrapped. Often the most beautifully colored wood lies right next to the sap and it, of course, must be preserved. The layout and sawing of the slabs into blank form is possibly the most important part of the process of turning a tree into gunstocks because cross-grain through the wrist of even the most beautiful blank will render it useless. (Note in the photos how frequently the darkest black is right next to the brightest yellow sap wood.)

Each end of the rough-sawn blank is sealed by dipping the end-grain in a melted paraffin/beeswax concoction to retard the drying of the wood. Having the ends sealed forces the moisture out of the blank's sides and edges and the longer drying time largely prevents "checking" or splitting of the end grain as the wood dries.

Blanks are then stacked in piles with slats of wood between to allow air circulation all the way around each blank. About half of the moisture will come out of an English blank in the first six months of drying. About 10 percent of all blanks will be lost to checking and splitting or warping and bending during the process.

Preslik's only air dry (as opposed to kiln-dry) their wood and figure a two-year minimum to complete the job. They use a sophisticated moisture meter and want to see the moisture content down to 10-12 percent before they will sell a blank. The meter has three contact points and is very accurate reading clear through the blank. It is so accurate in fact that Ed says if you take a reading while moving your hand along the off side of the blank, the reading will rise noticeably from your body fluid.

"One year per inch of thickness" is the old saying for drying wood. Thus, a 2-1/2-inch blank is dry in about 30 months. Time spent aging after this is known as "curing" - a concept that some people attach more importance to than drying. I know many stockmakers don't feel comfortable using a blank that isn't at least five years (2-1/2 years drying, 2-1/2 years curing) off of the stump. The curing time will lessen the chance of the buttstock shrinking away from the metal a few years down the road.

I'm getting more concerned about curing as more green blanks appear on the market. I'm willing to pay a premium for older blanks. I do try to buy my (dried) wood at least a year before I intend to use it. I also like to let a rough-shaped stock sit around the shop for a while before I pare it down to final dimensions. This allows the wood a final chance to relax before I complete the project.

Though all wood changes dimensions seasonally, English walnut is considered the most stable wood for gunstock. I'm more concerned about a gunstock that is stored in a dehumidified safe or locked in a car trunk in the summer than I am about taking my gun out in the rain. Intense heat or a prolonged absence of moisture will cause even a 150-year-old stock to shrink. A week in coastal Alaska shouldn't cause a well-sealed and finished gunstock to swell unless it was already baked bone dry.

In my own experience of moving from damp coastal Oregon to high and dry Montana I saw wood movement in action. All of my stocks shrank and these were guns that had been completed from five to 15 years prior to the transition. My sugar-maple stocked flintlock fowler showed the most dramatic change with the buttplate slightly proud of the stock within the first six months. Two years later, after a prolonged wet spring, summer and fall the wood had swelled almost back to normal.

My English walnut rifle and shotgun stocks shrank, but not nearly so much as the maple. This seasonal variation is part of the reason that custom stocks are finished with the wood slightly proud of the metal. (This bit of extra wood also allows for future refinishing.)

When the 10-12 percent moisture content is reached, the Presliks plane the rough blanks, saw the waxed ends off and coat the sides with Varathane to protect them and showcase their beauty. This is how a stock blank looks when I buy it. I store my stock blanks by inserting a screw eye in the small end and hang them up.

Shotgun stocks can be made from "two-piece" blanks. That is, the blank is purchased with a buttstock

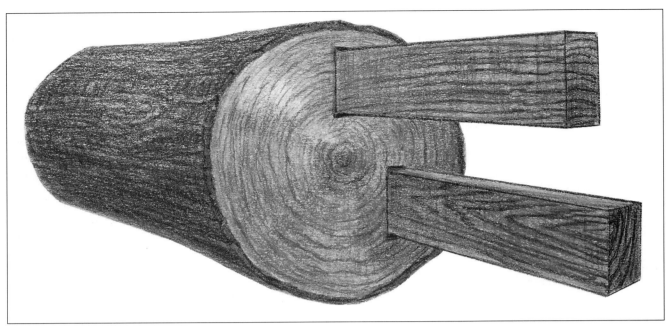

The easiest way to tell whether a blank is quarter-sawn or slab-sawn is to look at the end grain. Quarter-sawn end grain is horizontal and the sides of the blank usually show straight lines that nearly match side to side. Slab-sawn shows angled to vertical end grain and the sides are often different and show a V-shaped grain. Illustration by Thomas L. Eversman.

and a separate forend piece. A sporter, or rifle blank, is long enough to accommodate a bolt-action rifle stock. To achieve a perfect match of wood color and cut, it is best to buy a rifle blank. These will run about 25-50 percent more in price than two-piece blanks because it is harder to find a premium piece that large.

Occasionally, when making a straight-grip shotgun stock I can finagle my way into a buttstock blank big enough to yield a splinter forend as well. Of course personal selection of blanks is best but not always possible so one must rely on the wood sellers choice - and forend to butt color match - when dealing mail order.

How the slabs are cut from the tree (see diagram) will determine whether on not a blank is quarter-sawn or slab-sawn. The way to tell is by looking straight on at the end of the blank. Quarter-sawn wood will have the annular rings of the end grain running side to side across the thickness of the blank. Slab-sawn wood will have the growth rings running from heel to toe. Some blanks can be described as "nearly quarter-sawn" but in fact, they either are or they aren't. Only the center cuts, a very small percentage of the tree, will be 100 percent quarter sawn.

The term "quarter-sawn" comes from a time when logs were cut or split into quarters along their length before being sawn into boards. Craftsmen have long preferred quarter-sawn wood because it shows the least warping during drying and is the most stable when cured. Quarter-sawn wood also shows off fiddleback best on the sides of the blank, where as slab-sawn wood shows the figure on the top and bottom. The black lines of English

walnut will be thinner and nearly uniform from side to side on a quarter-sawn stick making the wood appear plainer than slab-sawn wood. Slab-sawing shows the black lines as if they were split open and spread across the sides of the stock enhancing the marbling effect.

For these reasons stockmakers tend to buy quarter-sawn wood, whereas customers lean towards the flashier slab-sawn blanks. Virtually all heavily marbled English walnut is slab-sawn. These blanks are more prone to being "one-sided", having better color on one side than the other. All stock blanks run the risk of going up or down one grade during the shaping of the stock. One never knows what the grain looks like on the inside nor how it will show with the finished stock's contours. Slab-sawn wood is more prone to changing appearance during shaping because it is possible to rasp away a whole band of color as the stock is thinned. Of course it is possible to expose an unseen band of color as well.

Making a rifle stock a few years ago, I watched a whole band of marvelous swirling black smoke disappear as I rasped the side of the stock to its final thickness. In contrast, another rather plain stick of quarter-sawn wood had the bands of black broaden and deepen during the rounding of the grip, comb and toe-line. It is interesting to note that the "disappearing" stock was supplied by a client who paid twice what I did for the "upgraded" quarter-sawn sleeper.

My oft photographed Fox gun presents a rare combination of quarter/slab wood. In the front, at the action, the wood is very nearly quarter-sawn with similar grain running back through the wrist. At the comb the grain starts a 180-degree turn and is completely slab-sawn at the butt. One side of the butt is noticeably fancier, although most folks don't object.

One would not want grain twist in the grip or the forend of a stock. When it occurs behind the grip, the stock may not be quite as strong but it's sure to be a whole lot prettier.

Grain twists can paint a pretty picture on the sides of a blank, but they can make shaping the wood with edge tools dangerous. The tools want to dig in and split the grain rather than cut along it. This is another reason that stockmakers prefer quarter-sawn wood: The corner quadrants can be easily peeled off with a drawknife during the shaping process.

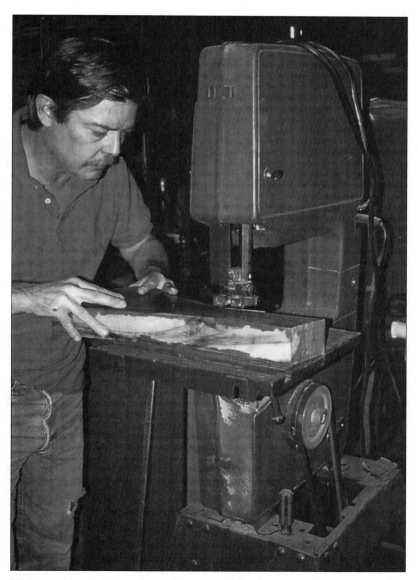

With much trepidation the author cuts with a band-saw a very expensive English walnut stock blank to profile. Note the quarter-sawn grain at the head of the stock.

As more blanks are being sold directly to clients, it is prudent that buyers should know what stockmakers are looking for. The first thing to determine is grain flow. Look at the pores of the wood - the small, elongated holes that form the cellular structure. The pores determine the direction of the grain flow, so following their trail by connecting the dots will draw the map of the blank. When viewed from the side, the grain flow should angle up and forward from the butt and remain parallel through the length of the grip. For a pistol-grip stock, it is even better if the grain follows the curve of the grip. The black streaking of English walnut is usually, but not always, a good indicator of grain flow.

Next look at the top and bottom edges of the blank. The grain flow should be straight at least through the grip area and preferably the length of the blank. While you are looking at the pores, note their relative size. Smaller pores mean denser grain and better quality wood.

Again, my Fox can be used as an example. Observant viewers will note that the angle of the grain a the head of the stock is less than perfect. On the left side the wood grain meets the action at a slight upward angle. The right side has a "wow" of upward angling grain that shows some "run-out" up towards the tang. In other words, the grain is not perfectly parallel through the wrist.

This stock is particularly dense throughout and is perfectly bedded, and I'm not too worried about it cracking. For perfect "layout" there would be no run-out, as the grain would have met the action straight on. (I admit that I chose this blank for it's flashy marbling and density.)

This term layout means how the profile shape of the stock fits onto the side of the blank. I use Plexiglass templates approximating the shape of the gunstock and have been know to fuss around for an hour or more, choosing the most perfect layout before using a band saw to cut the profile of the stock. Most wood merchants provide templates to help with layout and often draw a proposed layout on the sides of each blank.

Grain flow and layout are just as important at the toe of the stock. How many guns have you seen with a chip out of the toe? It is visually pleasing if the grain curves down from the heel to the toe (as on a lot of English made shotgun stocks.) For a checkered butt it is imperative that the wood has proper end grain, without any upward run-out at the fragile toe. After all, this is the end you set the gun on, and there will be no butt pad or plate to protect it.

So here's how I pick a blank:

Using a template nearly the shape of the proposed gunstock, I check the layout for straight grain through the wrist, with little or no run-out. I look for pin knots, bark inclusions or flaws in the template area. If I find some, I check the end grain (quarter-sawn or slab-sawn) to determine where the knots or flaws run through the blank. The wrist and head of the stock should be flawless. I am also sure to locate the template at the same location on each side of the blank to check for one-sidedness.

I then look at the size of the pores. Smaller pores mean denser wood, which is good at the head but will only add weight at the butt. Once I have picked out a few structurally sound blanks with good layout, I use color, figure and cost to make a final decision.

The cost of English walnut as risen steadily over the past decade. These days I am paying from $600 to $1200 for a fancy two-piece blank with excellent layout. Good wood can be had for less money but there are a few caveats to remember.

Because of the demand (and presumably the fast pace of this world) more and more wood is being sold green or just barely dried. There is nothing wrong with buying green wood as long as you know that's what your getting. The purchaser is in for at least a year of drying time and at least some risk that the blank will warp or check as it looses moisture.

High prices and great demand always introduce greed to the marketplace. I am willing to pay more for a stick from an established wood merchant especially if the wood has been cured for several years. Buying a blank at a local gunshow can be a crap-shoot. If there is professional stockmaker in your vicinity he may be a source or may know of a source for good wood.

Many wood dealers will sell blanks contingent upon the approval of a stockmaker. Some send color photos (be sure to get a photo of each side with a template drawn on) and some will send a selection of wood if you are willing to bear the freight charges. By far the best way to purchase wood is at the seller's location, or a gunshow where he has a large selection. For a real education, ask your stockmaker to show you a selection of blanks (even if they are not for sale) and rate their pros and cons. It will be great fun for sure!

To my eye, English walnut is the most beautiful wood in the world. The historically proven fact - both in terms of traditional choice and survival rate - makes English the best wood for gunstocks.

Working a blank of fine English is a sensual treat. Freshly cut, the wood has an intriguing, spicy aroma. The wood cuts so cleanly one can almost hear the curling cuts of a razor-sharp edge tool. The sensation of feeling the wood peel away with a drawknife is a joy. English is inspiring to look at during the entire process. The fifth sense, taste, is experienced when even one tiny chip lands in the coffee cup; that is the bitter side of the sweetness of walnut.

Chapter 2

Blueprinting Your Stock

A fellow brought by a brand-new Spanish double the other day telling me it was custom-made to fit and I asked him about the stock dimensions. He had a professional stock fitting and had ordered the gun from the fitter who verified the dimensions prior to shipping the shotgun.

"Do you remember what they are supposed to be," I asked?

"Yes, 1-3/8 inches at the comb, 2-1/4 inches at the heel, with an eighth-inch cast to the heel and a quarter-inch at the toe."

"Let's take a look".

I laid the top rib flat on my bench-top with the bead just off the edge and pulled a 6-inch scale from my tool box. I measured from the bench to the comb and to the heel.

"That's all there is too it," he asked?

"Yup, and the comb is about a sixteenth high, end to end."

It occurred to me that it would be helpful the relate all of the various pertinent stock dimensions, have them in one place, and explain how they are determined so at least you could know when a so-called professional is giving you the straight scoop on your stock. Many shooters have a particular shotgun that fits them very well but may not be sure of the actual dimensions so that they can be duplicated or used as a basis for comparison.

The basic premise of instinctive game shooting is to have a stock that fits your body and shooting style well enough so you don't have to contort yourself to fit the gun. It is amazing how we can compensate for an ill-fitting gun and how well some folks can mount and shoot that way.

Several years ago I agreed to build a custom shotgun for a fellow starting with a fine continental boxlock. I asked him about stock dimensions and he said, "Copy the stock the way it is, I shoot very well with it."

When I received the gun I noticed that a one inch recoil pad had been mounted without shortening the wood and the length of pull was about 15-1/2 inches. I asked the client how tall he was and he told me 5-feet, 7-inches. How he mounted that stock is a mystery to me, even shooting quail in a T-shirt. I figured it to be at least an inch too long.

Before the project was completed he had two different sets of measurements from two different stock fitters as well as a set given to him over the phone. Although I don't fit stocks, I asked him his height, relative neck length, sleeve length and about his posture and build. Combining this information with the original stock measurements and the fitters dimensions, I made the stock. Upon receipt, he killed the first 17 wild birds he shot at.

I don't like to do it that way and am a big believer in professional stock fitting. Unfortunately, there are many variables and few professionals in certain parts of the country. If the fitters teach different shooting styles you will get different dimensions from them. If two folks have exactly the same bodies but their stance or mount is different they will need different dimensions. Take a shooting lesson while you're being fitted to make sure your mount and style match his dimensions.

An O/U gun will be fit differently than a SXS. Try guns are a wonderful tool but are often heavy, ill balanced and unlike the gun you shoot back home. Some fitters use modern laser sighting devices and some never have you shoot a gun.

To compound the problem it seems like everyone is bending stocks these days. Another fellow came in recently to have me verify stock dimensions on a recently bent gunstock. He had asked for given dimensions for drop at heel, drop at comb and more cast at the toe than at the heel. The bender got the comb right but the heel was still too low. The client wasn't informed that to achieve the correct drop at heel the stock would have to be bent radically upward and the comb dressed down to suit. Besides, the cast at heel and toe were still 1/16 of an inch less than requested.

With the bead over the edge of a table top, anyone can determine drop measurements with a 6-inch rule.

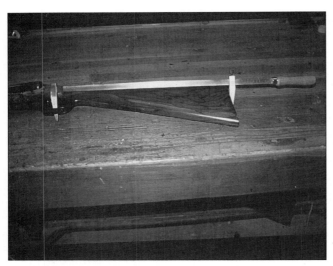

A "length-behind stick," or pull gauge, is the most accurate way to measure the length of pull.

This fellow paid me for an hour of shop time and I taught him how to measure his guns at home.

(Many people don't realize that when a stock is bent there is always a certain amount of spring back. A good bender accounts for this during the process but some stocks will continue to return to their original form. Because of the wood grain, a quarter-sawn piece of wood will bend easily up or down and a slab-sawn stick will bend side to side but you will have to fight them to bend them the opposite way. There are vague limits to what can be done by bending a stock, not the least of which is the opportunity to break it.)

The most obvious stock dimensions can be accurately measured by anyone with a few simple tools as I just described. The 6-inch stainless steel scale, grad-

uated in 32nds and 64ths of an inch (as used for the drop dimensions) is one of the most-used tools in my workshop. It is slightly flexible, accurately calibrated and, with bifocals, remarkably precise. They can be had at any good auto parts store.

With a thin tape measure one can determine the length-of-pull (LOP) quite handily. Hook the end of the tape over the center of the trigger (the front trigger for a double-trigger gun) and stretch it back to the middle of the butt, between the heel and the toe. Anywhere from 12-1/2 inches for a small woman to 16 inches plus are typical LOP dimensions.

To make precise measurements for length of pull one must use a "length-behind stick" as Jack Rowe calls it. This is essentially a huge set of calipers that measure from 12 inches to 18 inches. Galazan markets a fine quality length-of-pull gauge. The long staff has two perpendicular standards. One rests against the trigger and the other is thumb-screw adjustable to directly read the length measurement in 1/16ths of an inch. This is an expensive but remarkably precise and professional tool.

Likewise, one can determine the British version of a stock's pitch by measuring the length from the trigger to the heel, the trigger to the middle of the butt and from the trigger to the toe. These three lengths will correlate with the angle of the butt in relation to the top rib and sighting plane. Most checkered wood butts have a slight to moderate "bump" at the heel and a rounded off toe. The peak of the heel, and toe, are where the pitch lengths should be measured.

I prefer to measure the pitch by the American method: Lay the top rib down on a flat surface with a small wood block under the muzzles (see photo). Place a 12-inch carpenter's square behind the butt and slide

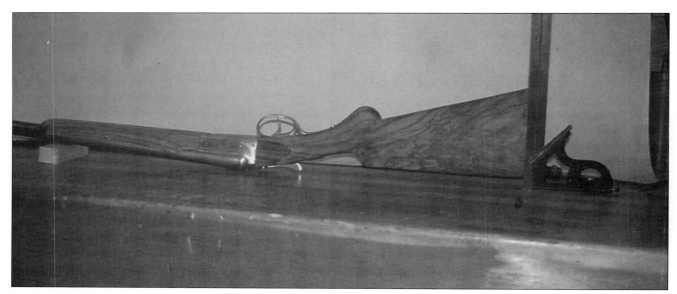

By elevating the muzzles with a wood block and squaring the butt to a flat surface, the American measurement for pitch is easily determined.

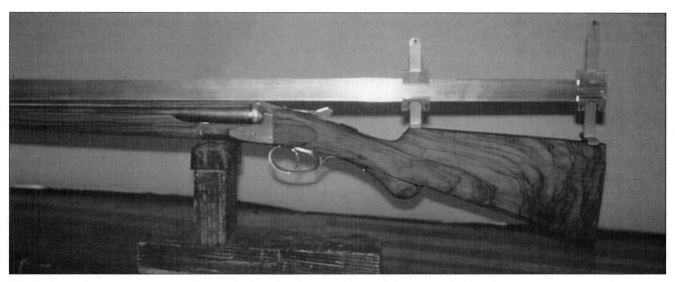

The Galazan drop gauge is a precise, professional and convenient tool for measuring bend.

the block towards the action until the flat end of the butt is flush with the square. Then measure the distance between the rib - at a point 26 inches from the breech (the shortest standard American barrel length) - and the table-top. This pitch measurement would be written as: zero to about 3 inches at 26 inches.

(When making a new stock I use this same method to layout the pitch. The LOP is marked on the side of the stock, the muzzles are elevated to the correct amount of pitch and the square is used to draw a line on the side of the stock blank. This straight line is perfect for recoil pad installation while a curved template is used to layout a wood butt.)

Two inches of pitch (at 26 inches) for a 15-inch LOP would translate to 15-1/16 inches length to heel and 15-3/8 inches length to toe in the British nomenclature. (I don't know of any conversion tables, I simply measured a stock.) Some folks refer to "degree of pitch" which can be determined with a protractor by measuring the angle where the butt would intersect a straight edge from the top rib. If the angle is 90 degrees, there are O degrees of pitch. In this case 2 inches of pitch would convert to about 4 degrees of positive pitch. (Negative pitch is not used for a game gun because the angle will interfere with gun mount.)

While the shotgun is bottom up we can check the drop at comb (DAC) and drop at heel (DAH) as I did at the beginning of this chapter. I work wood to a tolerance of plus-or-minus 1/64 of an inch (or 1/32 of an inch overall) although rarely are stock dimensions supplied this exacting. Nominal tolerances are 1/16 of an inch and I suppose that Spanish gun was just at the edge of a 1/8 of an inch tolerance. How finicky you are determines who is going to make your gun.

Normal DAC dimensions are from about 1-3/4 inches for an older American double to about 1-1/8 inch-es for a high comb target gun. For many years 1-1/2 inches was the American standard - just measure almost any pump gun. The DAH measurement will vary from a dogleg 3 inches or more to a high of about 1-1/2 inches, with factory pump guns about 2-1/2 inches.

(The first shotgun I learned to shoot really well was a Winchester Model 1912 measuring 1-1/2 inches by 2-1/2 inches by 14 inches. The side-by-sides I shoot now are higher at the comb and heel, a half-inch longer and have some cast. I made up for lack of cast by placing my cheek on top of the lower comb rather than along side it as I now do.)

Some folk like to add the drop-at-face dimension. This is the approximate location of where your cheek lays on the comb, but I've got 10 inches of comb and 4 inches of cheek so I'm not sure where that exact spot is. The only time this measurement makes any sense to me is on a stock with a Monte Carlo or raised comb which is completely out of vogue except for radical competition guns. For a standard straight comb stock the DAC and DAH dimensions will suffice.

For many years I measured the drop by first placing the gun in a stock cradle then laying a true-flat 4-foot ruler edge-up along the length of the rib and projecting out over the butt. The trusty 6-inch ruler was used to measure from the flat edge down to the comb and down to the heel. This method is very accurate although one could use a third hand.

Now that I can afford good tools I use a "bend stick". (Bend is the English term for drop as in "bend at comb" and "bend at heel".) Galazan offers a truly professional drop gauge with a 48-inch long by 1-inch wide by 3/8-inch high main staff of milled aluminum bar stock. Unlike the table-top method this gauge can be laid on a rib with double-beads because it is slotted to cover them both.

The de Pentheny cast gauge employs a clear plastic bar and a plumb-bob for accurately measuring cast.

A couple of T-shaped standards with wing-nuts, project at 90 degrees from the main staff and drop down to the comb and heel. Although these are only graduated in 1/8-inch increments, they are relieved to accept the 6-inch scale for close work. The forward standard can be slid back and forth to locate the comb nose or drop at cheek dimension. This is a precision instrument, and to take advantage of its accuracy be sure hold the gun in a stout cleaning tray or cradle.

Without a doubt the most difficult stock dimension to determine is cast. Cast is the amount the stock is angled right or left at the shooters cheek. Cast-off has the stock angled away from a right-handed shooter and cast-on is opposite and suitable for lefties. The idea here is to off-set the butt so that the master eye aligns with the sighting plane without the shooter having to cant his or her head over the stock comb.

Cast is easy to see; just look down the length of the top rib from the muzzles towards the butt. If there is any significant cast you'll see that the butt is angled to the right or left of the top rib and barrels. Looking down the bottom rib will show the cast to the toe and, with a bit of practice, you can determine whether there is more cast to the heel or toe. Many guns have more cast to the toe or a bit of a twist to the stock so that the butt rests more naturally in the shoulder pocket. Typical cast measurements will be from 1/8" to about 3/8", although many stocks will have none and some as much as 5/8".

Accurately measuring the cast of a finished gunstock can be a bitch. For years I used a 6-foot length of light monofilament fishing line with a loop tied in one end. With the loop over the front bead I would stretch the line over the center of the breech and extend it back to the heel. With a fair amount of practice at visually aligning the fishing line, I could measure the cast at the heel with reasonable accuracy. I could only guess at the cast at the toe, however.

The Galazan drop gauge can be used to measure the cast at the heel and the tool is calibrated for this in 1/8-inch increments. But because the rear standard is only 4 inches long and doesn't extend down to the toe, you must still guess at this lower cast measurement. To complicate the situation, it is difficult to align the staff perfectly on the top rib for a precise measurement.

California gunstocker Hugh O'Kelly (aka. Pentheny de Pentheny) has developed a cast gauge (available from Galazan) that allows precise measurements. The tool is something of a contraption and an improvement on the old fishing line method. It employs a 4-foot length of clear plastic that lies on top of the barrel rib.

To use the gauge, first lay the gun in a cleaning-box cradle and level the barrels side to side. Place the cast gauge on the top rib with its length extending just off the butt end of the stock. Align the gauge on center at both the breech and the muzzles - it is scribed with a center line. A plumb-bob can be adjusted to hang down to the depth of the toe.

The gauge is incrementally marked in 16ths of an inch, so it is quite easy to see and precisely determine the amount of cast at the heel and, more importantly, at the toe. Be sure the barrels and gauge are level side to side.

It is a snap to align the gauge with the center of the rib because one can see right through the clear plastic. The wide blade lies flat on the rib, allowing both hands and eyes the freedom to measure and mark the amount of cast.

I should mention that the amount of cast at the butt is only important in relation to the amount of cast at the face, where your cheek is placed Some stocks have the cast starting at the head of the stock and some at the back of the top strap, or tang. Some stocks have such a thick comb that even a great deal of cast will not align the eye with the rib. Furthermore, some stocks have an off-set comb that is dished, or pushed over more than the cast line. With the Pentheny de Pentheny gauge this is all very easy to see.

Any used gun dealer that is interested in an honest descriptions of his wares ought to have these gauges. Likewise the de Pentheny cast gauge should be a must-have tool for the stock bender. You might be surprised to find out how few fellows who regularly bend stocks can accurately measure cast.

Here is a capsule view of what these dimensions do and a bit on how they are determined.

Length of pull: Determined by arm length and muscles, should be as long as possible without snagging under the arm when mounting the gun.

Drop at comb: Locates the eye slightly above the sighting plane by the cheek placement on the stock. Partially determined by facial mass.

Drop at heel: Positions the butt in the pocket of the shoulder and helps with eye/sighting plane alignment. Determined by neck length and shoulder posture.

Pitch: Affects gun mount and contact of the butt to the shoulder.

It is important to note that changing any stock dimension (as in adding a recoil pad to lengthen a stock) will change all of the other measurements because it changes the relationship of the body to the stock.

Try out some of these methods on the guns you shoot regularly. They will give you great insight on how differently your guns measure up and what dimensions actually feel right and shoot well for you. Wouldn't it be good to really be your own measure of judgment?

Chapter 3

Get A Grip

Your trigger hand grips the "wrist" of the gun - in America, anyway. In Britain the wrist is called the "hand" - whereas the "grip" locks the barrels to the action. Somewhere in the world, wrist and grip and hand are each appropriate terms to describe the smallest part of the buttstock.

There are basically three styles of grips used on shotgun stocks: Straight-grips, semi-pistol-grips and pistol-grips. (The British know these straight-hand, half-hand and pistol-hand stocks; to add to the confusion, one of my Italian texts refers to a straight-grip as an English stock and mentions semi-pistol hand stocks.) The straight-grip is just that - straight lines top and bottom, joining the action to the butt. The traditional game gun has a straight-grip following the form of flintlock fowlers. This style provides a lean look, quick to the shoulder handling characteristics and is most appropriate with double-triggers for instinctive game shooting. I've heard it said that the advantage of a straight-grip

stock is that it places both hands in a nearly parallel line. Another belief is that a straight-grip helps the hand slide rearward when using double-triggers.

A semi-pistol-grip has a slightly curved top line and a concave curve for the lower section of the grip. Typically the grip has a lengthy, open curve that terminates in a "ball", "bag" or "round knob" where it joins the toe line on the bottom of the stock. This grip was popularized by American double-gun makers in the beginning of this century, and early Browning Superposed and Auto-5 shotguns have a variation of this style.

Another variation of the semi-pistol-grip is the turn of the century "Prince of Wales" grip. This one has a long open-curved pistol grip with a flatter angle at the grip cap. Many Woodwards were made in this configuration.

The full pistol-grip has a more pronounced curve and is usually flat on the end with a steel, horn or hard-rubber pistol-grip cap. This grip is often used with a single trigger. I would say that a pistol-grip in any form

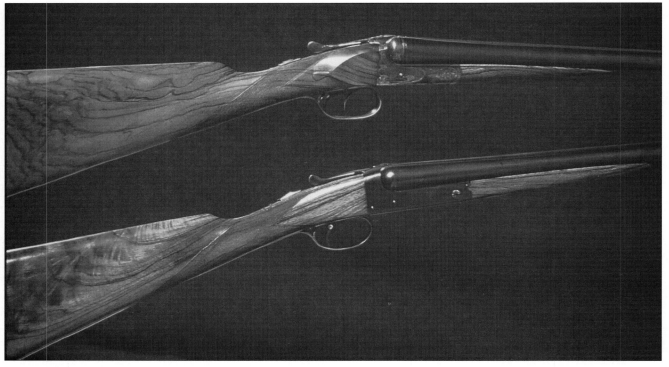

The straight-grip Fox has stock panels and drop points while the M-21 action has been shaped with a "round body" and stocked without panels. Both guns are from the author's bench.

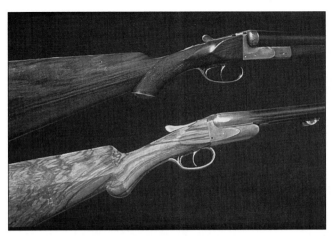

The French boxlock has pointed stock panels and a capped pistol-grip. The rough-stocked Fox has a bench-made guard, oval stock panels and a semi pistol-grip.

adds a greater degree of control for more precise aiming of a shotgun. If you're inclined to shoot game birds instinctively, the straight-grip/splinter forend combination may be advantageous. If, however, clay target shooting is your focus, a pistol-grip stock and perhaps even a beavertail forend might help break more birds. Determining the kind of target and type of shooting is the first step in choosing the grip style of a shotgun.

When making a stock there are several other decisions and determinations necessary to shaping a comfortable and attractive grip. The "height" of the grip is pretty much dictated by the distance between the upper and lower tangs. When restocking an existing gun this can be altered somewhat by bending or straightening the tangs. The top and bottom lines of a straight grip should form a slight taper from the height of the action rearward. (Please note that any alteration to the tangs can open the worm can requiring alterations to the sears/trigger relationship and the safety. This is not for the uninitiated.)

The thickness of the grip is always less than that of the action body. The circumference of the grip (as measured around with a tape) is the sum of the thickness, height and is influenced by the cross-sectional shape of the grip. This dimension should be matched to the relative size of the shooter's hand and the size of the action, which is determined by the gauge of the gun. (Gough Thomas writes that a straight grip 12-bore game gun ought to measure 4-1/8 inches around. Personally, I find this a bit small.)

A grip's sectional shape is usually referred to as round, oval or diamond. (I would add "slab-sided" to that list, which is the way many early Continental and American grips appear when viewed from above.) A round section grip may look and feel bulky, but just rasping away the corners to create an ovoid shape slims the lines and provides a better handle.

A diamond grip has sharp crease set out from the centers of the stock panels that almost form ridges down the middle of the wrist. In it's subtlest form, the diamond grip probably looks and feels the best on a straight-grip stock, although some semi-pistol-grips are shaped in this manner. It has been written that a diamond grip will position the hand properly so there is less chance to cant the gun.

When viewed from above it is easy to understand the gunstocker's dilemma of tapering the thickness of the grip. With a 12-bore gun having an action width of about 1-5/8 inches, a grip of about 1-1/4 inches or less and a butt thickness that nearly matches the action, both ends must taper towards the middle. This means that a collective three-eighths of an inch should come out of the grip width, yet it should be so subtle as to appear minimal.

Thank heavens for stock panels and drop points.

The stock panels of boxlocks and the lock panels that surround sidelocks are where this narrowing be-

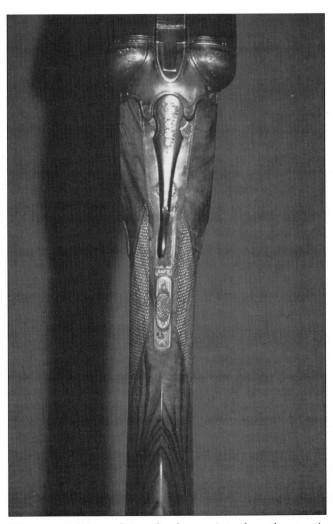

When viewed from above, the drop points show the transition from the stock panels to the grip thickness. As seen from the side, they appear as detail carving.

gins. As you look down at the top of many quality side-by-sides you will note the action body is shaped with a rearward taper. In the case of sidelocks, the taper continues in the lockplates and into the shelves of the lock panels that surround them. At the tail of the lock panels is where the thinning to the wrist begins, and drop points provide the transition for most of the rest of the drop (which may be why they're called drop points.)

When viewed from the side, drop points look like a nice little architectural detail that some stockmaker dreamed up to show off his skill at carving. Gander down from the top and you will see that they allow a delicate step down from the lock panels to the taper of the wrist.

Because this taper begins over a couple of inches on a sidelock, the step of the drop points needn't be too severe. The short length of a boxlock action, however, and the shorter length of its stock panels means the taper in the action body must be greater. Although it may not be immediately apparent from the side, many boxlock drop points are thicker and show a greater step down to the width of the wrist than sidelocks.

Almost every British or Continental boxlock has tapered action sides and tapered stock panels. Side-plated Lefevers and L.C. Smith guns have tapered actions too, but most American boxlocks don't, though their stock panels may have a great deal of taper. An eighth inch or more is the norm.

Stock panels that terminate in a point or an oval shape - without drop points - must be carefully sculpted to visually minimize the step down to the wrist. Pointed stock panels often stretch the crease farther rearward to begin a diamond-shape grip. Oval-back stock panels have a tapering concave shape that blends the transition into the wrist. Shaping and blending the square, hard-edged flats of the action into the pleasing-to-hold oval of the grip is the most difficult part of contouring a shotgun stock.

Round-action, trigger plate guns exhibit another style of grip shaping. Because their entire working mechanism is mounted on the trigger plate, the action body is more solid and stronger than other boxlocks. Consequently the action width and height can be relatively smaller (for the intended gauge). Therefore, the action-to-grip width requires less dimensional transition. The rounded corners of the action preclude hard-edged stock panels and begin the taper to the thin part of the wrist.

I might as well get it out right here: I can't stand the so called "round-action sidelocks" that are coming back into favor. Although some may say that these guns are smoother handling without the sharp corners surrounding the sidelocks, this is not where one handles the gun. Round action sidelocks are purely cosmetic and do not, in any way alter the function of the gun. All of the internal parts are identical to any similar sidelock.

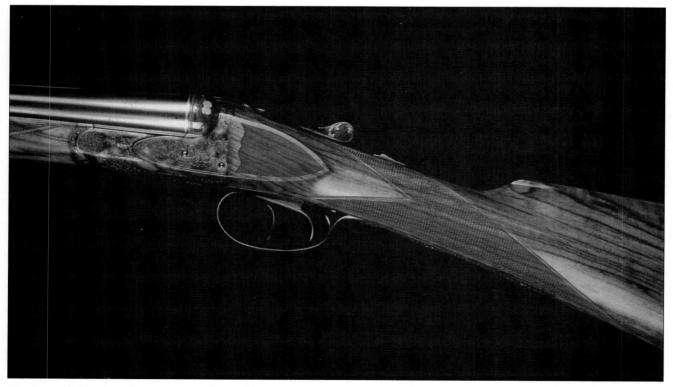

The lines of this Fox 20-gauge are enhanced by point-pattern checkering following the length of the grip and subtle comb nose fluting nearly parallel with the comb line.

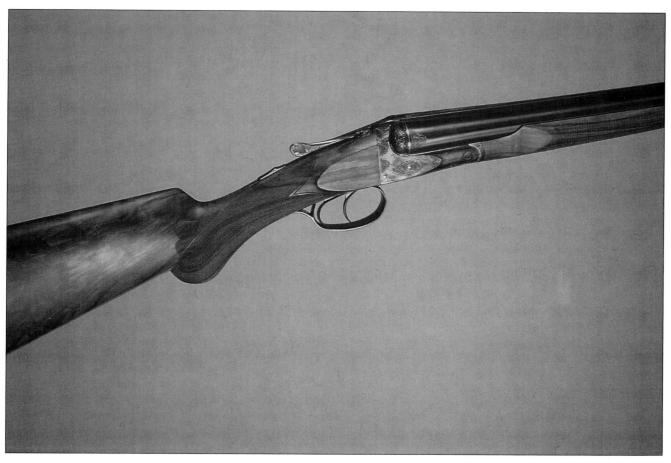

The checkering pattern follows the shape of the ball-end, semi pistol-grip of this Fox 16-bore. The open-curved grip allows comfortable use of the double triggers.

They are nothing new, Boss was building this style at the turn of the last century. They look to me like the stocker was lazy and filed the lockplates and panel edges off in 10 minutes. To my mind, sidelocks should have sharp-edged lock panels following the contour of the locks and ending with finely shaped drop points. These round-action sidelocks look worn smooth when they are new.

As opposed to the quick taper from the back of the stock panels to the narrowest part of the wrist (typically an inch or so, depending on how the panels are terminated), the taper from the width of the butt forward to the grip is much easier to spread over a foot or so of length. Likewise, blending the rounded shape of the butt to the oval wrist is much more natural. Generally speaking, you should be able to lay a straight-edge nearly flat on the side of the stock from the thickest part of the butt to the thinnest part of the grip. But many stocks have a slight bulge in between.

A stock with a significant amount of cast presents another visual effect. Cast is noticeably visible by looking down the length of the bottom of the barrels and out to the toe. If the cast was formed by heating and bending

the wood, you may be able to see the actual point of the bend. If it was carefully built into the stock one can still see it but it appears uniform and gradual.

As with tapering sidelocks, fine British guns have the beginning of the cast built into the upper and lower tangs so it is possible to shape the grip thickness nearly even, side to side. Unfortunately, no American double I know has the tangs formed to begin the cast. The clever stockmaker must shape the stock a bit thicker on one side of the wrist, a bit thinner on the other and still make it look symmetrical.

The long rear extension of a straight-grip trigger guard can help or hinder this process. This is when the stocker's brain shifts from left to right and the measuring sticks are traded for intuition and the eye. When making a trigger guard, I like to shape the taper of the rear extension so that it is slightly off-set towards the direction of the cast. I also inlet it as close as possible to one edge of the lower tang to give the wrist the appearance of uniformity straight out to the toe of the stock.

A semi-pistol or pistol-grip stock has the advantage of tending to confuse the eye because the grip interrupts the straight line. The bag-gripped (semi-pistol, round knob) Fox I'm building, as this is written, has considerable cast to the heel and even more at the toe. I did all of the little tricks with the guard extension and am now shaping the toe line to look like an artfully twisted custom stock.

The transition of the grip's top and bottom line is another matter. The wrist-to-comb line can be graceful or awkward with any style of grip. However, pistol-grip guns, especially the modern ones, do tend to be a bit fatter throughout.

When designing the profile of a stock, I like to think of the profile of the comb nose as a couple of circles with a straight line between. A larger radius forms the transition from the wrist into the comb nose and a smaller circle from the comb nose into the top line. Varying the size of the circles and the slope between them can significantly alter the appearance of the stock.

I personally prefer a crisp transition and dislike combs that appear rounded off on top. If there needs to be a great deal of rise in the comb nose because of a very high comb (the ski-slope effect), the appearance can be minimized by starting the rise well up on the wrist. In other words, use a larger circle below.

How the comb nose is blended into the top of the wrist varies greatly. The most common design looks like the bow of a ship, inverted on the comb. I like to shape the comb nose with a sharp crease that starts at the comb and disappears into the top of the wrist.

The term "comb nose fluting" refers to the concave hollow below the comb that allows room for your thumb. Typically, modern shotguns with thick combs have a major divot, with a 45-degree ledge, that does nothing for the lines of the gunstock. The comb nose fluting of late percussion and early breechloading doubles, have a small but distinct ridge just below the comb that nearly parallels the top line and blends into a sharply creased comb nose. I find these very attractive and often employ this design when a fuller-combed stock is in order.

The arc of the pistol-grip can be drawn with a compass after the distance from the trigger to the base of the grip is determined. However, the radius may need to be tapered to blend into the lower tang line. And for Pete's sake, let's try not to let the angle or the thickness of the trigger guard's rear extension interrupt the natural curve of the pistol grip. Some custom shotgun stocks have an extra crescent where the guard enters the grip, which ruins the lines.

The angle of a grip cap has a great effect on the look of the gun. To visualize this, lay a straight edge along the bottom of the grip cap, towards the butt, on any profile photo of any pistol-grip gun. The grip cap angle you see most often intersects the comb several inches forward of the heel. Woodward's have a very flat angle

at the cap that helps define the styling of the Prince of Wales grip. The angle of the Woodward nearly intersects the heel and is nearly parallel with the barrels.

The shape of the ball end of a semi-pistol-grip varies a great deal from gun to gun. Some are nearly circular, some are round in front and flatter in back and some are just a straight-grip with a bump on the toe line. My objection to many bag grips is that the checkering border doesn't follow the radius of the ball. Fox guns don't, and I was just looking at a semi-pistol-grip Holland, in an auction catalog, that has a flat checkering border with a ball-end grip. Yuck!

Although seemingly simple, how the bottom line of a straight-grip blends into the overall lines is extremely critical. If you can imagine a flintlock fowler with a graceful, concave arc from trigger guard to toe, you will begin to see what I mean. If the toe line is convex, it is called "perch belly," and that's what it looks like. If it is slightly concave, so slightly that a straight-edge is the only conformation, it looks straight, lean and sexy. Try laying a ruler on profile photos of straight-grip toe lines and you'll understand.

When restocking, or making a custom gun, it is a good idea to plan the checkering pattern during the design stage as checkering usually diminishes the visual mass of the grip. A well-designed checkering pattern adds greatly to the lines of a gun and a poor one ruins them.

The classic straight-grip is checkered with an open V-forward, point pattern that ends in a checkered V behind the guard tang. The forward V frames the stock panels and drop points. The long, straight rear line accentuates the straight grip. The point behind the guard helps diminish the visual affect to the cast.

There are also some special considerations to keep in mind, especially with modern competition guns: The tightly arched pistol grips significantly affect the length of pull. If the location of your trigger hand is determined by a sleep grip angle, the important measurement is from your hand to the trigger. Think about it.

I feel that a palm swell is a fine idea for a competition gun grip. But it isn't necessarily going to fit your hand on a factory stock. Pay some sharp stockmaker to alter it to fit and then nicely checker the stock.

There is one last point to make about the grip: This is the weakest part of the stock, regardless of the gun or the type of grip. All grips are hollowed for the tangs, triggers, tang screws or pins and the safety mechanism. Those long iron tangs may give the gun an appearance of greater strength but in fact the absence of wood makes the stock weaker. So pick your wood with straight, strong grain through the grip - or the wrist or the hand or whatever you want to call it.

Chapter 4

The Balancing Act of Dynamic Handling

The first consideration for designing a custom shotgun is the overall weight and how it will be balanced. These determinations can effect all other decisions from gauge to barrel length, stock design to wood selection. Because I typically begin with a complete shotgun, I can weigh it, determine the existing balance point and direct my work to effect and alter the weight and balance to achieve the intended handling qualities. Talking with the client about how the gun will be shot and about his shooting style helps guide the decisions. Recent projects included a 20-gauge quail gun for a slightly built long-distance walker and a 16-bore intended for pass shooting doves in the hands of a 6-foot, 3-inch fellow who likes to shoot a lot of shells. Each required a very different approach toward the goal of creating a dynamic-handling shotgun.

There were many differences between the two guns: 4 inches of barrel length, 5/8 inches in length of pull, one was splinter/straight-grip and the other semi-beavertail/semi-pistol-grip. The quail hunter requested that I "add more lightness" and the dove shooter wanted me to add weight. The light gun was requested to balance on the hinge pin while the heavier double was to be 5/8-inch weight-forward. The way I see it each gun should fit and feel like a favorite pair of hunting boots.

Where does one begin to determine the proper weight of a gun or its balance point? How do these definable features impact the gun's intrinsic handling qualities?

Many years ago a well-read client suggested the 96:1 ratio, a concept I wasn't familiar with at the time. The theory goes that a gun should weigh 96 times the weight of the shot charge. In other words, a 6-pound gun ought to shoot an ounce of shot, or vice versa. (1-1/8 ounces X 96 = 6-3/4 pounds; 1-1/4 ounces X 96 = 7-1/2 pounds.) Much to my surprise, the old saw works out very well and I've adopted it as a beginning point for hypothetical gun design. It mirrors my own tolerance of felt recoil with a hard-butted gun and felt recoil is the first consideration of gun weight.

My custom Fox 12-gauge weighs 6 pounds 10 ounces and I never shoot more than and 1-1/8 ounces of shot. Shooting clays, I prefer 1-ounce loads as (to my chagrin) I am prone to 100-shot headaches. How much a gun is shot in a given time period is another weighty factor.

The 20-bore quail gun will seldom see more than a box of 7/8-ounce cartridges in a day of hunting. Conversely, the dove gun might eject four times that many 1-ounce loads during a strong afternoon flight, with little felt recoil. The small bore will be carried afoot while the dove shooter sits stationary. How far the gun will be carried is the third consideration of its weight.

After a couple days of hard hunting, my Fox starts to feel like it weighs 8 pounds. So, on one trip I decided to shoot my lightweight (6-pound) back-up gun on the third day. Right off I noticed how much lighter it carried, but I had a bit of trepidation about shooting effectively. This gun balances a bit muzzle light and the problem was long shots requiring more follow-through, which the lighter gun didn't provide. I had to consciously push the barrels to kill the birds.

Properly balanced weight improves the swing. To project the proper weight of a gun start with the 96 rule, measure the ground to be covered then consider the number of shots fired in the course of a day's shooting. Also consider if the gun is to be shot instinctively or deliberately, snap shooting or pass shooting.

How that weight is balanced is the trick to making a gun that seems to shoot itself rather than one that feels dead in the hands.

"Balanced on the hinge-pin" and "weight between the hands" are the most common cliche's and, as with all generalizations, there's some truth and some misconception. My own perspective is based on workshop experience and dealing over the phone with folks that need a certain reference point. Except for guns with extra long or short action flats (like the M-21 Winchester) balancing on the hinge pin gives a reasonable perspective for the average shooter. Besides, if the owner says he wants this gun to balance on the hinge pin, no other gun matters.

How do we determine the balance point in the first place? I suppose using the top of your index finger is appropriate for a casual discussion, but I prefer to be more precise. I locate the balance point of a gun with a block of wood shaped as a long triangle clamped firmly in the bench vise. The knife-edge is slightly rounded and sanded smooth. Take care when trying this as some guns will sit perfectly on the edge of the wedge and some will want to topple over onto the floor. Sometimes turning the gun upside down, resting on the rib, will work best. (Some think it best to insert dummy rounds of shooting weight in the chambers to simulate shooting circumstances. *Don't try this with live ammunition!*)

Where do you start this balancing act? At the hinge pin of course, as most British or European side-bys will level out within a 1/2 inch of this location.

Another term related to balance begins to explain why it is so important: dynamic handling. Couldn't we all lust for a shotgun that feels DYNAMIC in the hands?

In his excellent text *Shotguns And Cartridges for Game and Clays*, Gough Thomas attempts to analyze and define dynamic handling as it relates to balance. He makes the suggestion that a gun's balance point is only important to handling as it relates to the distribution of weight. He writes about a gun's "half-weights" referring to the places fore and aft of the balance point where the weight is centralized. In other words, approximately half the gun's weight should be between the hands, one quarter behind the grip and one quarter beyond the forend. (A gun could have a third at the ends and middle, balance in the same location and handle like a bridge timber.) He believes the more concentrated the weight is towards the balance point the livelier the gun will feel. Because the front trigger locates the shooting hand, he states the balance point

should not exceed 4-1/4 inches in front of the trigger or the gun will start to feel muzzle heavy. His engineered tests confirm this assumption and my own experience agrees.

Anyone who has handled numerous fine shotguns can tell you that a well-balanced light gun will feel heavier than it is. And a well-balanced heavier gun will weigh more than you imagine from handling it. When my quail hunter client took delivery of his 20-gauge he was delighted and surprised to find it only weighed 5-1/2 pounds, thinking it felt heavier. When the dove hunter called, I asked him how much he figured his gun weighed he said, "a bit over 7 pounds". In fact it weighs 6 pounds, 12 ounces. Handling my Fox, most folks imagine it in the neighborhood of 6-1/4 to 6-1/2 pounds; always less than it tips the scales.

How does one get a gun properly balanced? What transpires in the gunsmith's shop to make it that way?

First of all, I contend that if a shotgun balances somewhere between 4-1/4 inches and 4-5/8 inches in front of the trigger it is going to handle well regardless of where the lead hand is positioned. But some guys might like a little more weight out front and so be it. I think it more important that a tall shooter use a gun with long barrels, perhaps 30 inches, to counteract the additional weight of a longer stock. Conversely, a diminutive woman might start with 26-inch or shorter tubes. The gun-

To determine a gun's balance point, the author uses a triangular wooden block clamped firmly in a bench vise.

smith is in for a real treat when he is sent a gun for balancing that has 30-inch barrels and a 13-inch length of pull. (My first inclination is to saw four ounces off the muzzles, but I know that isn't what you had in mind.)

Taping weights to the barrels to experiment in shifting the balance point forward is perhaps a good exercise, but your gunsmith is more likely to bore out the butt. When done correctly by a professional, the gun is sure to feel livelier than if you added weight in the wrong place, deadening the dynamics. Your gunsmith will be taking weight out of the right places - spicing up the dynamics.

Gunsmiths have only three options to alter balance: 1.) Boring, or in extreme cases hollowing the butt to shift the balance forward; 2.) Adding weight to the butt the shift it aft; or 3.) Adding weight to the forend. Thankfully, the most frequent desire is to bring the weight forward because boring the butt is the easiest to accomplish. I prefer to bore a couple of shallow holes rather than one deep one because the further back the weight is reduced the greater the effect. Visualize a fulcrum and think of the half-weights.

Although I weigh the stock before, during and after the process, the amount of weight reduction is not so important as its effect on the balance. If I get the balance and dynamics right you'll think it heavier or lighter than it actually weighs.

If a gun is of marginally light-weight and the balance needs to go forward, sometimes small lead ingots can be installed in the forend. Splinter forends are delicate in mass and one must be very careful removing any wood from them. Furthermore, lead is so heavy it must be securely installed to prevent its shifting and cracking the wood. (And don't try pouring molten lead into the stock for fear of burning or splitting the wood.)

There really isn't any way I know of to lighten the front end of a splinter forend shotgun. Most game guns have thin-walled barrels, so back-boring them is out of the question. Removing any appreciable weight by striking (filing) the barrels can have a serious, or dangerous, effect on barrel-wall thickness. When the balance needs to be shifted rearward one must add weight to the butt. Here again, where the weight is added greatly alters the half-weights of the gun. A small amount of weight at the extreme butt end will shift the balance sharply, but any appreciable amount could make the gun feel sluggish. If more than an ounce is needed, I prefer to bore a relatively deep hole and position the lead further forward and actually lighten the butt end with the bore hole. The point is to concentrate the weight as centrally as possible.

In the case of the quail gun, I started with light 26-inch barrels and I extensively hollowed the butt. The dove gun had a couple of holes bored under the recoil pad and a couple of ingots installed in the semi-beavertail forend. The weight increased while shifting forward. Both stocks had dense wood, a disadvantage in the first case and a plus in the second.

In speaking with many gunsmiths I find that some are simply not shooters and may take a mechanical rather than esoteric approach to balancing a shotgun. Furthermore, many factory-made American doubles began life with no inherent handling qualities whatsoever, so you can't expect miracles.

If your desire is to shoot a truly DYNAMIC gun you've only a few choices: Order a high-dollar bespoke gun from a high-brow English or European maker; develop a custom gun project with a sympathetic and knowledgeable American gunmaker; or find a used gun that feels very nearly perfect and requires little alteration. And if you ever do get the shotgun that carries like a feather and seems to shoot itself, for gosh sakes hang on to it, with both hands!

Chapter 5

The Lead-Hand Handle

The typical "Double Guns For Sale" ad reduces the forend to one of three words: splinter, semi-beavertail or beavertail. Of course these indicate nothing more than small, medium or large. But as a unit removed from the barrels, the forend is much more, consisting of a wood stock, forend iron that mates to the action, a latch mechanism and sometimes an escutcheon to anchor the metal to the wood. A couple or three screws hold the works together.

In a nutshell, the forend holds the barrels on the gun and gives the shooter's lead hand a handle of sorts. The wood stock houses and protects the ejector and latch mechanisms that are attached to the forend iron. The forend wood is but a nutshell, as I will explain later.

(Before removing the forend and barrels of any double gun, it is good to cock both the hammers and the ejectors by simply opening the action. Some guns can't be reassembled unless they are cocked.)

Splinter forends are the small ones and the most aptly named. Wedge shaped and petite relative to the rest of the gun, they really do look like splinters, especially when the iron is removed. They are widest where the wood joins the forend iron and then taper in width and thickness to the front, or forend tip.

There is absolutely no standardization of splinter forends. Their lengths and thickness vary among guns in the same gauge, even by the same maker. Generally speaking, American splinters are smaller and more radically tapered than British splinters, which, when viewed from below, show the least taper and have rounded or oval tips. Earlier American guns have the shortest and thinnest forends with the small-bore Fox about the tiniest of any double gun.

On the opposite end of the size scale is the beavertail forend. It is hard to put the finger on when and how the beavertail came to be or who slapped the

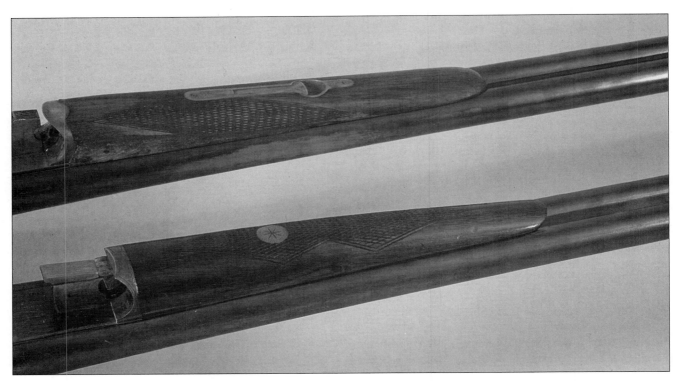

A J.P. Sauer splinter forend (top) with a Deeley pull-down latch is being prepared as a pattern stock. The small-bore Fox Sterlingworth forend (bottom) is recognized by its splinter look, ejector escutcheon and lack of visible latch. The front end is beveled to help "pull-off" the forend.

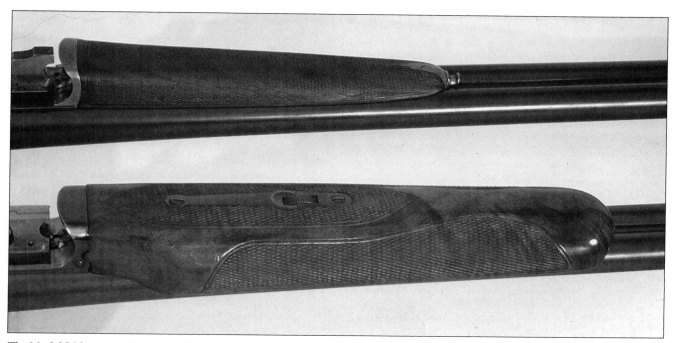

The Model 21 beavertail forend (with rotary latch) dwarfs an English-style Anson push-button release forend on a French boxlock.

name on it. I can't recall ever seeing one on a hammer gun, but that doesn't mean it wasn't done.

A reader wrote to say that the first reference of the term "beavertail" he has found was in a 1925 Ithaca catalog. That was the last year for the Flues Model, on which the company offered a beavertail forearm as a $25 option on Grade 4 and above guns. L.C. Smith offered their "Double Barrel Trap" in 1920 along with a massive beavertail forend, although they didn't call it that. One style had a flared tip, or schnabel, that I find particularly grotesque.

The 1929 Parker catalog introduces that company's new handle: "The specially designed Parker Trap Model Forend provides a large and comfortable grip, fully protecting hands and fingers from the heat of the barrel and will be fitted to old or new guns on all grades except Trojan." Looks like a beavertail to me and if you have one on a pre-1929 gun it may be a retrofit.

McIntosh, in his book *A.H. Fox*, notes that 1930 is the date that the first beavertail forend appeared in a Fox catalog. This Fox entry is the first reference to the term that I have seen.

It is interesting to note that although Winchester introduced the Model 21 in 1930, the company did not offer a beavertail until 1933, with the introduction of the Trap Grade as a model designation. Winchester offered four different style beavertail forends for the M-21, taking their development farther than any other maker. The Trap beavertail was a full 11 inches long and extended about a quarter inch above the barrel center-line. The Skeet and Field beavertails were about 1-1/2 inches shorter with the Skeet fuller than either of the others.

The Hessian, perhaps the rarest, is really a semi-beavertail and the most elegant to my eye.

Each of these makers was responding to an increasing interest in competitive trap shooting. Other features appeared during this era such as vent ribs, Monte Carlo combs and even a few cheekpieces. Each option was touted to lend some competitive edge.

As the gunmakers switched from splinters to beavertails, shooters found the larger forends cracking and breaking. Whereas splinter forends had simply slid through the hands during recoil, the greater mass of wood with beavertails allowed the shooters to grasp the handles more firmly, resulting in more resistance - and thus breakage - during recoil.

The answer was fitting additional support to tie the forend and forend iron more firmly together. Most often, a long machine screw entered from the forend tip, extended through the length of the wood and screwed into the forend iron. This sucked the wood tightly back onto the iron and added support through the stock. Winchester solved this problem on their M-21 with a flat steel anchor plate inlet about 1 inch in front of the iron. A machine screw pierced the anchor and entered the iron, pulling it forward for added support. (The same through bolt, or anchor system, is required when a custom stockmaker converts a splinter to a beavertail.)

The beavertail forend is purely an American invention, near as I can tell. Common knowledge suggests that the only beavertail forends found on British guns were ordered by Americans or made for the American market. One such was the Webley & Scott

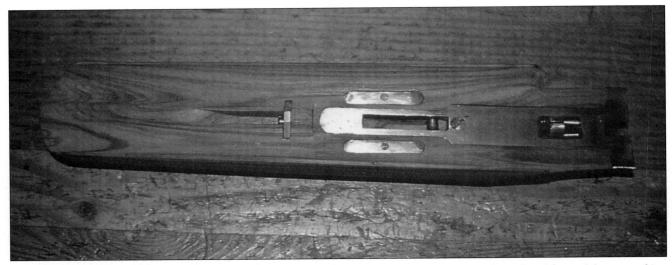

To convert this Fox 16-gauge forend from splinter to semi-beavertail, the iron was lengthened and tapped for a machine screw which enters through an anchor plate in front. (Note the twin lead weights next to the iron added to increase weight and shift the balance point forward.)

Model 702 produced from 1951 to 1979. Holland & Holland currently offers a beavertail forend as an option, but the only one pictured in the color catalog is on a sporting over/under. It is pretty much the same story for European and Continental guns; the ones made for Americans may have the massive frontal wood. Parker offered their Skeet Gun in all grades (VHE to A-1 Special) with a beavertail, straight-grip and single-trigger as standard features. The L. C. Smith Skeet Special was outfitted in a similar manner as were skeet guns from Lefever and Ithaca. Fox offered beavertail forends as an option on any grade.

My 1939 Stoeger Catalog illustrates an interesting perspective. Although all of the American makers presented beavertails on skeet guns, only one European makers did, Zephyr. Powell, H&H, Woodward, Grant and a few Continental brands are represented for the American market, but nary a one offered a skeet gun or a beavertail forend.

The typical beavertail forend matches the width of the forend iron at the rear. The sides flair up and out to wrap around the barrels - creating visible gaps (when viewed from above) if they come up more than halfway on the barrels, contrary to fine gunmaking principals. The flared-side transition can be accomplished quite artfully with distinct oval shapes, but rarely is. The bottom line of the beavertail is usually a straight taper from the iron to a rounded tip a half inch or more below the barrels. In its ugliest form, the forend will bulge down from the iron to gain greater mass underneath which distinctly interrupts the lines of the gun. Horn inlays, steel tips and flared Schnables often accentuated the over-done look.

Of course makers wouldn't be building these contraptions without some pragmatism. Again it goes

back to the competition gun stock and the perceived advantage of controlling the gun for that type of shooting (aiming). The beavertail will protect the hand from the heat of the barrels but the only guy I know that still shoots a side-by for trap also wears a glove. (It is interesting to note that trap guns had beavertails and pistol grips but skeet guns had beavertails and straight grips.)

These large forends go hand-in-hand with several other features. I think the Winchester M-21 is a perfect example and perhaps the most elegant combination of beavertail, pistol-grip and single-trigger. (I still don't like a vented rib on a side-by-side).

A semi-beavertail is less of the same thing. For those that don't like a splinter forend, the semi-beavertail makes some sense and can be quite attractive when mated to a semi-pistol-grip stock. The wood usually flares less in width and only rises halfway up the barrel. This medium-sized forend is most often seen in custom stocking or on European guns made for the American market. I can't think of an American gun company that provided a semi-beavertail as a standard feature (O/U guns excluded). Where they are found, British beavertail forends are usually of this size and style.

(I'm just finishing a semi-beavertail and semi-pistol-grip gun for a client who knows exactly what he wants. A dove gun. While I was a bit reluctant to accept the commission, I have fallen in love with the gun and the concept. It is a 30-inch barrel, ejector Fox weighing nearly 7 pounds. The gun offers a slightly weight-forward balance, long graceful tubes and controllable handles. I can just dream of swinging it on a 40-yard dove. The twin triggers offer instant selection of the custom choking.)

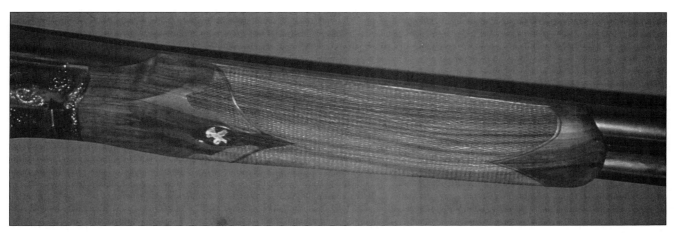

As finished, the Fox semi-beavertail has an oval escutcheon plate and a fill-in checkering pattern with panels and ribbons.

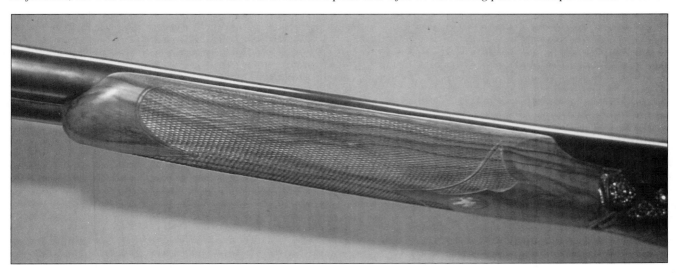

The British quite commonly shoot with leather hand-guards that slip over the barrels at the front of the forend. In essence, they are a slip-on semi-beavertail that protects the hand from heat, adds length and width to the forend and protects the barrel bluing from sweaty palms. For the British style of aimed shotgunning, driven pheasants, the added control is an advantage. These are all the right reasons to have a semi-beavertail and retain the elegant look of an English splinter.

The forend is held to the barrels by some sort of latch that grips the "loop" - an archaic term that dates to the muzzleloading era. On the front-end loaders, a "U" shaped loop was soldered between the barrels and a "key," or wedge, slid through forend and loop, side-to-side, to hold the forend on. (The stock was protected on both sides by slotted, two-screw escutcheons that I find immensely attractive. This "keyed" forend attachment is seen on some early break-open breechloading shotguns.)

Since the turn of the century forend loops commonly consist of an "L" shaped bar sitting on a block that is contoured to fit between the barrels of the side-by-side. When the forend is installed, the loop extends through a slot in the center of the iron. The rear surface of the loop on the barrels and the slot in the iron correctly position the forend to mate with the action and the latch. The "key-hole" in the iron locates the forend so the iron moves freely without binding on the knuckle of the action.

The notch, or bite, of the loop (the short leg of the "L") is engaged by the hook of the forend fastener. The hook and the notch have slightly tapering surfaces to take-up wear. The front edge of the loop is rounded to slip easily over the latch when installing the forend.

Lefaucheuxs' early French breechloaders used a simple lever at the forend tip that swung sideways to release the forend latch. This type is referred to as a "grip fastener." In the period of double gun development (1860 to 1900) dozens of different types of forend fasteners were patented for double guns.

Since the turn of the century four basic systems have endured; the Anson sliding snap bolt; the Deeley and Edge pull-down lever; various rotating latches; and the pull-off, or spring-tension, forend.

The Anson push-button latch (patented in 1872) is the most common on high-grade British and Continental guns. It employs a spring-loaded plunger at the forend tip that is slip fit in a tube on the front of the iron. Depressing the button and pulling on the forend releases the forend unit from the barrels. Inside there is a slotted, rectangular bolt that slips over the latch to engage the bite of the loop. The bolt looks a lot like the Purdey under-bolt that is the primary locking system for many of these guns.

I find this the most elegant latch because there is little or no metal inserted between the iron and the tip. It also provides the graceful movement of depressing the button with the index finger and pulling the forend down and off. Some guns will have a small oval or diamond inlay in the center of the forend, and all Anson latches have an iron forend tip or "pipe" surrounding the button. (Another lovely old term, "pipe" refers to the entry pipe, or thimble, that protected the wood where the ramrod entered the stock of muzzleloading guns.) A screw from the iron to the inlay and a screw from the pipe to the iron secure the metal to the stock.

Anson latches are easy to use, self-compensating for wear and the coil spring mechanism and tapered sliding bolt help snug the barrels, action and iron together. Rare is the rattling forend with an Anson latch. They also have the greatest number of parts and require the most hand-fitting.

In 1873 J. Deeley and J. Edge were issued a patent for a pull-down lever fastener. This system has become a classic for many British, American and European shotguns. It is commonly called the Deeley latch. Housed in a long forend plate, it has a concave cup that allows the forefinger to grasp the top of the lever. As the lever is pulled down, it rotates a leaf-spring tensioned hook that disengages from the bite of the loop. This motion is the most natural of any fastener for removing the forend, and the lever gives some leverage as well. Deeley latch plates are usually secured with two screws through the forend from the iron. Although the Deeley latch compensates somewhat for wear, loose forends are found with this mechanism. Fox, Parker and Lefever each used a pull down latch and I've often wondered if Mr. Deeley got anything out of the deal.

The rotating latch is commonly seen on M-21s and L.C. Smith guns. Rotating the latch with your thumb or finger-tip releases the hook from the barrel loop. Although the M-21 system works quite well, I have always found these awkward to manipulate. It is easiest to remove the forend using both hands, but that doesn't leave one to hold the gun. A tight fitting forend on an M-21 can be difficult to remove.

Parker Trojan, Fox Sterlingworth and many L.C. Smiths have snap on, or spring-tensioned, forends. These have no latch at all and are secured by mating a leaf spring or roller and coil spring which is compressed to snap the forend into place. (Actually the M-21 has a similar arrangement with the external rotating latch.)

You will note that the Trojan and Sterlingworth guns were the blue-collar grade, as were most of the "Elsies." These spring-tension fasteners required the fewest number of parts and the least hand-fitting. They work quite well and the forends almost never come loose. The constant spring tension on the loop may loosen it from the barrels after long use, and that tension can disguise a loose fitting gun if you're not observant.

That is the simple side of forends. If you would like to delve a bit deeper, just remove the wood from any ejector forend. *(Don't bugger the screws!)* The first thing you'll notice is a complicated mechanism your not used to seeing. And you'll see how little wood surrounds those moving parts.

The wood, back near the iron, is less than 1/8 inch thick on the forends of small bore Foxes. Any shotgun with Southgate ejectors (most British and Continental guns have this type) will be similarly thin. Winchester M-21's have even less wood, in spots, between the latch plate and the mechanism. And this is not the only fragile part of the wood.

Most all the edges of the buttstock are rounded or capped by some metal part. Look at the forend. Every time you remove it to break-down the gun, all of the wood's hard-edges are exposed to chipping or other damage. Beveled tip, pull-off forends are weakest right where you pull them off. A steel forend tip may look stronger, but wood had to be removed to install it, so the wood is actually weaker. There is almost no wood between an Anson push-button release and the forend pipe.

A large beavertail forend is not supported by the barrels even when assembled, the thin edges can be broken. If the wood is figured, or anything but perfectly straight-grained, the risk of damage increases, greatly. Splicing new wood to replace a chip or break is difficult, to say the least. Please be careful, especially when the handle is removed from the barrels. And although it sounds snappy, don't slam the forend back on the barrels.

Think of the forend as a nutshell that you hold in your hand. Inside is part of the meat of the gun, only a thin fragile shell surrounds it.

Chapter 6

Closest To Your Heart

Whether you're restoring a shotgun, having a custom gun built, or simply dreaming about a made-to-measure stock, having to chose what caps the butt end can be an enjoyable dilemma. You might consider historic precedent, what is practical for durability and ease of gun mounting, or just what you will find most pleasing. In any case, the butt is what contacts your shoulder, nearly to the heart of the matter.

I hate to admit it, but a recoil pad is without a doubt the best protection for the end of a buttstock. Considering where that butt is likely to be set down - on logs, rocks, shaky gun club racks, soggy creek bottoms or cactus spines -- a pad is the best answer for a field gun. Add the advantages of recoil absorption,

easy replacement, and the fact that your gun won't shift around on your shoulder, and one wonders why anything else is even considered.

Rubber pads don't slip out of gun racks, they come in a variety of thicknesses - which makes it easy to change the length of pull - and they can be shaped ideally for best gun mounting. There are scores of combinations of different colors, configurations and degrees of softness. And there are adjustable pads, interchangeable pads and even crescent shaped pads for pre-mounted shooting.

Despite the seemingly infinite variety, rubber recoil pads can be separated into three basic groups for sporting shotguns: standard, super-soft and traditional.

There was a time when the standard recoil pad was an inch thick, ventilated, red rubber contraption with white and black lines where it met the stock. Nobody I know uses this kind of pad anymore. The new standard pad for good guns is arguably Pachmayr's "Old English" model which can be had in red, brown or black with a black base or the currently unstylish white-line base. It comes with a "leather" face (which describes the rubber surface and not the material). The Old English model is well rounded at the toe, heel and sides, and it's probably your best choice for replacing a pad or adding one to a field gun.

Several makers are offering super-soft pads for those who are particularly recoil sensitive. These are quite spongy, with about twice the give of a standard pad, and most are either black or brown in color. Pachmayr sells their Old English in a "Decelerator" or super-soft version. They also have a soft Sporting Clay model with a harder heel insert to slide smoothly over clothing.

Traditional style pads are typified by the Silvers pad, imported from England. This is the pinkish-red

Checkered wood butts are the most elegant treatments for a shotgun stock. On the left, a 20-gauge gun, checkered 16 lines per inch with flat-topped diamonds. The 12-bore gun sports heel and toe clips made at the author's bench and 26 lines per inch checkering in between. Both butts have been hollowed for balance and plugged with 1-1/8-inch X 2-1/4-inch oval holes. Can you see the plugs?

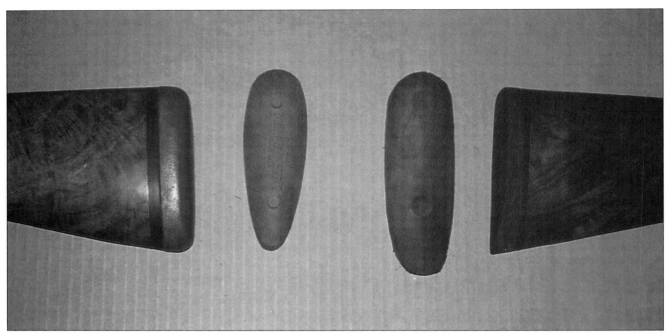

A M-21 stock has a mediocre leather-covered recoil pad. In the center are a red Winchester and a black super-soft pads from Galazan's. The black Pachmayr Old English pad compliments marbled English walnut.

pad found on most British guns as well as many older American shotguns. They are about an inch thick and have two rubber plugs that cover the screw holes in the back of the pad. Jack Rowe brings them into this country in two styles. One style has a pointed teat on top and the other does not. This teat - or nib as Jack calls it - is inlet into the heel of the stock, which in my opinion looks quite attractive. Silvers pads are favored by many gunsmiths for their classic look and the fact that they can be ground to any conformation and smoothly finished with less hassle than other pads.

Galazan is the leading maker of traditional pads in this country. They offer a Silvers clone, with teat, that is said to have a more authentic orange/red color than the modern Silvers pad. This one is a good replacement pad for older guns. They are available in either a 1-inch thickness or, for short stocks, 1-1/2 inches thick. A similar black super-soft pad of theirs comes with the teat which can easily be ground off if you don't want it. Also from Galazan is a traditional solid red pad (not orange/red) and original style Winchester and Hawkins pads complete with the proper logos on the back.

If you don't like the look of a recoil pad (and I, for one, don't), you can have it leather covered, which the British have been doing for decades. Mind you, this will somewhat nullify the rough usage advantage of having a pad in the first place, but if you want that classy look, Jack Rowe and Dietrich Apel (New England Custom Gun Service) are just two of the many craftsmen who offer leather-covered pad installation.

They will definitely want to replace your pad with a new one as part of the service.

Traditionally, the leather is reddish-brown pigskin which is wetted and stretched over a slightly undersized pad and then left to dry in place. The leather is tucked around the hard side of the pad with V cuts to keep it from bunching. All is glued down with epoxy and lightly ground to provide a flat surface to fit to the stock.

Slits are cut in the back of the cover and the leather is glued down into the mounting-screw plug holes. The plugs themselves are covered with matching leather and inserted into the plug holes after installation. Super-soft pads can also be leather-covered but the repeated extra stretching will cause the leather to deform more rapidly.

A good leather pad job will have the surface of the leather just barely above the wood and none of the edge of the stock showing. As a finishing touch, many craftsmen burnish a couple of lines into the leather where it meets the stock.

Lately I've seen a few leather-covered pads that did not have any plugs in the back for mounting screws. I asked Apel about this and he said some folks request them that way for a cleaner appearance. In such cases he installs the pad with blind wood pegs and epoxy. Personally, I don't permanently attach anything to a stock except the monogram plate. The idea of having to remove a pad with a bandsaw is foreign to my way of thinking.

All of this entails quite a bit of expertise and costs at least a couple of hundred dollars in most

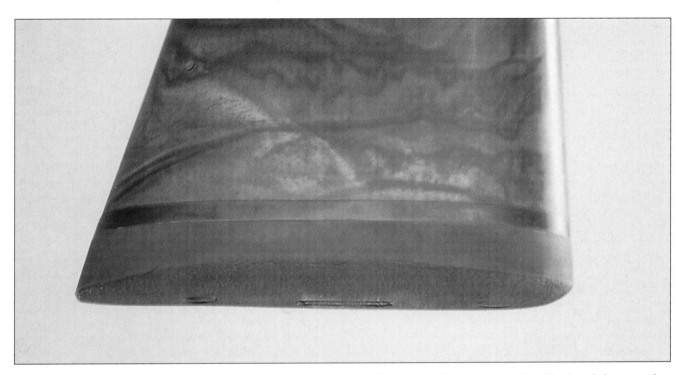

Pachmyr's Old English pad well-fit to a stick of very high grade English walnut. The author prefers black pads because they seem to complement the black streaking of the walnut.

shops. If well done, a leather-covered pad looks very classy, and it certainly slips past the arm pit when mounting the gun. Some shooters dislike the leather because it is *too* slippery and tends to slide around on the shoulder. As with any quality leather product, the pad cover deserves regular cleaning and conditioning, especially if it is subjected to wet weather.

If your stock doesn't already have a pad, some amount of wood will need to be cut from the butt. This is the opportunity to change the length of pull and pitch of the stock. A typical pad is three quarters of an inch or 1 inch thick so one-half to three quarters of an inch can be gained. When shortening the LOP, think twice before sawing the butt. A shorter than normal length of pull will reduce the value of a shotgun. An accommodating gunsmith can incrementally shorten the stock and let you try it on for size.

Changing the pitch can have a significant impact on gun mount. Generally speaking, the more pitch, the more likely the heel will get hung-up during mounting. With the right amount of pitch the gun will mount smoothly and fully contact the shoulder.

Recoil pads weigh more than wood and this added weight will alter the balance of the gun. A careful (and more expensive) gunsmith will weigh the gun before installation. The butt can be hollowed to remove enough wood to return the original weight and balance. Likewise, this is a golden opportunity to change the balance. A larger, deeper cavity will lighten the

gun and shift the balance point forward. To add weight, a lead ingot can be formed and tightly inlet into the butt. (This ingot should be held firmly in place with a wood screw so that it doesn't shift in recoil.) Don't let anyone pour molten lead into the butt because the stock can crack during the process or years later. Because these weight changes are at the extreme end of the gun, just a few ounces, either way, will alter the balance point. (All this work is hidden under the pad, making the tasks vastly easier than altering and finishing a checkered wood butt.)

There is a great range in quality of recoil pad installations, as well as price. The low is probably about $35 (plus pad), up to $250 or more for a leather-covered pad with changes in balance. A good job will show the pad following the heel and toe lines, and the plane of the sides of the stock. The base should be almost perfectly flush with the wood, but the pad being a tiny bit proud is better than seeing wood at the joint. (An absolutely perfect joint is only possible when the wood and pad are sanded together as when refinishing or making a new stock.) The rubber should be smooth and free of grinding marks, the pad should appear centered when viewed from the rear and the screw holes shouldn't show at all unless they are covered with matching rubber plugs.

A poor quality pad installation is easy to see. And if it doesn't look good, who's to say the LOP or pitch is correct, either. Boring the butt requires clamping the

Steel skeleton buttplate and heel and toe plates from Stan McFarland are the finest available.

stock very securely and using a large wood bit to make the hole. Lack of experience, or care, will result in a damaged, cracked or thin-walled stock.

The once common buttplate is rarely used on shotguns anymore. Parker, Smith and Fox all used hard rubber buttplates and the Parker dog's-head is almost legendary. (Part of that legend is that a dog's-head is rarely seen that is not chipped or cracked or broken.) Galazan offers more than 20 different styles of reproduction factory buttplates, including replacement buttplates for Parkers, Smith, Foxes, Bakers, Ithacas, Lefevers and several others.

Most older European and continental shotguns have genuine buffalo horn buttplates. They are serrated, checkered or have a basket-weave pattern on the back. I've always found them a pleasing way to protect the stock. Import regulations make it difficult to find them these days, which I suppose is good for the buffalo.

British muzzleloading double guns were invariably fitted with curved steel buttplates (some with long, elegant finials running up the comb). This feature seems to have died out around the turn of the last century, when fashion changed completely and eliminated the buttplate altogether. I suspect this follows the trend towards less weight and better balance in British gunmaking. A steel buttplate can add a nearly half-pound, just where it has the greatest affect on balance.

A checkered - or chequered in the British vernacular - wood butt became the norm in this century. The end of the stock was curved to fit the shoulder and rounded over at the toe, heel and sides. A noticeable break-line joined the rounded edge to the sides of the stock and a small but distinct "bump" was left on the heel. The butt was usually bored out to balance the gun, and the hole plugged with matching wood. The finished butt was checkered in one style or another. (Close examination will usually, but not always, show the plug.)

Some guns have side-to-side serrations or grooves cut in the butt. Some are checkered coarsely with flat-topped diamonds. When done in this country, the checkering often matches the grip of the stock in lines per inch, with sharply pointed diamonds.

A plain serrated butt is likely the most practical as they serve the intended purpose of roughening the surface to stick to the shoulder. Fine line, pointed diamonds are the best looking and show the beautiful end grain most advantageously, but pointed diamonds are more likely to be broken off or packed with dirt. Course, flat-topped checkering is a good compromise in my opinion. No matter the style, the bump at he heel should remain smooth for ease of mounting. (An old, soft-bristled tooth brush is the best tool for cleaning a checkered wood butt.

Any gun with a checkered butt must have perfect stock grain layout. There can't be *any* angled grain or runout at the fragile toe and heel of the stock. I've seen too many chipped-toe stocks - even guns with buttplates or pads - to risk poor end grain with no protection.

I am not a big fan of checkered butt guns. I suppose this is because I worry about the stock toe chipping or the diamonds breaking off, and I imagine having to repair them. Some folks won't have anything else. My 5-foot, 18-inch-tall buddy, JP, told me he's going to have a wood extension fitted to his new/used British boxlock, with a checkered butt. I suggested a thick recoil pad and a black spacer, but he wouldn't have any of that; got to have that smooth-sliding, elegant wood butt. I opted for steel heel and toe plates for my own gun.

Although I don't know how or when it happened, steel heel and toe plates were a natural development. Sometimes called heel and toe clips, these are fit to the top and bottom of the butt to protect the most vulnerable edges. With hand filed scalloping and checkering in between, these offer substantial protection and are perhaps the most elegant treatment possible. Unfortunately, one must turn the gun upside down to see them so they rarely command the appreciation they deserve. (The photo shows my Fox gun with shop-made heel and toe plates, and slightly recessed checkering. After four years of shooting and hunting, there is nary a chipped or broken diamond and I still can't find the plug, even with magnification. But, I do think about those diamonds nearly every time I set the gun down.)

To the best of my knowledge, skeleton buttplates were an American invention. They are *de-rigour* for today's custom rifles and often make the transition to custom shotguns. Historically, the earliest guns I've seen with skeleton buttplates are high-grade Parkers. I don't know when or how the style developed, but they make sense as an evolution of the heel and toe plate rational: Now the edges of the butt are protected as well.

Typically made of steel, they have the normal upper and lower screws, and two small flanges along the inside edges are drilled for smaller screws. To finish off a nice installation, the exposed wood within the buttplate is checkered with a bordered pattern.

Hand-fitting a skeleton buttplate is one of the most challenging tasks facing the stockmaker. It may add $650 or more to the cost of a custom stock. If the price is much less, it is either machine fitted, has a wood plug fitted separate from the stock or you're dealing with a less than professional stockmaker. It will take three or four days of intense work to prepare the buttplate, inlet it and install the four fitted screws - with the slots aligned - and then finish and checker the wood.

Stan McFarland makes the best skeleton buttplates as well as heel and toe plates. I believe that Parker Reproductions sells the skeleton buttplate used on their guns as an aftermarket part.

Before you chose a skeleton buttplate, consider the experience of a good friend of mine who has one on a Parker Repro, "Steel Special." He uses the gun for waterfowling and constantly worries about the ele-

gant, but impractical skeleton buttplate. I've about got him talked into sawing it off and adding a pad.

Even on good guns, the butt end of the stock is all too often buggered. The scenario goes like this; a short, recoil sensitive fellow has his stock cut down and a 1-inch-thick recoil pad added. This makes the length of pull, without the pad, about 12-1/2 inches. The next owner, who is six feet tall, buys the gun because it was a good deal thinking, I'll just have it restocked." He finds out that the price of a new stock is not only going to nullify the good deal but is going to put him in the hole on the gun. The practical decision is to add spacers. In this case, two inches or more will be needed. Plug ugly!

In England the common fix is to fit a piece of walnut to the butt which is nicely finished and checkered. Most of these British patch jobs show fine craftsmanship. (I always imagine the gunsmith spending hours - as I have - digging through his scrap box to find that never-quite-matching piece that's been cut off some long gone stock blank.)

In this country the quick-fix is more likely. One sees 1-1/2-inch recoil pads and/or thick black spacers made of ebony or black plastic or sadly mismatched walnut. (I saw a lovely Woodward sidelock, recently bought at auction and imported from England, that had its butt capped with two half-inch black spacers and a full-size Silvers recoil pad. The customer wanted to know about having another spacer added and the whole works covered with leather. I can't imagine two and a half inches of leather looking any more elegant. I suggested a new stock.)

In my opinion, all of these spacers look like hell. But I'm spoiled and seldom swayed by the pragmatic quick-fix solutions. As stockmaker Jim Greenwood says, "They always tell their buddies how the gunsmith fixed the stock for them, and that's the last thing I want to be known for." I like to buy these ugly guns for custom projects.

When one orders a gun or has one restocked, the height and width of the butt can be built to suit. The height can vary from about 4-3/4 inches to 5-1/2 inches. The width is usually between an 1-3/8 inches and 1-5/8 inches. To a certain extent, the longer the length of pull, the taller and wider the butt. The intended weight and gauge of the gun will be determining factors as will the size and build of the shooter. A lightweight 12-bore, for a person of small stature will be quite different than a pigeon gun for Hulk Hogan. And don't forget that a larger butt will offer more recoil surface. For these reasons I always factor in the intended shot charge (ie: 7/8-ounce, 20-gauge vs 1-3/8-ounce., 12-guage) when designing a gunstock.

So the choice is yours. Whether you're customizing and personalizing a shotgun or having a multi-thousand dollar special project made, think about the part of the gun that will be closest to your heart. You will feel it every time you shoot and think about it every time you set the gun down.

Chapter 7

Checkering: The Cutting Edge

When it comes to custom gun work, some countries' craftsmen simply do things better than others. For example, in the category of overall design and construction, who could deny that England's gunmakers hold the crown? For bulino engraving, would you credit anyone but Italy's tradesmen as being Number One? What about intricate and precise mechanisms? Why, the Germans are tops, of course.

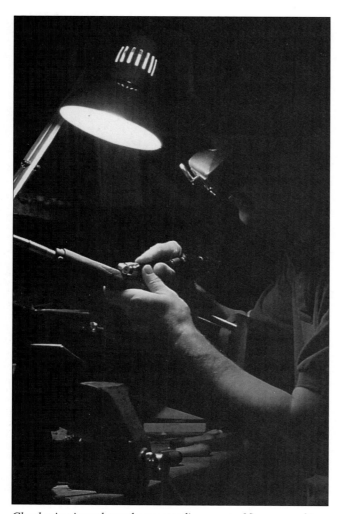

Checkering is perhaps the most tedious part of fine gunmaking.

Well, believe it or not, you'd be hard-pressed to find a foreign gun with checkering comparable to that done in the good old U.S. of A.

How can this be, you ask? Texas stockmaker Paul Hodgins knows how. He served a five-year apprenticeship with Holland & Holland in London, but never once checkered a stock there. Because H & H employed "finishers" to checker stocks, Hodgins only learned the rudiments before coming to this country. He says that some other factories had the "stocker" doing the checkering, but many smaller shops employed "outworkers" for this task. Regardless of who did the work, each craftsman was allotted a certain amount of time per job and the quality of the work depended upon the individual's skill and experience.

In the U.S., gunstock checkering has become a form of applied art. Many of our custom stockmakers first taught themselves to checker and then later to make stocks. I suspect that the American penchant for perfect and precise checkering developed with the hobby aspect of stockmaking. A contemporary custom gun without high quality checkering is as acceptable as one without a barrel.

As for American checkering Hodgins says, "I like it. I modeled my own skills from the work found on the best American rifle stocks. But it is inconceivable for someone trained in Europe or England to spend as much time checkering as you Americans do."

I know just what he is talking about as I am in the middle of a fairly straight forward checkering job. The twin grip panels and wrap-around forend panel will consume more than 25 intensely focused hours at the bench. That's 25 hours, if everything goes well.

It is not unusual for a custom stockmaker to spend 40 or more hours on a complicated fleur-de-lis and ribbon pattern for a high-grade rifle stock. And most use a power checkering tool to speed-up the work.

Let's look at the history of checkering and define some terms before we go any further. Cutting incised, cross-hatched lines in gunstocks seems to have come into fashion in England during the 1770s. This early work was very course, having only a few lines-

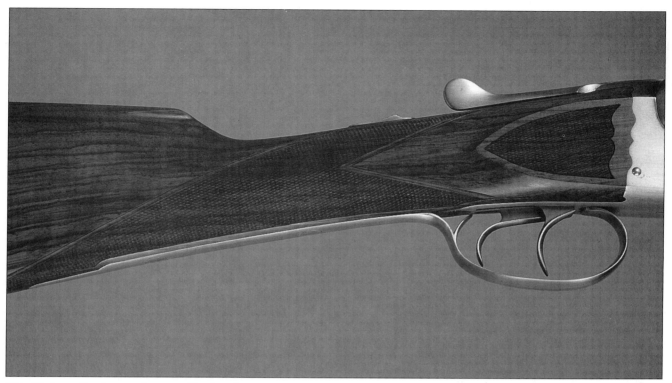

This 20-bore Fox is complemented by fine-line checkered (32 lines per inch) stock panels that mirror the action scalloping. The grip is done in a point pattern, 26 lines per inch, with mullered borders.

per-inch (lpi) with dots punched on top of the individual diamonds. At that time the cabinet trade called this decorative carving "diaper work" a term that has, thankfully, fallen from favor.

The fact that checkering (or chequering in British terminology) was applied to the grip of the gunstock leads some credence to its pragmatism. This point of practical application versus decoration has been debated ever since.

By the 1780s the patterns were down to about 16-18 lpi and the dots dispensed with, although the borders were left as rough X's. According to my research, the use of "mullered" or concave grooved borders appeared on London flintlock guns in the 1790s. Mullered is a pleasingly archaic term meaning molded. In this country mullered borders have come back into fashion in the past 10 years although the British have always found them an attractive way to finish off a "point pattern." The point pattern is the most common checkering style found on straight-grip guns. In the wrist area, it ends with a two-point (sometimes three) open V forward and a single-pointed V aft. These points are created by the individual lines of the pattern.

The ratio of the point-to-point measurements (length: width) of the diamonds themselves will change the appearance to the pattern. The earliest checkering had diamonds that were almost square. The ratio was actually about 1-1/2:1 or 2:1, making the Vs at the end of the pattern rather blunt.

Most modern checkering is designed at 3:1 or 3-1/2:1 ratio. Stockmakers use layout templates that are celluloid diamonds 3-1/2 inches x 1 inch and 7 inches x 2 inches to aid in layout. These shallower angle ratios present deeper, sharper-looking diamonds and longer Vs at the ends of the pattern. On the rear border of a straight-grip pattern, the line will run halfway to the toe of the butt. (Very sexy with a long-tang trigger guard!)

The other type of checkering pattern is called a "fill-in" by today's stockmakers. With this type, the entire border is cut in first, the master lines laid out in the middle, and the checkering cut to fill in the center. These are known as "borderless" patterns because the diamonds run right up to the edge, with no borders outside them.

The *fleur-de-lis* (flower of the lily) is a three-petal design commonly done as a borderless fill-in pattern. Naturally, the motif can be attributed to the French and it has been used for firearms decoration since the beginning. *Fleur-de-lis* is a standard for American-made custom rifles and often finds its way on to pistol-grip shotgun stocks made by these same craftsmen. All of the early American double-gun makers used one or another form of *fleur* pattern on their high-grade guns. The highest grades often had ribbons - narrow uncheckered bands - running through the patterns. Parker A-1 Specials and Fox F grade guns used

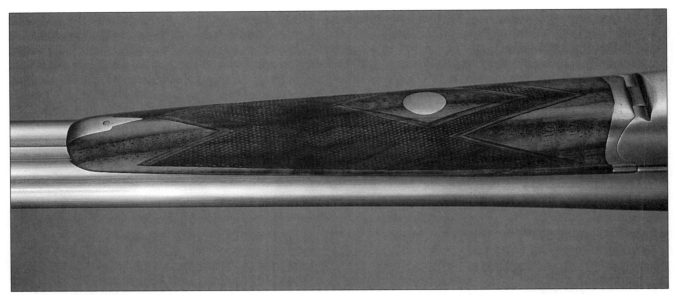

A traditional six-point pattern nearly covers the splinter forend. The diamond ratio is 3-1/2:1, and the lines 26 per inch. An open diamond captures the escutcheon and mullered borders surround the pattern.

a combination of fluer-de-lis, ribbons and cut or carved borders for some of the most elaborate and attractive checkering jobs you are likely to see.

Recent publication of Charles Semmer's, *Remington Double Shotguns*, shows some outstanding early checkering. The highest grade guns have the most complicated fill-in patterns - with fleurs, ribbons and organically shaped borders - I have ever seen. They certainly rival the finest American custom bolt rifles which have the best checkering ever accomplished.

All of these high grade American guns had pointed diamonds (not to be confused with point patterns). Flat-topped checkering - checkering with unpointed diamonds - is often found on field grade American guns as well as older London "best" guns. On the economy models, the maker simply quit checkering with the V-shaped tool before any of the diamonds were pointed. By contrast, early English flat-topped checkering was cut with a parallel-sided tool much like a small back-saw. (This is arguably the most difficult kind of checkering to do well.) Keep in mind that all checkering eventually wears down to a flat top and this may cause some confusion with older guns.

In the trade, we call the unpointed diamonds around the edge of a freshly cut pattern "shiners," as their tops are still flat and show the shine of the stock finish. They are to be avoided. Which brings us to evaluating checkering for quality workmanship. Those shiners are caused by not "pointing-up" (or completing the depth of each line) right out to the edge of the pattern. Few patterns by even fewer craftsmen have all of the diamonds pointed because doing so will add several hours to an already ridiculously time-consuming endeavor.

I might as well get it off my chest: When I read about "flawless checkering" in some magazine gun review, I don't believe it. That is to say; unless names like James Tucker, Jerry Fisher, Stan and Max McFarland or a few others are mentioned as the craftsmen. There is almost no such thing as flawless checkering. When evaluating even the best, its a matter of how tiny a nit you want to pick. This attitude drives the English crazy. But it also make our checkering the world's best.

So in the perfect checkering job, all of the diamonds should be sharply pointed. All of the grooves should appear to be the same depth. The straight lines should be truly straight with the pattern ending at equal locations side to side. To determine if the lines are straight in the middle of the pattern, don't even try to look down them individually. This is especially true under the curve of a pistol-grip gun where the lines *must* curve a bit.

Look across the tops of the points, perpendicular to the direction that the lines are cut. It is easy to see if the points are wavy. Try it, you'll see. By the way, a slight wave across the points *is* acceptable.

The diamonds are never perfectly uniform in size as they vary slightly running around the curves of the stock. But they should be of equal size in each similar contour area. If they are not, the spacing wasn't done accurately.

Do the edges of the pattern follow the lines of the gun? Are they equidistant from the edges of the metal throughout? In a pattern interrupted by an inlay or ribbon, does each row align properly on each side of the interruption?

The Italians have a penchant for cutting the front V borders, or the long rear border of a point pattern first. The rest of the pattern is checkered fill-in style so

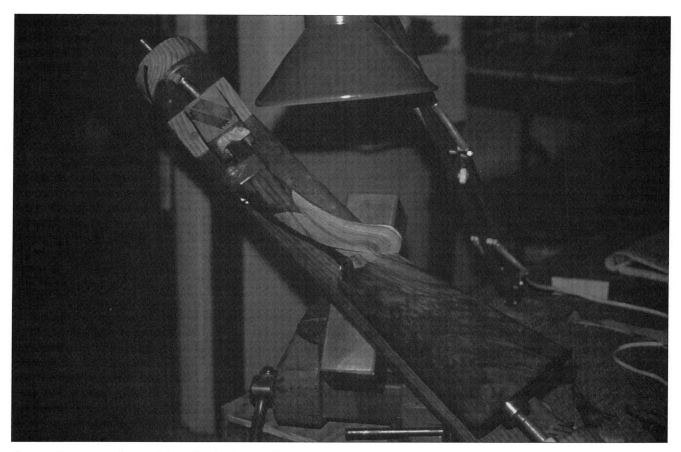

Custom jigs secure the stock in a checkering cradle.

that the border lines run contrary to the checkering lines. In other words they do a fill-in point pattern; an oxymoron for sure. This drives me crazy!

They also cut shallow 30 lpi or finer checkering which serves no purpose what-so-ever, besides wearing out very rapidly. You will find both of these quickie methods on some fine Italian guns. (I have to note, the finest imported shotguns made these days show distinctly improved checkering. Sophisticated American clients and the craftsman's pride have raised the standards.)

Not having to worry about where the points are going to come out certainly speeds thing up. And although some people drool over very fine-line checkering, the fact is that it takes about half the passes - read that half the time - to cut to full-depth checkering. American stockmakers cut fine-line checkering with a 75-degree cutter, rather than a 90-degree tool, for deeper cuts and taller, sharper diamonds.

As for lines-per-inch, 16 to 20 lpi is what you'll see on a factory shotgun stock. Finer, 24 lpi is about standard for British and American high-grade work. I like 26 lpi which is about as fine as is practical for actual gripping. The finest - 30 to 32-lpi work - should be reserved for decorative stock panels and handgun grips. This is show-off stuff, and if all the diamonds aren't perfectly pointed, it spoils the effect.

A full-page advertisement in a recent magazine showed a new British "best" with obvious run-overs at the borders of the checkering. These are caused by the tool cutting right on past where it was supposed to stop. A $30,000 gun! It is enough to drive American stockmakers crazy. (Maybe this essay will make them take note!)

Understanding the tools and the techniques used to checker a stock will give you a better perspective for evaluating the work.

Until the middle of this century all cut checkering was done entirely by hand. The myriad of today's commercially available tools would make earlier craftsmen stutter in confusion because most of them filed their cutters from spring steel. My checkering tool chest has about 18 hand tools I use regularly. There are four handles that work with interchangeable cutters. These cutters vary from single-line fine to course cut, convex cutters for mullered borders, concave for the beaded variety and multi-line tools to space 18 to 32 lpi.

A wonderful innovation to modern checkering was the advent of carbide cutters. Rene' Doiron pioneered their manufacture and his son Jon (J & R Engineering, Athol, MA) continues to supply them. The carbide cutters last so much longer than hardened steel tools that it's nearly impossible to calculate the

The author's associate, T. Harms, lays out a fill-in pattern on a semi-beavertail forend.

difference. Carbide, as well as tool steel cutters, are available in lengths from 1/4-inch to 5/8-inch for use in tight spots, tight radius curves or the wide open spaces. They can be had with 90- or 75-degree angle for short or tall diamonds. Most are available with fixed shanks and handles or as inserts.

Special tools include 60- and 90-degree veiners (V gouges) for cutting borders, jointers that are 1-1/2 inches long for straightening wandering lines and open bowed handles that allow the user to see the back edge of the cutter. Regardless of these commercial tools, many stockers I know still make at least some of their own tools.

I use a $1,000 electric checkering tool with a $100 carbide cutter for spacing. It is a miniature circular buzz saw with a spring-loaded guide parallel to the cutter. The guide is adjustable for spacing (lpi) and the depth of the cut. A variety of carbide cutters can be had in different angles and widths for fine to production-type checkering. I'd give up checkering if I had to give up my electric tool. (For many years all electric checkering tools ran off a hand-grinder with a flex-shaft. Another Doiron innovation was an electric tool attached directly to a hand-held motor that eliminates the felt torque of the flex-shaft for greater control.)

The gunstock is held firmly in a checkering cradle, on centers so it can be rotated 360 degrees. The base of the cradle is slotted and mounted to a block with a large machine screw and wing-nut. When the block is clamped in a bench vise, the base can be swiveled, moved back and forth and tilted in the vise.

During the checkering process the stock is swapped end for end to accommodate the working qualities of the wood grain. The stock is rotated and the base swiveled as the cutters follow the curve of the stock's contours. Infinite adjustment and freedom of movement are essential to the process. Numerous jigs and fixtures, a different one for nearly every different gun, are individually made to hold the stock or forend in the cradle. They must be held very securely without fear of that expensive stock slipping out of the fixture.

Before explaining my techniques, let me say that while I applaud the amateur who decides to checker his own stock, he is entering deep water. The "starter" checkering tool kits don't have any of the same tools I use, the wood on that un-checkered factory stock probably isn't going to "hold checkering well," and there are so many little tricks that no written explanation I've seen will get you where you want to go. Better to start on a filled and finished scrap of flat walnut, then advance to re-cutting a worn pattern before taking on a good gunstock.

I'll explain my methods, which I'm sure are at least similar to others'.

First, the stock must be very nearly or completely finished with the pores of the grain filled and level with the wood surface. I know that some English craftsmen cut the checkering before the oil finish is applied, but they are neither fanatical about filling the pores nor perfecting the checkering.

Next, designing and laying out the pattern on the stock is paramount to a good job. As stockmaker Larry Brace once told me, "It's never going to get any better than the layout, so you'd better get that near perfection".

In the case of a straight-grip shotgun stock, one cuts the border lines along the guard and upper tangs first with a V-shaped gouge called a "veiner." For a fill-in pattern, all of the borders are lightly cut with this tool.

The two "master lines" are the first actual checkering lines cut in the pattern. Each forms one angle of the diamonds. All of the other checkering lines are cut by spacing off of these master lines, so they damn well better be perfectly straight and laid out at the proper angles. The diamond template is used to trace them onto the stock.

For the most perfect layout of a straight-grip stock, the V underneath and behind the guard tang forms the master lines with one going up to the top tang on each side. The trouble is one never really knows if the lines will stay straight to form the V's at the front of the pattern in the correct location. If you take a look at a gunstock and imagine all of those lines being spaced from the ones in the rear, you'll see what I mean.

For this reason many stockers, including myself, prefer to layout the most visible front Vs as master lines and then just run one line and a border to connect as a point behind the guard tang. If the checkering continues behind the guard tang with this type of layout, the diamonds won't match at the toe line. A thin, carved line down the center will separate the two patterns.

The master lines are cut to about half depth. Then each individual line - going one direction - is cut by spacing off of the master line. I use the electric checkering tool for spacing.

Hobbyists and some professionals cut each line with a hand tool which can be described as a 3/8-inch V file with a shank attaching it to a handle. Hand spacing is done with a two-line cutter that has no teeth on one V and is made for the correct lpi. Some use multiple-line tools to space two, three and even four lines at a time. When all of the lines are spaced in one direction, the stock is turned around and all of the lines going the other direction are cut. This second direction forms the diamonds.

Most stockmakers hold the wood firmly in a checkering cradle that allows the stock to rotate as one cuts around the curves. I checker in a dark room, with a single 100-watt bulb held closely to the work, wearing a set of 3X magnifiers in front of my eyes. The strong light casts a good shadow and the magnification helps to distinguish each individual line. Try that sometime - working 6 inches from the subject, for eight hours at a stretch. Yoga, Geisha girls or strong drink are the only known restoratives.

(Cathy Forester, who checkers gunstocks for a living, sent me a full-spectrum light bulb to try out. It gives a natural light that is a bit less stressful on the eyes and shows the wood colors more realistically than incandescent bulbs do. I don't know if it makes a great deal of difference to the psyche after a long day checkering, but I like to think so. It sure makes the wood look better!)

I'll make a second pass with the electric tool to deepen the lines, but from there on, at least in my shop, it is all done with hand tools. Other stockmakers manage three or even four deepening passes with the buzz-saw.

After all the spacing is complete, I'll wet sand the stock with 400-grit paper twice and 600 once. The sawdust/oil mud left during the wet sanding will be pushed into the edges and borders of the checkering. This material is easily cut out of where you don't want it. This can also serve to fill in the occasional run-over (not me!) or scratch made by a tool slipping.

Then I'll rub in the final finish coats of oil onto the entire stock before completing the checkering. From this point on the stock cannot be dinged, scratched or marred in any way without having to repair the screw-up.

Pointing up the diamonds by cutting each line to the proper depth is a huge part of the job. Several passes with the hand tools are required, swapping the stock end for end to accommodate the grain flow. Again, eliminating the shiners at the edges adds hours of fussy work. I go all the way around the pattern, cutting the last three diamonds at each end of every line with a veiner to point them up.

Twenty to 30 hours after starting, a couple of coats of stock finish brushed into the checkering completes the job. It makes me tired just to write about it and I've still got that half-checkered stock out in the shop.

As for an honest gun review; Mike McIntosh once said about my own work, "...I can see a few imperfections in the checkering - but on the other hand, perfect ... checkering (is) as hard to find as perfect dogs and writers." I can live with that, on all three counts.

Chapter 8

Fanatic Finishes

Whenever stockmakers gather, a conversation about wood finishing is inevitable.

These individuals have probably experimented more with different products and application techniques than with any other single aspect of their craft. The reason? Simple: Americans are fanatics for fine finishes.

I can't pinpoint the origin or inspiration of this fanaticism. I suspect that it's the product of a situation and a goal. In this country we are more apt to use firearms in extreme terrain or inclement weather. Also, American custom gunmakers lavish such patience and detail on their stockmaking that they want the finished appearance to reflect that attitude.

It should be pretty clear that wood needs finish. Without protection a gunstock is just a semi-hard sponge. The cellular makeup will readily absorb moisture and without a harder outer shell, will easily dent and scratch. The desired properties of a gunstock finish are resistance to moisture, abrasion and solvents in a medium that will

enhance the beauty of the wood with a process that doesn't require a month to apply. Towards the end of this story I will reveal the "secret" of a fine stock finish.

Linseed oil is the traditional stock finish. Urethane is the popular modern substitute. Just the word *linseed* conjures up the hallowed look of a "dull London oil finish." The coined words "urethane" and especially "polyurethane" bring to mind the top of a shot-and-a beer Western bar. Neither is quite true.

Former Holland & Holland stocker Paul Hodgins tells me that a blend of linseed oil, paint dryers and wax has long been the standard mix for the London finish. As used for who knows how long, multiple coats of this concoction are applied to fill (mostly) the stock pours - those minute openings in the wood grain. Drying agents speed up the drying time considerably. After wet sanding and drying, top coats of the same mix are hand-rubbed until tacky, then wiped off and left to dry. When three or four thin coats are built up the finish is rubbed

The look of a London dull oil finish is replicated on this J.P. Sauer stock. The wood has been filled and finished with a ure-thane/tung oil blend and top coated with linseed oil.

out with rottenstone - a very fine pumice powder - lubricated with oil. The result is a light sheen, rather than a bright shine, that presents the walnut in a subtle and enchanting manner. This is known as a "slackum" finish and is usually accompanied by a red toning agent.

Older London guns usually show the wood pours quite prominently. This is partially because the oils continue to sink into the wood over time; it also demonstrates that British makers were not concerned with completely filling the pours. And, from what I've seen and heard, rare is the British gun that has any finish applied to seal the stock's interior inletting.

Many German makers subscribe to the "one coat" method of stock finishing. The finish is applied by completely immersing the stock in a vat of moderately heavy, colored oil. After the residue has run off, the stock is rubbed down with a drying agent to harden the surface oil. Even today many German stocks show a dead, dull and open-poured finish that does little to enhance the wood grain.

As German trained gunsmith Dietrich Apel says, "They never fussed with stock finish."
(By the way, Apel *does* fuss and has long since adopted American finishing techniques.)

Word around the trade has it that commercially available American stock finishes are becoming popular in Europe. Several stockmakers have chuckled when telling me of their "old world" contemporaries who are very interested in what we are using over here.

Remember, *we are the fanatics*. And, many of our clients who have grown accustomed to fine stock finishes are high-dollar consumers of imported guns.

Before I tear the "London oil finish" to doll rags (which I'm sure will bring some comments) let me unequivocally state that it is a gorgeous *looking* finish and that *look* is a worthy achievement.

Data reported in the *USDA Wood Handbook #72* states that boiled linseed oil rated 20 percent in moisture protection while oil-modified polyurethane rated 75 percent. (Zero was bare wood and 100 complete resistance.) Linseed passes water like an old crew sock. It is also a known fact that without some building-up of finish on top of the wood, there is less resistance to direct contact with water no matter the finish.

Have you ever seen an old British gunstock that was so dark in tone the color and figure of the wood was hidden? This is because linseed never really dries and, in combination with the wax, continues to pick up dirt and darkens over time. (As I wrote this a client called and told me of an old London gun he recently had refinished. The stock was so black that neither he nor the craftsman noticed the 1-inch walnut extension at the butt until the linseed finish had been stripped.) Also, because the linseed and wax is a soft, in-the-wood finish, it offers little protection against abrasion or denting.

The most common problem with well-cared-for British guns is oil soaked wood at the head of the stock (where it meets the action). Because the wood

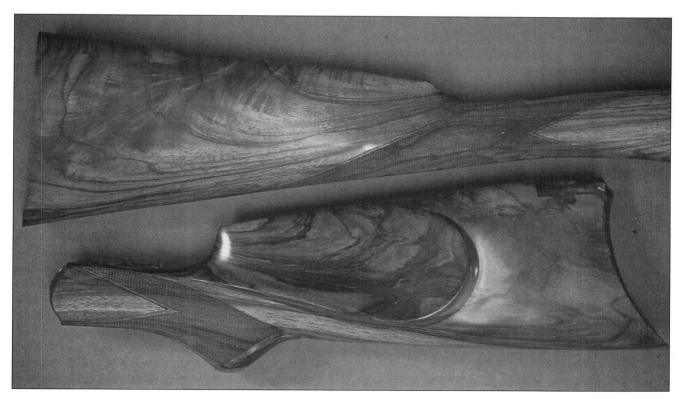

The M-21 stock on top, shows a low-gloss sheen while the rifle stock has a shinier built-up finish.

is not sealed, lubricating or rust-preventing oil is freely soaked up by the end grain of the wood. This is not only the most porous part, it also mates to the action. As the gun sits, muzzle up, waiting for next season, well-oiled gun barrels provide lots of surface area and firing pin holes act as funnels to direct the oil to the head of the stock. If the wood of your stock is darker at the action it is inhaling oil and *will* rot. Even if it is coated with linseed it is not protected.

In their defense, the natural oils have some beneficial characteristics that the synthetics don't. They are much more elastic and will stretch and shrink with the wood's seasonal/dimensional changes. Because they are soft, spot or touch-up finishing is very easy as is rubbing them down annually with additional finish. (Tung oil is probably the best natural oil for gunstocks because it rapidly dries hard, resists moisture and is only moderately shiny.)

A straight polyurethane finish will harden to the point that the surface can crack and craze when the wood moves. Touch-up is a major chore and the look is as flashy as a Colorado spinner. Yuck!

The best modern gunstock finishes are a blend of natural and synthetic oils that are formulated to give the better properties of each. What follows are exactly the properties the fanatic wants from a stock finish.

All of the stock pours should be filled level with the outer surface of the stock. This creates a hard and uniform surface that won't trap beads of water or dirt particles. All of the inletting and unexposed surfaces of the stock - under the action, locks, forend iron, trigger guard and butt pad - should be sealed with at least two coats of a penetrating finish. This prevents lubricating oil from migrating and softening and rotting the wood, as well as retarding the intake of moisture which can swell the wood and cause the closely fitted moving parts to bind.

A slight to moderate build-up of finish on top of the wood protects it from moisture and offers a surface that will take minor scratches and abrasions before they reach the wood's surface.

The "look" of a stock finish is just as important as its other qualities. What good is a durable, water-resistant surface if it doesn't show the beauty of the wood? As I've alluded to earlier, there are two basic types of surfaces: an in-the-wood finish and a built-up finish. Either requires top-coating after the wood pours are filled.

"French polish" - a mixture of orange shellac, linseed and a dryer - has long been employed as a top coat. It is applied by hand and rubbed until the friction-heat sets it up. The look is moderately shiny and pleasing but the finish will show scratches.

Linseed with a coloring agent such as alkenet root will add a fine sheen with a touch of reddish tones. High quality waxes such as carnauba make a great annual treatment for gunstocks. One must be careful not to apply the wax too heavily on unfilled wood because

Wet sanding the Sauer stock. Note that all metal is in place and the action and pad are protected with masking tape.

it may dry as white specs in the pours. The shiny look of wax may also bring out any scratches or dents in the stock. Shine shows flaws.

(I avoid any wax or gun oil that has silicon. The stuff is insidious, and, in the case of refinishing, cannot be removed with normal strippers. Nothing will stick to it. One must use a special agent to remove any silicon before doing anything to a stock or metal finish.)

English walnut often has a rather light-yellow background color and can stand to have some color added. Older English and American stocks usually have a reddish tone that brings out the richness of the wood. I'm a big believer in adding a red tone to the walnut but have had limited success in accomplishing the process.

The traditional toning agent was most assuredly alkenet root steeped in linseed oil - often referred to as red-oil. I have used red-oil imported from Germany, but it is dries extremely slowly and must be rubbed daily with a drying agent for as long as a week. It penetrates well and works well for in-the-wood finishes. One must be very certain it is dry before applying any finish on top or you'll wind-up with a sticky mess that will never dry.

Red-oil finishes don't work well with complete pore filling and wet sanding. The number of sandings needed and having to sand right down to the wood surface tends to remove the color and leave a patchy look to the stock.

Before any finish is applied, surface preparation of the stock, in the form of diligent sanding, sealing and thorough pore filling is the prerequisite to a top-drawer finish. During dry sanding the wood must be wetted and rapidly dried to "raise the grain". This exposes and lifts the crushed and compressed wood fibers. If the grain isn't raised or "whiskered," before the finish is applied, the first time the stock gets really rain wet, the fibers will lift right up though the finish. Guaranteed.

Following is the method of sealing and filling that most American stockers employ. The stock must be whiskered and dry sanded to 220-grit - with the metal in place to prevent sanding it below the wood surfaces. (I like to raise the grain once more after final sanding to clean and open the pours.) All of the metalwork is removed and a water-thin coat of stock finish is liberally mopped on all of the surfaces, inside and out, with much emphasis on the end grain at the head and butt of the stock. These surfaces will literally drink up coat after coat of the thin sealer. When the wood will take no more, the stock is hung in a temperature-controlled drying cabinet that speeds the drying, keeps the dust off and protects the fragile stock from accidental damage. As this sealer coat dries it freezes what's left of the raised grain which will be removed with the first wet sanding.

The wood takes a lot less finish when a second coat of sealer is applied the following day. This is enough for the inletting - unless one is using very porous wood such as black walnut. When the second coat dries there will be a bit of shine, which is oil drying on the surface. The unfilled pours will be evident as dull spots on the stock.

This M-21 custom stock receives the final hand rubbing with linseed oil and rottenstone.

The metal goes back in place, where possible, and the external surfaces get a third and sometimes a fourth coat of finish. These coats will begin to build up on the surface.

There are two different methods to complete the pour-filling. What is known as the "sanded in finish" relies on wet sanding the stock with 320-grit wet and dry paper, lubricated with thinned stock finish (most finishes thin well with mineral spirits). The sanding slurry of oil and dust is worked into the pours and a light coat is left to dry on the surface. The other method is similar but the stocker builds up successive coats of finish, then cuts them back to the wood surface by wet sanding. With this method, all of the slurry is wiped off as it accumulates. Using either method, it will take at least three wet sandings with 320-grit paper to fill the pours of close-grained English walnut.

Wet sanding is a sticky, slow and messy chore that is essential to proper filling. The use of paste fillers, common in finishing furniture, is shunned by custom stockmakers. We don't like the silica filler, the color, nor the inferior adhesion.

Holding the stock up to the light will help show unfilled pours, and these spots can be re-coated and wet sanded again. When the pores are completely filled the stock is wet sanded with 400-grit, allowed to dry, wet sanded with 600-grit and then sometimes with 800- or 1,200- grit. These fine wet sandings serve to polish the finish. At this point I like to let the stock sit for a week or so to cure and harden.

The stock is usually checkered at this stage. A couple of light coats of thinned finish is all that is needed for the checkering. Just enough to seal the wood without making the checkering shiny. I paint this on with a fine brush and wipe the excess off the stock with a rag.

For the final finish, my preferred build-up is two or three coats of the same finish thinned like the sealer. Each minute coat is applied by hand and rubbed until it is just tacky. Extreme care must be taken to prevent dust (or springer spaniel hairs) from sticking to the finish.

When all is dry, there is a thin but even film of finish built-up on the filled surface. Again I let everything cure, and then work it with a very fine rubbing compound to polish and even the surface. This rubbing will break down the gloss considerably. If I want a semi-gloss finish I'm done. If I want a London finish I do what they do in London: fine polishing with linseed and rottenstone. A couple or three go-rounds and I have the hallowed look, with just a bit more hard finish on top of the wood.

As far as time goes, the complete stock finishing of a small, 20-bore, straight-grip, splinter-forend Fox consumed nearly 11 hours by my log book, over about two weeks. And that, my friends, is the *secret*: patience and thoroughness until the job is complete.

Nearly every stockmaker that I know, regardless of experience or years in the trade, is still looking for a better finish and/or method of application. Gunsmith Dennis Potter says, "Looking over at my finishing bench, I'll bet there are 40 bottles, vials or 35mm film cans full of commercial finishes or some concoction that I've mixed-up as an experiment. Next year there will be a few more."

For those of you who are buying imported doubles, new or old, I've got tip. If you want to take them out in a real Oregon rain or expect the stock to last for your grandson, send the gun to a competent 'smith and ask him to remove all of the metal and seal the inlets with a quality finish. I recently repaired the cracked stock of a 10-year-old Spanish sidelock. It was no surprise that the high-quality gun had no finish at the stock head and was already showing signs of punky, oil-soaked wood.

Truth be told, I have little experience with refinishing stocks. The vast majority of the work I have done is with new wood. When refinishing, my approach is usually the same except that the old finish is first removed with a commercial stripper. Dents are steamed out with a soldering iron placed on a wet rag on the dent. Sanding is kept to the bare minimum and must be done with the metal in place. Extreme care is necessary so that the wood is not sanded below the metal surfaces, and, at the same time, the metal is not scratched or marred.

Stock refinishing for restoration is even more touchy as one must understand the original finish and application techniques in order to duplicate them. As mentioned, stain or toning are often needed to duplicate the original appearance. I wouldn't suggest attempting a true restoration as a first project.

If you want to dress-up a stock 10 minutes before taking it to a gun show, rub on a light coat of Old English furniture polish Scratch Cover. The stain in the stuff will darken the flaws, and the sheen will certainly improve the look - for a little while anyway. That is the only quick and easy tip I know about gunstock finishes.

AUTHOR'S NOTE:

I can recommend two commercial stock finishes that I have used extensively. *Pro Custom Oil*, clear gloss, which is marketed under the GUN SAV'R label. A mixture of tung oil and urethane. (For filling, use the multi-coat method.) This one has a greater percentage of natural oils and is easier to use.

Permalyn (sealer or finish) made by Laurel Mt. Forge is linseed and urethane. It is more difficult to apply but gives a very hard finish. Use the sanded-in method of filling and wait no more than 48 hours between coats for good adhesion

Section 2

Gun Metal

Chapter 1

Mikes, Pulls and Gauges

To start this section about shotgun metalwork it is important to understand how gunsmiths arrive at the numbers which translate to the various pertinent measurements that make up your gun. I'll show how the cold, hard steel is measured so that you can understand the tools and techniques used to arrive at those numbers. Tiny tolerances can be quite important, so these tools and gauges are exacting and precise.

I've often heard folks relating barrel and gunsmithing dimensions in tenths, hundredths and thousandths of an inch. But make no mistake: We who earn our living at the trade deal in only in thousandths of an inch. If you want to sound well-informed and speak the same language as the gunsmith, it's easy to remember. Everything is in thousandths and the numbers behind the decimal are the number of thousandths.

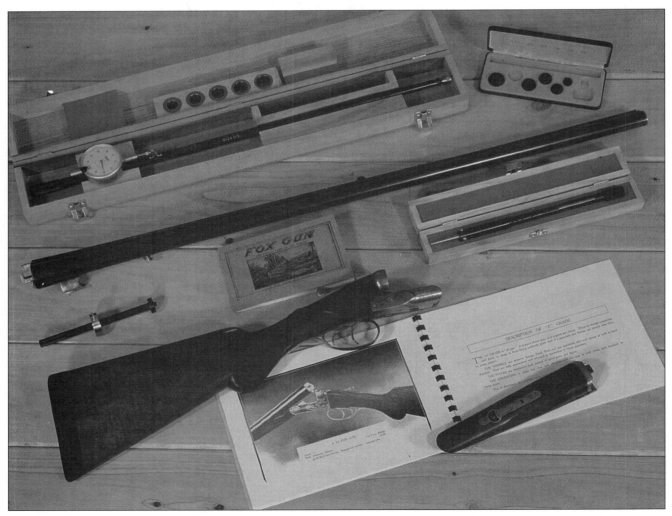

Fully researching this fine old Fox A Grade requires measuring tools and instruments. The chokes are full and fuller, the chambers have been lengthen to 2-3/4 inches and the bores mike .731 inches. Old catalogs help determine how the gun came out of the factory.

(From top) Dial calipers, an outside micrometer and inside dial calipers are all used to measure gun metal in thousandths of an inch.

An example: .001" is one thousandth of an inch, .017" is seventeen thousandths and .729" (nominal 12-bore) is expressed as 729 thousandths. (A gunsmith would say, "It 'mikes' seven twenty-nine"). An outside micrometer will be found in the apron pocket of anyone who does extensive machine metalwork. Although largely replaced by dial calipers for convenience, if I want to know what the exact measurement is, I use a mike.

Even when speaking of "points of choke" as the English say, we still talk about thousandths of an inch. That is: 40 points of choke equals .040 inches which is expressed as 40 thousandths.

Most all shotgun metal dimensions are expressed this way, and typical gunsmithing tolerances are an included .001 inches (plus or minus one-half thousandth .0005 inches). To give you a relative idea of how thick this is, typing paper measures, or 'mikes', with a micrometer, .004 inches (four thousandths).

Backing away to some coarser measurements and their importance, it is easy to run a tape measure or ruler from the barrel breeches to the muzzle to find out the barrel length. For an American shotgun this will usually measure within 1/16 of an inch of 26, 28, 30, or 32 inches. If they measure 27 inches you might want to check to see if there is any choke left, as the barrels may have been shortened - or perhaps, special-ordered.

Continental guns, on the other hand, are measured metrically. The two I have at hand measure 68.10cm (26-13/16 inches) and 69.85cm (27-1/2 inches). (Inches times 2.54 will give you centimeters.) Because so many British guns were custom or individually made, barrels from the UK can be about any length but are usually to the even inch.

Switching from inches to pounds and ounces, let's check the trigger pulls. It is surprising how few folks know what the triggers of their pet gun actually break at. A few years ago I had a double in for custom work and suggested to the client that I ought to lighten the trigger pulls. When he asked why, I explained that the front trigger was firing at more than 10 pounds and the rear at nearly 17. He had been shooting the gun like that for a couple of years.

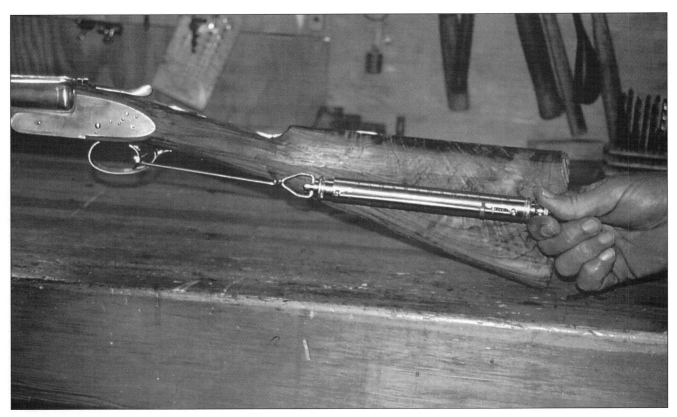

With the gun held securely, the recording trigger pull gauge is used to check the weight of pull in pounds.

There are two types and several variations of trigger pull gauges. Certainly the most accurate - as used officially for NRA rifle and pistol competitions - are the trigger pull weights. A set consists of a long rod that holds 1-, 1/2- and 1/8-pound weights. By placing the rod with the weights on the floor, hooking the upper end over the trigger, lifting the weights with the gun and adding weights until the tumbler drops, we get the trigger pull weight within 1/8 of a pound.

These are also a pain in the ass. One must have several weights of each increment and stack them until the trigger trips. It's also relatively easy to scratch or mar the stock in the process.

Nearly as accurate and certainly more convenient is a quality spring gauge. (And I mean *quality*, don't waste your money on the $20 model.)

Brownells, of Montezuma, Iowa sells all varieties of pull gauges. Above my bench is a lathe-turned brass version that sells for about $75. The spring gauge is adjustable and records each measurement up to 12 pounds.

The recording feature is a major bonus. Trying to read the gauge at the moment the trigger breaks is very difficult, to say the least. A neat little tally marker slides along with the pointer as the weight increases. When the sear breaks and the pointer snaps back, the marker is left right on the mark to accurately record the weight of pull.

For shotgunners, Brownells offers these gauges in 6- and 12-pound models. I have the 12-pounder so I can also hang a custom gun by the trigger guard to weight it as I stock or work on it.

Using the proper method for measuring trigger pulls is as important as having accurate gauges. The gun *must* be held securely for starters. In my shop this means the gun is clamped in a well-padded vise with the muzzles and toe of the stock supported. The hook end of the pull rod is carefully centered on the trigger shoe and the gauge is held in a consistent lateral position for each measurement. I like to flop a clean rag over the side of the stock to prevent dings and scratches.

I take four or five measurements of each trigger and average them to arrive at a pull weight. The rear trigger requires a bit more care as its curved radius is harder to find the center of, and one has the tendency to pull a bit upward rather than to the rear.

When creating a custom shotgun, I like to judge the finished weight within a couple of ounces before I start the project. This estimate comes from weighing the gun I start with, weighing its individual components - barrels, stock, action etc. - and a large dash of workshop intuition. While I don't keep a record of barrel weights like some do, I have a penchant for weight as it pertains to the gun's balance and the shot charge.

A couple of cast-lead ingots have been inlet and installed next to the forend iron of a dove gun. Hollowing the butt and adding the weights shifted the balance towards the muzzles.

Gough Thomas, in his excellent text, *Shotguns & Cartridges*, gives a ratio of 96:1 as a good benchmark. In other words, a one ounce shot charge is right for a six-pound gun. (1-1/8 ounce X 96 = 6-3/4 pounds.; 1-1/4 ounce X 96 = 7-1/2 pounds.) This ratio works out very closely to what I can stand in the way of felt recoil.

When balancing a custom shotgun, I often alter the weight and balance by boring or hollowing the butt to reduce the weight and shift the balance forward. A recently completed project called for a 7-pound, 16-gauge gun with a slightly weight-forward balance. With its medium weight, 30-inch tubes and dense walnut semi pistol-grip stock and recoil pad, I was very near the correct weight. But the gun was a bit butt-heavy so I bored a cavity under the pad and cast two small ingots of lead that were inletted and secured in the barrel channels next to the forend iron.

The shooter can feel the heft as the left hand holds the semi-beavertail forend. The gun was designed and built for pass shooting doves and the extra weight for a 16-bore coupled with the weight-forward balance should make it a pleasure to shoot all day.

I use a simple old-fashioned spring shipping scale to determine the weight of guns. I've calibrated it to a gallon of water and get consistent results. But I'd sure like to have one of the nouveau electronic jobs.

Switching back to inches but shortening our measuring stick a bit, lets check the chamber lengths. Measuring chamber length is easy - with the right tools. Early American shotguns had chambers of 2-1/2 inches or 2-5/8 inches depending on the gauge. Pre-World War II British and Continental game guns were most often chambered for 2-1/2-inch shells. Pigeon and waterfowl guns often had 2-3/4-inch chambers, and there are a smattering of 2-inch chambered guns around.

Galazan offers a Handy Model chamber length gauge, which looks like an oversize set of feeler gauges. The six brass leaves span .410-bore to 10-gauge and can be used to measure 2-inch, 2-1/2-inch, 2-3/4-inch, 3-inch and 3-1/2-inch chambers. Each blade closely fits the chamber dimensions, so it will stop on the forcing cone and get a close-enough chamber length.

They also sell a Presentation Model chamber length gauge that comes in a leatherette instrument case. The set includes six blued gauge rings, a calibrated rod they screw onto and a brass collar. Definitely the high-brow set (which I have at my bench) although they are no more accurate than the pedestrian model. Just install the appropriate gauge ring on the rod, slip it into the chamber until the brass collar stops at the breech. Then you can easily read the depth of the chamber.

Galazan's chamber length gauge on the bench, in action measuring a 2-3/4-inch 12-gauge chamber.

Many folks wonder about choke dimensions. If you have a set of dial calipers you can easily measure the choke at the muzzle. Unfortunately this doesn't tell you much because the difference between the bore and the choke dimensions is what is important. One must reach in a bit further to measure both.

For many years I've been using an inside dial caliper to check chokes quickly. It reads in thousandths of an inch, like any dial caliper, but it has two arms about 3-1/4 inches long. It will reach past the choke and to the bore of most barrels. As the arms are slowly pulled out of the muzzle, the amount of constriction, or the change in constriction, from bore to choke can be measured.

Unfortunately the tool has three limitations. The most obvious is that it may not reach into the bore of some older, long-choke barrels. It really works best as a comparative tool because the dial must be calibrated to a known dimension to actually measure with the tool. The third limitation is that because the gauge only has two feelers, tipping it even slightly will give a false reading.

If one develops a standard of consistency, the inside dial calipers are a convenient and accurate gauge for measuring choke constriction. MSC Industrial Supply sells a good Internal Dial Caliper for about $90.

I should remind the reader at this point that choke constriction has little to do with the actual choke measurement. It has everything to do with the difference between the choke and bore dimensions. You must measure the bore and measure the choke, then subtract the difference. This eliminates all of the push-in-the-muzzle choke gauges for truly accurate

choke determination because you can't get the bore dimensions, only constriction at the muzzle.

Getting down to the gnat's hind-quarters, we have the bore gauges that are specifically designed and manufactured for measuring the inside of shotgun barrels. Again, these also vary in style and degree of sophistication.

For several years I've been using the bore gauge offered by Galazan. At a current list price of $395, this one is for the professional and it should instill confidence in any customer who sees it in his gunsmith's shop. Galazan's bore gauge works with three metal fingers arranged to expand and contract when a knob is turned on the opposite end. The instrument's dial indicator measures the bore in thousandths of an inch. Test bushings in 28, 20, 16, 12 and 10 gauges (set in a hardwood block) allow the operator to set the dial for the appropriate barrel. The works are housed in a wood-partitioned and padded case. The tool has a 15-inch reach so it is possible to measure any part of a 30-inch barrel working from muzzle and breech.

On the more affordable end of the spectrum is the Skeet's bore gauge sold by Brownells in the $90 price range. The measuring end uses three ball bearings that expand to fit the bore. This tool is offered in 12/16- or 20/28-gauge models, with just one test bushing for each. The dial indicator is calibrated in .001-inch units, the reach is about 12 inches and the shaft is aluminum, covered with a phenolic resin sleeve.

At the top of the heap of bore gauges is the CSP Digital Bore Micrometer also from Brownells. The

On the left side of the photo are two styles of chamber length gauges. The Sweet's bore gauge has a short 12"-inch shaft. Galazan's bore gauge is housed in a hardwood box and the CSP bore gauge is on the upper right.

complete set goes for about $620 and it's the one you will find in Bill Heckman's shop. Heckman Specialties offers sophisticated shotgun bore work and Bill has nearly 10 years' experience with the CSP gauge and recommends it highly.

The CSP bore gauge works on the three-ball system, has a 15-3/8-inch reach, comes with four gauge heads (.410, 28-, 20- and 12-gauge) and four test rings, and displays measurements digitally. Both 16- and 10-gauge heads and rings are available and the whole works comes in a padded hardwood box. For those that are metrically inclined, just flipping a switch will convert the gauge to read in millimeters, nifty!

The final instrument that I'll present is Galazan's Shotgun Barrel Wall thickness Gauge ($395) which is the only one of its kind available that I know of. Any professional that alters, sells or deals with double-barreled shotguns owes it to his or her customers to make the substantial investment in this gauge. Anyone who purchases or has barrel work done on a double gun should be ready to reject the deal if accurate wall thickness dimensions cannot be provided.

A few different types of wall thickness gauges have been offered over the years. The one to stay away from is the "tuning fork" variety. There is just no way an 18-inch-long tuning fork that is small enough to fit into a 20-gauge barrel is not going to flex. When it does the measurement is inaccurate.

I know of two shotgun specialists who have tried to used these gauges, without confidence, and have retired them to collect dust on a back-bench peg board. One fellow says, "you can get them to read whatever dimension you want, just push on the rod."

Galazan's, on the other hand, has a stout steel base and three reinforced upright shafts. The central shaft holds a dial indicator. The other shafts hold 12/16-guage or 20/28-gauge barrels. Each shaft has a thumb-screw collar that positions the barrel location to be measured and a spring-loaded plunger that secures the barrel to the shaft. The whole unit weighs nearly 15 pounds and is about as steady as they come.

In the next chapter, I'll tell some stories about barrels you might find floating around out there. We will learn how and why these instruments are used so that even if you don't own them you will know if and how your gunsmith or firearms dealer is giving you the straight scoop on the barrels of that multi-thousand dollar dream gun.

Chapter 2

Blue-Printing The Barrels

In the last chapter I left you holding barrel measuring instruments without telling you what to do with them. I'll cover that in detail in a moment but, first let's see why these gauges are so important.

Scattered through this book are a few of photos of a pre-World War I French boxlock I own and shoot. This 12-bore gun weighs just 6-1/4 pounds. and has 27-1/2-inch barrels. When I bought it I knew the barrels must be quite light and thin. Because I took my chamber length gauges and inside dial calipers to the gun show, I also knew that the chambers had been lengthened and I suspected that the bore and chokes had been altered as well. But the gun was lovely, tight and the price was right, so I bought it.

Here's what I found when I got it back to the shop: With a bore gauge I determined that the barrels

measured .731 inches and .732 inches inside. Because many Continental guns have tight bores, I surmised that the barrels had been honed to remove pitting, but they are well within tolerance (the nominal 12-bore measure being .729 inches).

The choke of the right barrel was .009 (nine thousandths, remember?) and the was left, .017. Looking at the barrel bottom and flats, I found Belgian proofs and the following markings: Both barrels were stamped *65* (chamber length in millimeters), with "*choke 17.8/18.4*" on the right and "*choke 17.4/18.4*" on the left. Many Continental doubles show choke and bore diameters in millimeters; the first number indicating constriction, the second bore diameter.

Because 1 mm equals .03937 inches, simple multiplication told me that the original chambers

With the barrel lump in a padded vise and the muzzle supported, the author measures a set of double barrels.

A professional-quality wall thickness gauge, such as this one from Galazan, if is vital for judging the relative safety of shotgun barrels.

back from the muzzle it "miked" .785 inches. Simple math would suggest that the minimum wall thickness is .0265 inches (.785 inches minus .732 inches = .053 inches, divided by 2 = .0265 inches). This would be well within the range of adequate wall thickness.

I marked the location of the smallest barrel diameter with a grease pencil and then took the barrels across the shop to the wall thickness gauge. The gauge was carefully dialed-in to zero and the barrels set-up at the proper thin-wall location.

The thickest part of the barrel wall is normally up next to the top rib and miked .030 inches. But at the typically thinnest part, out at the apex of the curve of the barrel farthest from the ribs, the wall measured only .021 inches. The other barrel told a similar story.

There is a lot to be learned from this exercise, much of which could have been deduced right at the gun show if I had brought along a bore gauge and a calculator (because I'm mathematically challenged). I wouldn't have been able to arrive at the exact wall thickness, but if I had known the calculated inside/outside wall thickness was less than .030 inches, I would also have known the barrels might be quite thin in spots because they always vary somewhat when measuring the actual thickness around the curve.

The .009-inch variation in these barrels is a bit more than normal but the gun was at least 80 years old and who knows how many times the barrels had been struck. The outboard surface almost always is the thinnest and I'll bet that's because it's the easiest part to get a file on. It is also the part that you *can't* measure from the outside with calipers because the rib is in the way. (An English trained gunsmith has told me that it was not uncommon to strike the barrels *after* proofing to lighten them to achieve weight reduction or balance. What is the easiest part of the barrels to work on?)

Opinions on safe barrel wall thickness vary considerably, not only from expert to expert but from country to country. I'm not going to stick my neck into the noose of liability by stating what a safe or minimum wall thickness is. Safety is a subjective word - even when inlaid in gold on the top tang.

What I will say is that the barrels on my boxlock are fluid steel, in fine condition inside and out, and I only shoot the gun with shells that approximate the pressures of cartridges the gun was designed for. I'm comfortable with that, especially because hotter loads would smack the hell out of me in a 6-1/4-pound 12-bore.

But what if I manage to even slightly dent one of the barrels, especially on the thin outside curve where it is most vulnerable? Pushing out the dent and striking the tube will probably remove enough metal to put it past the limit of reasonable safety. In this event I might chose to sleeve the gun.

measured 2.559 inches (65 mm X .03937) or a nominal 2-5/8 inches. The original bores were .724 inches (18.4 X .03937). The chokes were .701 inches (17.8mm X .03937) right and .685 inches (17.4 X .03937) left. In other words the entire barrel bores had been considerably altered - the chambers by 1/8 of an inch, the bores by .007 inches and the chokes by .021 inches and .030 inches, respectively. This is just the situation where the wall thickness gauge becomes a vitally important tool.

I measured the outside of each barrel with a dial caliper to find the smallest diameter. About 8-1/2 inches

A potentially more dangerous example is the reason *caveat emptor* is so frequently cited when buying used guns. A client sent me a Lefever G grade sideplate 16-bore to inspect. After purchasing the gun, he had read in Elliot and Cobb's Lefever book that most G grade guns were made with Damascus barrels. The barrels on this gun were nicely, but recently rust blued and had been represented by the dealer as being fluid steel. Overall, the gun appeared to be a fine piece that had been expertly refinished.

But a small dab of bluing remover under the forend at the breech end of the barrels started to reveal another story. The finger-print of the Damascus pattern became immediately obvious.

The chambers measured 2-3/4 inches, which I'm almost sure was not original because this model was only made until 1900, before 2-3/4-inch chambers were common. Measuring the bright shiny barrel bores I found them to be .009 inches and .010 inches over normal bore size. I then used the wall thickness gauge to mike the left tube at .030 inches at the thinnest spot and the right barrel at only .024 inches at the minimum.

Who is to say if the barrels were safe? I only knew that I wasn't going to shoot the gun. And what about the ethics question, about misrepresentation, maybe deceit? I know that my client wouldn't have purchased the Lefever if he had known the barrels were blued over and honed out Damascus with .024-inch barrel wall thickness. And this gun was purchased from a very well known dealer who should know better!

I really became frightened when I showed it to a gunsmith friend who isn't particularly familiar with Lefevers. I asked him what he though of the gun and whether it looked safe to shoot. "Sure," he said, "it looks really good to me." When I removed the forend and showed him the Damascus pattern, we both realized how easy it is to buffalo someone with outside appearance. Oh, and he changed his opinion about shooting it.

What to do with the gun? I don't know. I suggested that I return it to the dealer with a written summation, a bill for my inspection work and a note saying I didn't want to see it advertised unless the ad read, "G grade Lefever, 16 bore with sleeved barrels."

There are times when even the finest gauges can't tell you, or even a professional, about serious bore problems. I recently saw a DHE Parker, a beautiful gun, completely and expertly restored to "as new" condition. The wood had been care-fully refinished, the checkering recut and the engraving picked-up. The action showed beautiful Parker-toned case colors and the barrels and metal parts deeply blackened.

The gun wasn't shooting to point of aim because the barrels were slightly bent: not all that unusual. The gunsmith discovered the problem when he lightly honed the bores. After removing the ribs to straighten the barrels a serious problem showed up. There was some heavy rust between the barrels, under the ribs. The pitting was so heavy that there were actually some tiny pin holes right through the barrels and into the bores. The scary part is knowing that the both the client and the gunsmith had fired the gun.

The customer had purchased the gun from a dealer, who, in turn, had gotten it in trade from another dealer. Everyone wanted to pass it back to the last party and get their money back (the client had spent about $10,000). Another scary bit of reality; the client requested that the gunsmith solder the ribs back and re-black the barrels, as it was when he purchased the gun. The gunsmith boxed it and returned it not wanting to be a party to further deception.

Unfortunately, cases like this are apparently becoming more common. So, if you're a serious buyer of fine shotguns you're going to want to know how to thoroughly inspect barrel bores - or at least ask the gunsmith what kind of tools and methods he uses.

I've had calls from two other professional shotgun 'smiths lately asking me where all of these wrung out barrels are coming from. Where are they coming from? The demand for used doubles has intensified to the point that greed is a motivating factor. "That gun is

Exact determination of bore and choke measurements requires a precision bore gauge. Test rings, mounted in a wood block, calibrate the gauge. The three expanding petals at the working end of the shaft, sit next to the gauge block. A set of barrels awaits measurement.

pretty nice except for the bore pitting, so we'll hone 'em out 'til they shine." Which is too often done with grit paper on a slotted stick in a drill motor.

Personally I'm skeptical when I see an ad for a 70-year-old gun with "mirror bores". How many of these guys have invested in the expensive tooling to accurately determine what they are selling? Especially the greedy types. So you had better ask them. I know of at least one purveyor of used doubles that is as crooked as a bonsai tree!

Bill Heckman, of Heckman Specialties, and I came up with the following procedure to "blueprint" the barrel bores of a shotgun. Heckman offers this as a service to his clients for just the sort of cases profiled above.

To spec out a set of barrels, look first at the diagram of a barrel bore as shown in the accompanying drawing. (When blueprinting a set of barrels we have two of these diagrams set side-by-side.) Keeping the measurements straight between the right and left barrels is the trickiest part. For this reason, I like to clamp the lump in a padded bench vise and support the muzzles for the whole operation. If you're turning the barrels upside down and end for end you *will* get confused at some point.

Make sure the barrels are squeaky clean and very lightly oiled. Starting at the breech end with a chamber gauge, check and note the chamber lengths. Then zero the bore gauge to the appropriate size with the test ring.

Slide the bore gauge in from the breach until it is past the forcing cone and measure the bores in as far as you can reach. Record the depth and bore dimension on the diagram. As you slide the gauge towards the breech note any dimensional variations. There shouldn't be any until the gauge reaches the front of the forcing cone, which will be easy to feel.

Slide the gauge back and forth until you feel the exact beginning of the forcing cone and mark that location on the bore gauge rod with a pencil. Remove the gauge and measure the length from the pencil mark to the measuring end of the bore gauge (which will be feelers or roller balls depending on the model you use. By subtracting the chamber length from the length to the front of the forcing cone you will have a very good idea of the overall forcing cone length. Note this on your diagram.

From the front of the same barrel, slide the bore gauge past the choke and down to the place you reached into from the breech end. Slide the gauge

In use, the bore gauge is inserted into each end of the barrels, the adjusting knob - in the right hand - is turned to expand the petals, and the entire bore, choke and cones can be measured.

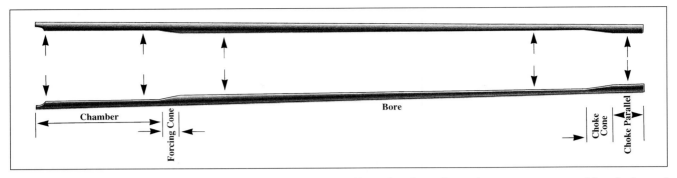

Using a diagram such as this is valuable for blueprinting a set of barrels. These dimensions are exaggerated for clarity and the diagram is not drawn to scale.

towards the muzzles, noting variations and bore size on the diagram.

As the gauge comes towards the muzzles it will again be easy to feel the beginning of the choke. Note the depth just as you did with the forcing cone, and pencil mark the shaft. Sliding the gauge towards the muzzles, you will now come to the choke parallel. Mark the depth on the shaft of the gauge. Remove the gauge and measure between the two mark to note the length of the choke lead, or cone. Then insert the gauge and measure the smallest point of the choke and mark it on the diagram.

By subtracting the choke size from the bore size you will note the amount of constriction or actual amount of choke in the barrel. At the same time, note the length of the choke parallel on the diagram. Complete all measurements for one tube before starting the other.

For wall thickness, follow the procedure outlined at the beginning of this chapter. Be sure to center and tension the barrels properly on the wall thickness gauge. Rotate the barrels and measure the wall thickness around the tube. Note the dimensions on the diagram.

It takes a bit of practice to develop the procedure, but with a good diagram to record the measurements as you proceed, it should become a simple operation.

If you are not able purchase and use these gauges, at least ask your gunsmith to let you watch while he does it (and pay him for his time to instruct you). If that's not possible, send the prospective purchase to an impartial 'smith for a thorough inspection.

I wish the marketplace was kinder and gentler, but it isn't. Asking the right questions prior to purchase and finding a gunsmith you can trust to evaluate an expensive dream gun before the culmination of the sale is your only protection from disappointment, financial distress or possible dismemberment.

Chapter 3

Barrels, Bores, and Resurrection

As we continue our discussion of the components of double guns, we're going to get to the soul of the matter; the barrels. After all, the barrels carry the shot charge and that is what enables us to "shoot flying."

We are very fortunate to have a couple of experts on shotgun barrel work to help us understand the nuances of the subject. Bill Heckman has 10 years experience with shotgun work, has done a tremendous amount of specialty barrel work for competition shooters and manufactures a barrel honing machine for the trade.

Kirk Merrington was trained at Churchill's in Birmingham, England and has more than 20 years experience in the gun trade. Merrington prefers to "work for the

bird shooters" while Bill's barrel jobs have consistently pulverized clay targets as well as feathered ones. Whether you're creating a complete custom double gun or just interested in the barrels and bores of the gun you're shooting, you'll find this knowledge enlightening.

Let's start with the common repairs that old double-barrels often need. Just last week I attempted to remove the bead from a Fox gun and the muzzle end of the top rib lifted slightly. What a surprise! I had "rung" the barrels with a brass rod, carefully inspected them and had been working on this custom project for a few months.

Ribs that are loose in one spot or another are quite common on older guns and I'm not above being fooled on occasion myself. I'll be sending these bar-

Sleeving is a relatively affordable way to save damaged barrels and create custom barrels at the same time. The breech of these barrels has been cut for a "mono-block," and is shown along with a burst barrel and a new tube. Photo courtesy of Kirk Merrington.

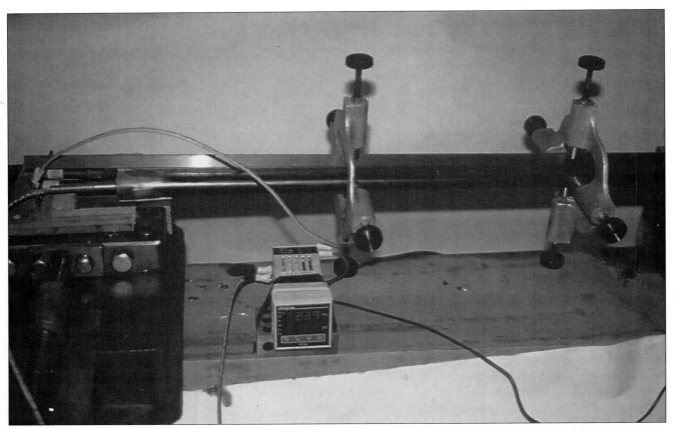

Using a modern digital thermocouple, with heating rods down each bore, these barrels are being soldered in the Heckman Specialties shop. Spring-loaded, four-way clamps secure the ribs and barrels in place.

rels out to have the ribs stripped from the barrels for complete re-laying and soldering. Spot repair - re-soldering one section of the rib - is too risky to guarantee, so it is rarely done.

Ringing the barrels to find out if the ribs are loose is a simple process that anyone can learn. Holding the hook of the lump on your index finger, suspend the barrels so that they are hanging freely. I use a small brass rod to lightly tap the sides of each barrel every few inches along their length. If the ribs are tight, the barrels will ring like a chime with a slightly different pitch as the wall thickness varies.

Unfortunately this is not any sort of guarantee the ribs are perfectly attached, as in the above instance. Maybe my pulling on the pressed-in bead tore loose the last remaining bit of solder holding the rib in place, I don't know. What I do know is when rust bluing I've found several sets of barrels with imperfect rib joints that had rung nicely.

Immersing them in boiling water will expose "leakers" with a trail of bubbles from the imperfect joints. When this occurs it is usually minor individual spots and not worthy of great concern to the shooter as 95 percent of the joints are sealed. It plays havoc with the blacking as oil migrates from under the ribs to spot the coloring. They must then be blown dry

with compressed air to remove any water from between the ribs and barrels.

There are two primary causes for loose ribs. Age and its attendant sufferings or caustic (hot-dip) bluing. Although I've heard it said that drilling a hole in the bottom rib will allow caustic bluing salts to be boiled out, I don't buy it. Side-by-side shotgun barrels should never be hot-dip blued. The buffed bright, mirror black finish is inappropriate besides detrimental.

A fair number of forend loops are soldered back onto the barrels of American guns with spring-loaded forends such as L.C. Smiths and Fox Sterlingworths. The spring tension of snapping the forend in place can put a good deal of strain on the loop. In this particular circumstance it may be possible to reattach the loop by soldering without completely stripping the ribs.

Another current problem is folks trying to glue ribs back down with modern adhesives. Epoxy and/or the so called super-glues will not fix loose ribs. Even if the adjoining surfaces could be completely degreased to assure any sort of adhesion (and they can't) spot repairs won't work because joining the ribs to the barrels requires cohesion throughout all of the surfaces. This super-glue idea sounds silly but any 'smith that solders ribs or blacks barrels will tell

(continued on page 81)

FINE GUNMAKING GALLERY

The making of the author's Hughes/Fox is described in Section Four.

A quarter-sawn Turkish walnut rifle blank sits atop two California "English" walnut buttstock blanks. The left stock shows feather-crotch which is exceedingly rare in English walnut. The two-piece stocks have fine layout for shotgun stocks while the rifle blank has a "wow" in the layout and would make a better shotgun stock.

This potpourri of English walnut from Hughes' scrap box shows many different background colors, grain patterns and figures. The stock blank has nearly perfect layout for a straight-grip stock. On top is a slab-sawn piece with heavy marbling next to sap wood and a quarter-sawn piece with many thin black lines. On the right are two pieces with reddish background color, one quarter-sawn and one slab-sawn with wavy black streaks. The two pieces on the bottom show quarter- and slab-sawing with a light background color. The upper left stick has fiddleback figure on a plain reddish background.

As fine a stick of English walnut as one can imagine. This blank shows perfect straight-grip layout, dense grain, heavy marbling and feather-crotch figure. Unfortunately there is no room for a forend from the same piece.

This gorgeous California English walnut stock blank shows deep black marbling on a honey-colored background with excellent layout and some figure in the butt.

Displaying a palette of colors this Hughes/Fox 20-bore has; a case-colored action, rust blued barrels, charcoal blued lever safety and guard, nitre blued triggers, pins and screws along with the rich tones of high-grade walnut.

A 16-gauge Fox with sparkling case colors and rust blued furniture. Engraving by Michael Dubber.

Freshly finished 12-gauge Hughes/Fox sports multi-hued case-colored action and forend iron by Doug Turnbull. Rust blued barrel, guard and escutcheon and nitre blued triggers, screws and pins from the author's shop.

A custom Model 21 Winchester 20-gauge from the workshop of Bruce Russell. The action was engraved by Eric Gold and cyanide color case-hardened.

A custom 16-bore J.P.Sauer with splendid case colors by Doug Turnbull.

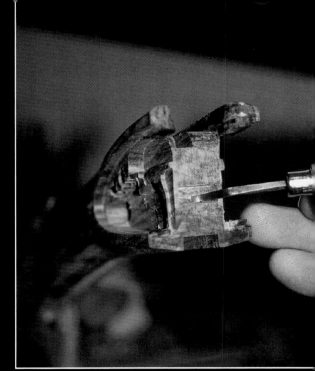

Checkering uphill, a 24 lines per inch fill-in pattern is executed in top-drawer English walnut. Note the fine ribbon that separates the two panels.

A tiny bench-made dog-leg chisel is used to inlet the locking bolt recess in a sidelock stock.

With a larger dog-leg chisel...

the author removes wood for the trigger guard tang on a custom M-21 stock.

A draw clamp holds the action to the stock as the trigger plate is inlet.

A sidelock project with assorted tools on the author's workbench.

Using a chisel and chasing hammer the author sculpts the fences of a sidelock action.

The chisel cuts a curl of steel as the fences are shaped

A custom shotgun project begins with complete disassembly, tuning and polishing all the working parts.

A template is used in shaping and refining a Fox action.

Stockmaker Jim Greenwood did a masterful job on this Beretta O/U sporting clays gun. The client was so pleased with the fit, finish and checkering he ordered a back-up gun to match. Both guns are shot extensively. on Blumb Photos

The 16-gauge Hughes/Fox — the lightweight quail gun, "smoothest of you handling and easy to Handling." It weighs 5-1/2 pounds.

A 20-pound Montana gobbler and the Hughes/Fox.

The author's 12-bore with chukar and Hungarian partridge in Idaho.

A custom M-21 16-gauge with an Idaho pheasant. The gun has been extensively lightened with sophisticated metalwork and stocked with high-grade walnut.

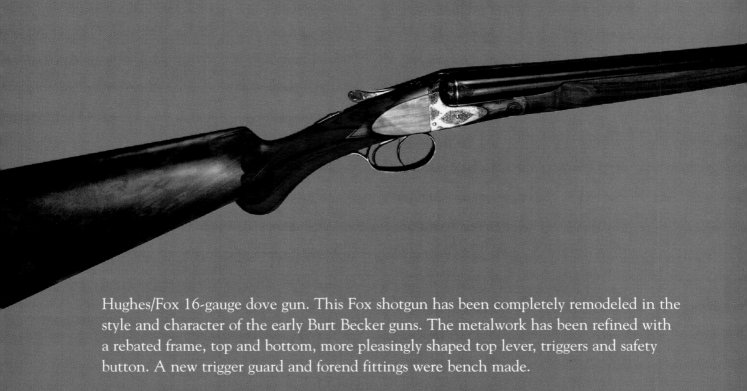

Hughes/Fox 16-gauge dove gun. This Fox shotgun has been completely remodeled in the style and character of the early Burt Becker guns. The metalwork has been refined with a rebated frame, top and bottom, more pleasingly shaped top lever, triggers and safety button. A new trigger guard and forend fittings were bench made.

The stock was made in semi-pistol-grip style with comb fluting. The forend is semi-beavertail and all is checkered 24 lines per inch with ribbons and borders.

Michael Dubber engraved the Fox with backgrounded English scroll and inlays of 24-karat gold as barrel-bands, safety and forend vignette .
Case coloring by Doug Turnbull. The barrels and hardware are rust blued and the screws nitre blued. About 250 bench hours were invested in the project prior to engraving.

The author created a 6 pound 16-gauge upland game gun starting with J.P. Sauer metalwork.

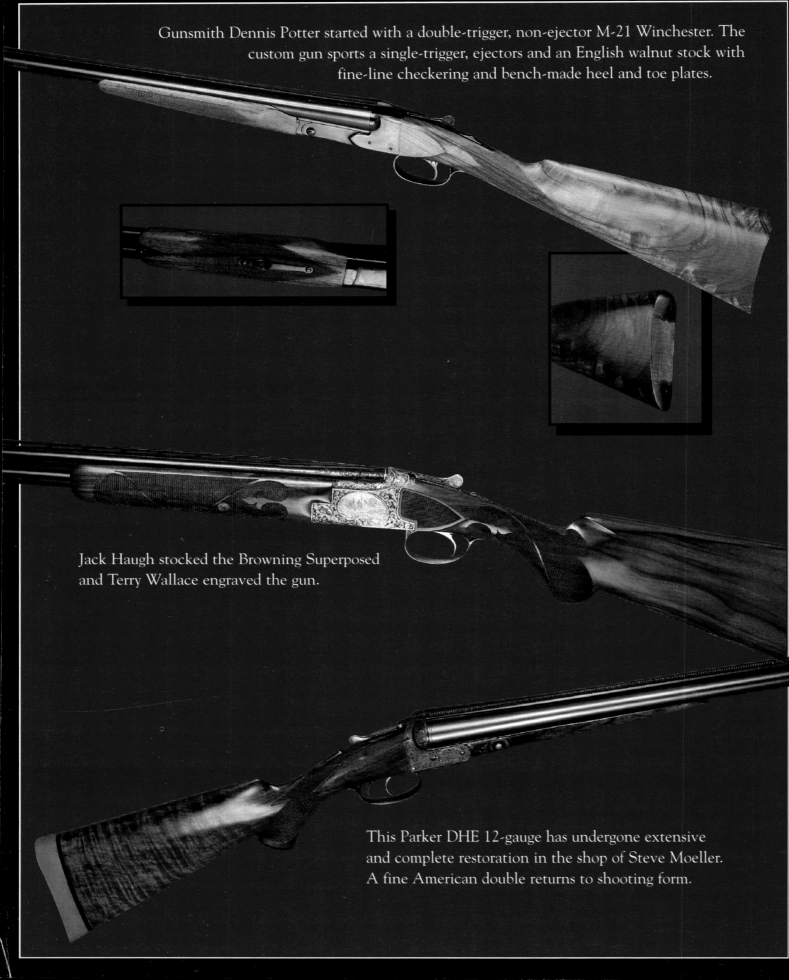

Gunsmith Dennis Potter started with a double-trigger, non-ejector M-21 Winchester. The custom gun sports a single-trigger, ejectors and an English walnut stock with fine-line checkering and bench-made heel and toe plates.

Jack Haugh stocked the Browning Superposed and Terry Wallace engraved the gun.

This Parker DHE 12-gauge has undergone extensive and complete restoration in the shop of Steve Moeller. A fine American double returns to shooting form.

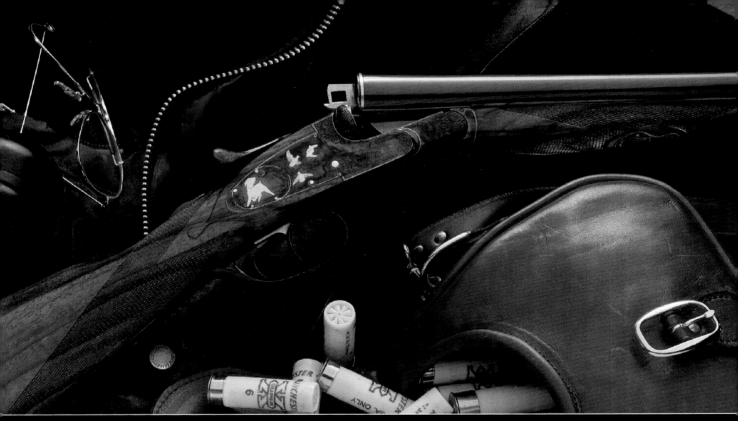

The American Custom Gunmakers Guild Project #10. The 20-gauge L.C. Smith is a joint effort of metalsmith Pete Mazur, stockmaker Steve Billib and engraver Bob Evans. Mustafa Bilal Photo courtesy ACGG.

Starting with English barrels and action this 12-bore gun was stocked, engraved and finished at Duncan Gunworks. The owner shoots and hunts this fine shotgun.

A Fabbri O/U engraved and gold inlaid by Winston Churchill. Winston Churchill Photo.

Described in the text, Churchill's Parker is a sight to behold. Winston Churchill Photo.

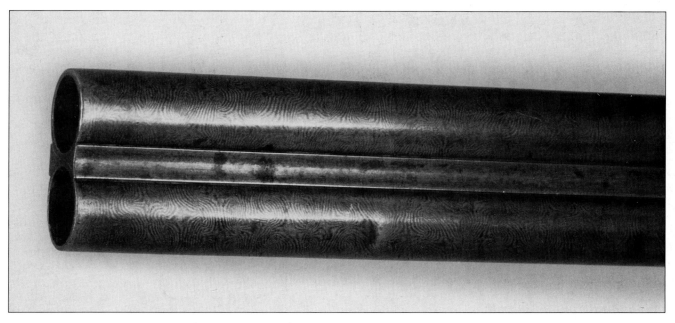

A set of Damascus barrels with several obvious dents. These must be removed before barrel honing. To properly complete the job, the barrels would be polished and browned.

you it is relatively common. Heat from boiling the barrels immediately loosens the glue and makes a mess. Don't even try it!

Re-laying ribs or soldering loops is a fairly major effort for a competent gunsmith and is definitely not something to entrust to anyone with a torch. The top and bottom ribs are removed with careful constant heat so the parts do not warp or twist in the process. Over-heating can raise hell with these oddly shaped, and closely fitted, parts. Surfaces where the ribs meet the barrels are cleaned as are the barrel walls where we cannot see. All solder is removed from all of the metal.

There is usually a spacer or two between the barrels that help align them over their length. These must also be removed, cleaned and reinstalled. Then the ribs are re-fit to the tubes and the adjoining surfaces fluxed and tinned with solder.

The traditional method of jigging the barrels and ribs for re-soldering is called "nailing the ribs." In the old days, nails were laid on the ribs. The tubes and nails were encircled with iron wire twisted tightly to apply side pressure on the barrels as well as top and bottom pressure on the ribs. Modern gunsmiths employ more sophisticated jigs to hold the parts together but still rely on twisted wire to tension the individual parts.

The barrels are slowly brought to temperature along their length, these days employing heating rods inside the bores and torch heat outside. Once the solder from the tinning starts to flow, more solder is run into the joints along the length of the top and bottom ribs. Non-corrosive flux is used throughout the process to prevent rusting between the barrels.

As you might imagine, the solder runs out onto the barrels and up the sides of the top rib making quite a mess. A good bit of the work in relaying ribs is spent cleaning up these surfaces to remove all traces of flux and extra solder. The barrels are polished prior to blacking or rust bluing.

It seems like I can't find an old gun without at least a few small dents in the barrels. A solid whack on a fence post can dent the thin-walled barrels of a fine British gun. Unless they are severe, they will come right out when entrusted to an experienced craftsman.

Dents are removed with the aid of a hydraulic dent remover. It is an undersize mandrill with a movable radiused section on one side. After marking the location of the dent in relation to the remover's mandrill, it is inserted into the bore with the movable section aligned with the dent. Pumping a handle puts pressure on the inside of the dent and pushes it out nearly flush. As you might suspect, a hydraulic dent remover is no toy and enough pressure can be applied to severely bulge the barrel.

Bulges can be a greater problem if they are bad enough to ring the bore on the rib side of the barrel. "Pimple" bulges are sometimes seen in the bores, almost always in the left barrel. These are caused by the first shot loosening the crimp on a handloaded cartridge in the other barrel. When the second shot is fired, the wad runs over the loose shot and pimple bulges the bore.

Bulges are peened down from the outside with a close-tolerance mandrill inserted in the bore to act as an anvil. After removing bulges or dents, the inside of the barrels must be honed and the outside polished and blackened to remove all traces of the work.

Occasionally, one barrel will shoot to a different point than the other. Often this is the by-product of a shoddy choke reaming job. Sometimes the barrels weren't aligned properly when the gun was manufactured and sometimes one or both barrels are bent. Depending on the situation, the cure is straightening the choke by precision honing, installing an eccentric choke tube or straightening the bent barrels. As with all barrel repairs, each job must be individually evaluated. Barrel men say that they can get most any set of barrels to shoot to the same point of impact, but it is up to the stockmaker and the shooter to place the shot on the target.

Now that our barrels are returned to a cohesive unit, performance alterations can be considered. These days much is made of backboring (enlarging the overall bore diameter behind the choke) and long forcing cones (elongating the taper in front of the chamber). Let's take a look at the chamber dimensions to begin with.

Many double guns have short chambers. Older American 12-gauge guns have 2-5/8-inch chambers, 16-gauge guns were chambered for 2-9/16-inch shells and 20-bores for 2-1/2-inch cartridges. Most pre-war British and Continental guns were chambered for 2-1/2-

inch shells. I've read various reports on the safety of shooting standard 2-3/4-inch shells in these guns and conflicting statements on the wisdom of lengthening short chambers.

My own opinion is that it is foolish to shoot modern-length shells in short-chambered guns and quite acceptable to lengthen the chambers in American guns in most instances. Extremely thin-walled barrels or rare collector's guns are the exceptions. Lengthening the chambers on English guns will take the gun "out of proof" and may detract from its resale value. Both Heckman and Merrington concur although surprisingly Kirk doesn't attach the value stigma to British doubles. He thinks that it is fine to lengthen a British gun's chambers when the barrels have substantial wall thickness. Merrington says it will lower chamber pressures if a 2-3/4-inch shell finds its way into the gun which, in essence, makes the gun with 2-3/4-inch chambers safer to shoot with reasonable loads. Neither fellow will even consider 3-inch chambers, reserving those for guns manufactured to shoot them.

Some reamer makers offer tools that are billed to lengthen the chamber and the forcing cone with the same operation. It is interesting that both Heckman and Merrington consider these separate jobs. They ream the chamber to length with a chambering ream-

Honing a set of side-by-side barrels at Heckman Specialties. Cutting oil flows through the bores during the entire operation to aid the honing stones and flush out the waste material.

er then lengthen the forcing cones with a different tool. Long forcing cones have been touted as a route to improved pattering and reduced recoil. Forcing cones of 1-3/8 inches to 2 inches seem to be the norm for this alteration. The angle of the taper and the bore size determines their length.

If I am having the bores of an older American gun reworked, I consider long forcing cones as part of the package. After all, once the chambers are lengthened it will make for a very abrupt transition for the shot if the cones are not stretched out as well. Many American doubles came out of the factory with steep-angled forcing cones and I believe it is a good idea to ease the shot charge along on its route to the target in any way possible. Longer, gentler angles will help.

Heckman is of the opinion that long forcing cones will lessen the stress on the barrels, locking mechanism and the shooter. Merrington asked his customers to evaluate the results of lengthening the forcing cones relative to recoil and patterning. After shooting their guns, half thought the results useful and half didn't notice the difference. Remember that Heckman has worked for clay breakers that shoot 20 shells for each one fired by Merrington's bird shooters.

(A note about my perspective on interior ballistics: Until someone invents a shrinking machine and someone else volunteers to ride a shot column down the barrel of a gun, no one will really know what goes on when the hammer is dropped on a cartridge. Externally mounted strain (pressure) gauges and rapid shutter photography can tell us much. Tried and true methods, tested on pattern paper is still the best way to judge barrel performance. If pressures are within a reasonable range, what goes on inside the barrel is not as important as what happens outside, at the target. Before and after patterning, with consistent factory loads, is the best test of barrel bore alterations.)

Backboring is another recently popular and controversial subject. By way of theory, enlarging the bore is beneficial to the shot pattern and lessens recoil. These are the same advantages attached to long forcing cones and not coincidentally, the most desired improvements to any shotgun's performance.

Backboring is not new and has been taken to the extreme of a 10-gauge bore with a 12-gauge chamber. Our two experts have very similar opinions about backboring. The best reasons to enlarge the bore of a side-by-side are to clean-up pitting or to put some

Heckman Specialties manufactures this barrel honing machine for the trade. Twin honing stones can be seen projecting from the muzzle at the left side of the photo. The dial on the other end of the machine sets the RPM, a foot petal turns the machine on and the carriage holding the barrels is moved back and forth by hand.

choke in a cylinder bored barrel. No matter the reason, the first consideration is the wall thickness of the barrels at the thinnest location, which is usually six inches to 10 inches behind the muzzles. This is not the outside diameter minus the inside diameter, but the actual measurement of the wall. The thickness will often vary from one side of the barrel to the other.

Merrington considers 30 thousandths of an inch (.030) to be a minimum for new barrels and anything .020 inches or less to be scrap. Both fellows told me of sectioning barrels to find one wall .050 inches and the opposite wall .020 inches. Needless to say, even a .006-inch backboring could render these barrels dangerous.

According to Heckman, taking a true 12-gauge of .729 inches bore diameter out to .735 inches or .740 inches will keep the barrel within modern specifications for wads and loads. He believes that a competition shooter will notice the difference of lighter recoil over the course of a 200- to 400-round day of target shooting. Merrington is of the opinion that backboring is paying him to "take some life out of the barrel" although he'll be glad to, if it is safe and if that is what you want.

Many shotgun barrels I measure are undersize to begin with. A recent L.C. Smith measured .726 inches, and a .003-inch honing would bring it up to modern specifications. Continental guns often have tight bores but they also have thin walls on occasion. All barrels must be judged on an individual basis. As for backboring to lighten barrels, or the gun, sure it will. But don't expect to measure the difference on your postal scale. Backboring to restore choke in a cylinder bore gun can be useful, but don't expect more than a .005-inch skeet choke although some thick-walled barrels may allow a .010-inch improved cylinder.

Seemingly the majority of older American doubles have 30-inch tubes. Frequently I am asked about shortening them to 28 inches or 26 inches. With a moderately heavy-barreled gun it can make some sense, especially if you want screw-in chokes installed as well. If you have a tightly choked, long-barreled gun it may be possible to open the chokes to the desired constriction, which will lengthen the parallel section of the choke. Then the length of the choke can be measured and the barrel shortened accordingly, still retaining the choking.

My own 28-inch Fox 12-gauge had Full and Modified chokes which were opened to .006 inches and .029 inches constriction. About 1-1/4 inches could have be cut off the muzzles still retaining a short parallel section of choke. There will always be a gap between the barrels on shortened guns and many folks think "bug-eyed" muzzles unsightly. The gap must be filled with lead or solder.

English guns were built to balance at their given length. Cutting the barrels changes the balance which is what a good British gun is all about. Merrington

comments, "You can say that a bloody limey says that it is bloody stupid to cut the barrels of a bloody good English gun!"

As for some Parkers, Heckman has seen a number of them "ringed" or bulged at the choke because of the unique shape of the choke cone done at the factory. Cutting them is a quick fix but not necessarily a wise move.

Personally I think radical alteration of a perfectly good gun is a bit short-sighted and selfish. Why not trade it for one that suits you better?

This leaves us chokes to discuss. Fortunately, the early gunmakers tended to put tight chokes in their double guns. We need the extra metal to work with as chokes can only be opened up, except for installing screw chokes.

Shotgun choking is the constriction of the bore, at the muzzles, that forces the leading part of the shot charge to speed-up, lengthening the shot string which holds the pattern together longer. The only important measurement of the choke is the amount of constriction from the bore diameter. In other words, the actual dimensions of the bore and choke are not as important as the difference between them.

Choke constriction is referred to in thousandths of an inch (Full choke equals .035 inches) in this country. In England the term is "points of choke" which fortunately means the same thing (35 thousandths is 35 points of choke). All of the other terms (Improved Cylinder, Modified, Full or quarter choke, half choke etc.) are relatively meaningless to the gunsmith. By all means, ask him to open your choke to Improved Cylinder or whatever, but also ask him what that dimension will be.

I just measured a 30-inch Fox gun made in 1920 at .035 inches in the right barrel and .039 inches in the left. This is what I call "full and fuller" and is ideal because it can be opened to any dimension and the wall thickness is suitable for screw chokes.

Opening the chokes is no great chore and many gun shops offer the service. How they do it and how the finished job looks, and shoots, is another matter. Just the other day I heard of another "choke reaming job" that left the muzzles rough and off-shooting. This is nearly always the product of careless reaming from the muzzle end.

Both Heckman and Merrington work from the breech end with piloted tools. Merrington reams to nearly the final dimension then finishes with abrasive honing. Heckman uses just the hones. Now I've heard some say this isn't always the best way to do the job because the barrels may not be perfectly straight and the pilot will push the choke off center. When I've got machining to do that relies on alignment, I use a piloted tool if possible.

I've successfully reamed them from the muzzle, but only with sharp tools, light cuts and extreme care. Because this work is always done blind (you can't see

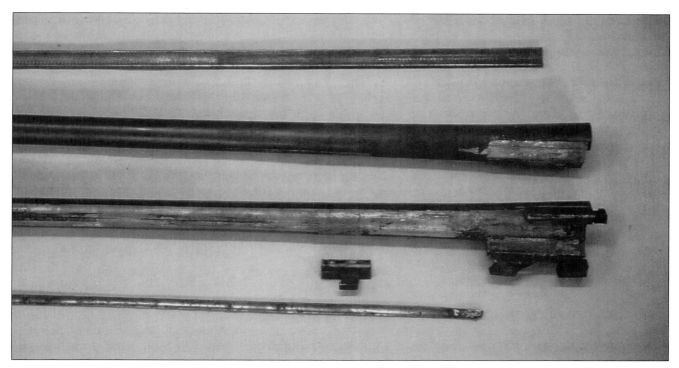

These Parker barrels have been stripped to show their construction. From the top down are the top rib, left barrel with integral bar, right barrel with rib extension and dovetail lumps still attached, the forend loop and the bottom rib. Normally barrels would not be disassembled this far because extreme heat is required to braze the breeches back together.

the tool) success is a matter of developing a feel for the technique and constantly checking with gauges as the work progresses. Regardless of the method used, or who does it, experience and care are the watchwords. These days I leave all bore work to specialists.

If your choke was poorly reamed (can you see any tool marks?) a professional can straighten it, remove the tool marks and measure and alter what is left.

Some gunsmiths will open chokes to a given dimension and "shoot-in" for a pattern percentage with a given load. The shooting part takes lots of time and can cost much more per tube as opposed to working from a given dimension. In any case, it is up to you to determine what chokes are appropriate for your shooting.

Screw-in chokes are interchangeable tubes installed at the muzzle and are offered in a great variety of constrictions. Let me first say that Heckman believes that a fixed choke will always give a better pattern, and theoretically, I agree. He offers screw-in chokes with stainless steel tubes available in .005-inch increments. There is no doubt that this system offers incredible versatility.

Merrington does not install choke tubes but refers his clients to Briley, of Houston Texas, who has the biggest name in the business. Briley offers a multitude of combinations including tubes for steel shot and eccentric choking.

Most of the guns that we are interested in have relatively thin-walled barrels and it is in your best in-terests to deal with someone having a great deal of experience and excellent judgment. Heckman says he needs a minimum of .805 inches outside diameter at the muzzle and even wall thickness to install screw-in chokes.

I must admit that until recently I considered it a heresy to install screw-in chokes in a classic side-by-side. I have amended that opinion to exclude the more common American guns that have already been altered from their original configuration. These guns are the best candidates for a custom project and if you want the versatility for different game or targets, by all means consider screw-in chokes. And be sure that they are the flush-at-the-muzzle variety. It gags me to see protuberances, or knurled rings, at the muzzles of side-by-sides.

Merrington adamantly points out the greater responsibility of screw-in choke users. "The chokes must be cleaned regularly and always installed fully seated. They must be inspected for clean and undamaged threads," he says. Ignoring this advice could lead to the muzzles parting company from your barrels.

What if you have a good gun with a really trashed set of barrels? I just bought a horribly pitted 16-bore Fox ejector gun that I will consider sending out to have the barrels "sleeved." Sleeving is the process for replacing the barrel tubes but retaining the original breech section. It entails removing the ribs and cutting the barrels off about 3-1/2 inches from the breech. New barrel tubes are lathe-turned to match the original contours. The breech section is bored out through the chambers of this "mono-block." New tubes are fitted through the mono-block, replacing the chamber metal as well. The ribs and forend loop are re-installed and all is soldered back together. The chambers and extractor recesses recut and the barrels blued.

In my opinion a quality sleeving job is cosmetically finished as well as structurally sound. I know of one "best grade" London gun that shows slight bulges in the chambers because the sleeves were not perfectly fit to the mono-block. This gun, and several others I've seen, shows mis-matched bluing on the outside as obvious as a leather elbow patch on a corduroy jacket. Others show an obvious solder joint and some are so poorly mated the joint is covered with chicken track engraving. I've also seen sleeving done so perfectly that the bluing was identical on both parts and the joints were so well-fit as to be invisible except under magnification. Sleeving is also referred to as "retubing" and, if done well, is a great way to resurrect an otherwise ruined gun.

A few years back folks were having Damascus guns re-tubed to shoot modern ammunition. These days, shooting "in proof" twist barrels, with black powder or moderate pressure cartridges, is becoming the rage. I do hate to see a fine set of Damascus barrels cut off.

At the time of sleeving the barrels can be lengthened or shortened, to add weight or lighten them. New ribs may be needed, the price increases accordingly. I am a big fan of this process for good guns that can be bought inexpensively because of bad or burst barrels. The notion of brand-new tubes will gladden the heart of those who want to shoot the hell out of an old gun.

There are a few barrelsmiths around the country who make complete double-barrel sets from scratch. I have tremendous admiration for the craftsmanship involved in melding all of the pieces and parts and then fitting them to an existing gun.

Galazan offers milled steel barrel ribs, bar tube barrels and even chopper lump barrel sets with ribs, extractors and forend loops installed. These must be individually constructed for a specific gun, then hand-fitted to the action and forend. Heckman Specialties has just begun making 12-gauge barrel tubes for sleeving and blanks suitable for boxlock barrel construction.

If you must have an extra set of barrels for your gun there are a few other alternatives. Sometimes barrels can be retrofit from another gun of the same frame size, but don't expect them to be interchangeable between guns. On mass-produced American guns the barrels may fit at the hook and hinge pin and even fit "on face" at the breech. The problems arise when fitting the locking mechanism which must be individually mated between the barrels and action.

London Guns of Santa Barbara, California is making Winchester M-21 barrel sets in .410, 28-gauge and 20-gauge for guns with 20-gauge frames. They duplicate the originals but are only sold through dealers who are capable of fitting, finish choking and bluing them. They are offered in-the-white with a solid rib and ejectors.

Whether you're fixing up an old double or creating a new custom shotgun, the barrels you've got could probably stand some improvement. At the minimum, the chambers should be full-length for the cartridges you shoot, chokes modified to your needs and the bores honed to as-new condition. The rest of the modifications are purely optional although I can see a fine custom gun with all of them. Barrel sleeving will bring a ruined gun back to life. No matter your choice, be sure to deal with a professional to avoid disappointing or dangerous results.

Chapter 4

Proper Repair vs. The Bloody Bodgers

Double-gunning is becoming so popular good used guns are getting hard to find. Many of the doubles that languished in closets for all those years that pumps and autos were in vogue have now been shot and hunted for a decade or more and are showing the signs of use. As a matter of fact, most guys I know who are buying used doubles, know the gun is going to need some work before it's right. Unfortunately, more often than not, it isn't the imagined stock bending or choke modifications. The guns are in need of mechanical repair to render them safe and functional.

As for custom shotgun projects, all of the functional aspects of the shotgun must be faultless before any other work is done. The juicy parts, altering and shaping the metalwork, designing and crafting the stock and embellishing with checkering and engraving, all come after insuring their function.

Although I have interviewed five full-time gunsmiths that specialize in double gun repair, I've yet to find any "problem" American side by side. (That isn't to say that there aren't problems with American guns, and some makes always seem to have the same problems.) Universally these fellows hold the belief that neglect, abuse and plain old wear are the prime factors contributing to guns needing repair. A close second was quaintly expressed by John "Jack" Rowe, an

A small-bore Fox action has a coil mainspring, hammer (with integral cocking lever in front) and sear. The left side of the action is still assembled.

English-trained gunsmith who said, "If the bloody bodgers could keep their hands off things we wouldn't have the work we do."

"Bodgering," and "tinkering," are just two of the many derogatory terms used by qualified gunsmiths to describe amateur work done by individuals who don't understand double guns. Each of the gunsmiths told me tales of peened lumps, filed ejectors, "trigger jobs" and basket cases that eventually ended up in an expert's shop for proper repair.

So do yourself a favor, don't try this in your garage. And before you drop off your Parker at the local gun shop, see how many doubles he has on the rack for repair.

All doubles have the same basic parts and same problems. With an overall understanding of the guns you can go on to learn specifics about the gun that you're most interested in. I'm going to confine this chapter to the more popular guns that are good candidates for general hunting and shooting.

Generally speaking, the firing mechanisms of all doubles have twin hammers, sears and their attendant hammer springs and sear springs. Some guns have separate firing pins (strikers) and some are integral with the hammers. All have mechanical levers of some sort that cock each hammer. These parts must function individually, but also in harmony with one another. In other words, if the timing is off on the left ejector, the problem could be way back in the action, caused by a short sear nose.

To hold the barrels to the action, all guns have a hinge pin that the barrels rotate on and a locking mechanism that locks them shut. Fox and L.C. Smith guns have a "rotary bolt" that locks a barrel extension slotted into the breech of the action. Most of the rest have some type of underbolt (under the barrels) that engages the "bite" or notch on the barrel lump. The

most popular British locking mechanism is the Purdey double-underbolt that engages two lumps.

(Most double gun terms are very graphic although the shear number of them, American, British and European, can be confusing. The "barrel lump", for example is the only thing on the bottom of the barrels except the forend "loop" which graphically describes itself. The "extension" extends from the back of the barrels behind the top rib and the "locking bolt" serves to "bite" into the notch on the lump. Are you with me?)

Parker guns have a single underbolt with the newer guns having a "bolt plate" in the bite that can be replaced to tighten worn guns. Winchester M-21s have an underbolt with a wedge-shaped end that engages the barrel lump with a simple stop-screw to adjust the engagement. Anson & Deeley (A&D) design boxlocks employ a Purdey double-underbolt.

The most common problem with double guns is described by the catch-all term "loose." This means that the barrels can be wiggled one way or the other. One of the problems causing a loose gun is described using the British vernacular; "the gun is off face."

"Off face" means that the barrel breeches don't fully contact the standing breech of the action, which is the face that the firing pins protrude through. This is usually caused by a worn hinge pin or "hook" (the hook-shaped part of the lump that contacts the hinge pin).

The other problem causing a loose gun is a worn locking bolt or worn bite on the lump, or barrel extension. If the locking bolt is appreciably worn it is obvious that the breech of the barrels won't be held tightly against the breech face of the action.

Although this general problem of looseness can relate to either the locking bolt or the barrels being off

The Fox rotary bolt, almost identical to L.C. Smith, engages the slot in the barrel extension to lock the gun.

face, the two are so closely related that curing one problem often cures the other. By and large, American gunsmiths prefer to work on the locking system and British gunsmiths work on the barrel hook or hinge pin. The different approaches may be because of way that the guns were originally manufactured (and the way gunsmiths in those countries were taught to work on them).

American guns, for example, were mass-produced. Tolerances were determined for the size of the hinge pin, barrel hook and the distance between the hook and the standing breech (which is the dimension that puts the gun "on face"). The parts were manufactured, checked for tolerance and assembled with the minimum of hand-fitting. One would like to think that the higher-grade guns had more hand-fitting but that wasn't necessarily the case.

All double guns have a locking bolt that fits with some sort of tapered arrangement to compensate for wear. The shooter can see evidence of this in a new gun that has its top lever slightly off to the right. As the bolting mechanism wears, the tapered surfaces compensates and the top lever moves closer to center. With some guns, the lever can be a bit to the left of center and the gun will still lock up tightly. With other guns, such as small-bore Foxes, other internal parts restrict the movement of the lever past center and the gun can be loose even though the lever is nearly centered.

In contrast, all of the better quality British guns were assembled and fitted by hand. Tolerances were judged on an individual basis, and were generally much closer than those found on American guns. When the barrels were fit to the action or "jointed", their breeches were smoked from the soot of a lamp to show where they mated. Then they were hand-filed to a very exacting fit. The English call the process "blacking it down."

If the barrels are determined to be off face, they are "rejointed" to fit them back on face. English-trained gunsmiths most often rejoint a gun by replacing the hinge pin or by "piecing the hook."

Most British and German guns have replaceable hinge pins that are screwed into the action. Some have caps over the pins. Oversize pins can be made and installed by top-notch professionals.

Parkers and M-21s have removable hinge pins and parts are semi-available. The fact is that seldom do either of these guns need rejointing.

Fox and L.C. Smith guns have solid hinge pins as do most Anson & Deeley-style boxlocks. These can be replaced with considerable difficulty. Old Smith catalogs boast that the guns "never shoot loose" but here are plenty of loose "Elsies" out there. If the pins can't be readily removed then the hook gets the attention.

"Piecing the hook" means inserting a piece of tough steel in the hook area of the barrel lump. This is commonly done by milling out the center of the arc and dovetailing in a new piece of steel large enough to cover most of the radius of the hook. The face of the arc is then very carefully dressed down to leave just a few thousandths of extra metal to set the barrels back on face. To do a "bang-up job" the breech is then "blacked down" tightly fitting the barrels to the action.

One might think that the hook could be welded to add metal. Since the barrels are held together with solder and sometimes the lump itself is brazed in place, British proof laws state that the barrels must be reproved if any heat is applied to the lump, so this is avoided.

Gunsmith Abe Chaber tells me that he has, on occasion, employed the services of an extremely talented TIG (tungsten inert gas) welder to build up a hook. He doesn't recommend it though, as there are few who know the proper steel alloys and can assure perfect heat control. Some Birmingham, England gunsmiths now use "spray welding" or "metalizing" to build up a hook

A Purdey double-underbolt sits on top of the lumps, just above the bites. Shiny spots on the bolt show the locking surfaces. The barrel loop, for attaching the forend is to the left.

Proper Repair vs. The Bloody Bodgers   89

The Anson & Deeley boxlock action is partially disassembled with the hammer spring, hammer, sear and sear spring on the bench. The same parts for the left side of the action are still assembled.

and this can be identified on recently imported guns by the yellowish tinge to the hook's working surface.

No matter the method, piecing or building up the hook and jointing the barrels should be left to the experts. When the barrels are set back slightly, the locking bolt engagement invariably tightens or as Rowe says, "you've got bite again."

Since American guns were seldom fitted to extremely close tolerance at the face, American gunsmiths often work on the locking bolt. The theory is that unless there is an appreciable amount of wear to the hinge pin, tightening the locking surfaces will bring the face back into tolerance and hold the gun tightly closed.

Abe Chaber will not repair a locking bolt but prefers to make and hand-fit a new one. Chaber apprenticed with a true "old-world" and "old-school" German gunsmith and I hold his techniques and approach in the highest regard. Unfortunately, hand-making parts can be quite expensive.

Rowe and Dennis Potter often "half sole" locking bolts to repair and renew them. This operation entails milling out a section of the bolts working surface, closely fitting a slightly oversize piece of tough steel, silver brazing it in place and hand-fitting it to the gun. If one has the skill, experience and good judgment that Potter and Rowe do, this can be an effective and permanent repair.

None of the gunsmiths I spoke with would half sole a Purdey bolt nor would they soak a client to

hand-make a new bolt for a beat-up Ithaca Flues model. Each fellow has the knowledge of, and respect for, the quality of the original manufacture of the gun and can be relied upon to judge the proper approach for each individual repair.

The next question on my gunsmith survey was about ejector problems. Contrary to my expectations, these fellows don't see many problems with the ejectors of American guns. Potter said he occasionally has to tune Fox ejectors but most often it is simply deburring them. Chaber added that a lot of Fox ejector problems are cause by cracked forends because the wood is so very thin.

Everyone said that Parker ejectors are overly complicated but short of an occasional broken spring they work fine. They are difficult to repair when there is a problem. More than one nitwit has hot-blued a M-21 forend iron without completely disassembling it. This will either soften the spring tension or gunk-up the works with bluing salts.

Chaber cautioned me that some of the ejector problems he sees are caused by the forend loop being slightly loose. Because a loose loop can be difficult to detect, folks seem to want to work on the ejectors instead, and oftentimes screw things up. In fact, each of these gunsmiths complained about having to fix ejectors that had been "monkeyed with." Here again, only trust these repairs to those who will ferret out the problem before breaking out the file.

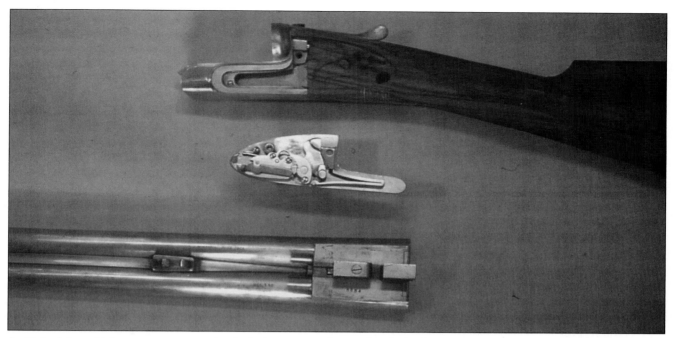

A sidelock has all the same parts as a boxlock, just mounted to a plate behind the action. In the works, this custom project started with a Bertuzzi metalwork featuring Holland style lockwork.

Sears and hammers are other mechanical parts. The sear is simply a lever rotating on an axis. The sear "nose" slips into the hammer notch (or bent as the English call it) and holds the hammer in the cocked position. When the sear "tail" (nose to the front, tail to the rear) is lifted by the trigger, the sear nose rotates downward disengaging the hammer notch, allowing the hammer to fall.

Needless to say, sears and hammers present the greatest liability to gunsmithing. Their engagement must be positive and their fit to each other and to the pins that they ride on, must be exact. If there is a problem with the sear or hammer notch, there is a potentially fatal flaw.

In the case of sear or hammer work, Abe Chaber's doctrine of "make and fit a new part" becomes universal unless factory parts are available.

The engaging surface of a sear nose is measured in thousandths of an inch. Likewise, the hammer notch of the Fox gun on my bench is but .020 inches deep. Not only do the surfaces need to be correctly mated but the relative hardness of each part must be equal. If the hammer is harder than the sear nose, each time they slip into engagement, the sear will wear on the harder hammer. If the sear is harder than the hammer, each time the gun is fired tiny bits of metal will be shaved off like wood under a block plane.

I recently saw this exact scenario in a fine English shotgun that was brought to me because one barrel wouldn't fire. The hammer had been welded to repair a crack. The heat of welding drew the temper out of the hammer, softening the steel. When I disassembled the gun, all that was left of the hammer notch was a little pile of oily slivers in front of the sear nose.

The owner is lucky that he didn't blow up a sporting clays station, or worse, when he closed the gun.

Springs power the shotgun. Hammer springs fire the gun, sear springs hold the sears in engagement and the top lever spring holds the gun closed and snaps the lever shut. The top lever spring holds the bolt closed when the barrels are down. Springs also power the ejectors and engage the ejector sears when they aren't needed.

The majority of American double guns have coil springs which present a mixed blessing. Coil springs seldom, if ever break or fail to function. (On the other hand, they always feel mushy and they will never display that art and mystery that is the heritage of European gunmaking). Unless they are loaded with dirt, badly rusted or subjected to incompetent disassembly, coil springs work. That's all there is to it. For replacing the occasional soft coil spring, most of us 'smiths hoard junker guns for the springs and other parts we seldom need.

Fox sear springs, old-style Parker top lever springs, all Parker ejector springs and most L.C. Smith springs are flat or V-type springs. Spring making was a specialty in England and their are still a few who enter "springmaker" as their occupation on tax forms. What I'm trying to say is that even British-trained Jack Rowe will send a complicated sidelock mainspring to England to be duplicated by a springmaker rather than make one himself.

The few gunsmiths that make sophisticated V springs are always reluctant to do so. If a gunsmith doesn't hesitate and caution you as to the complication and expense of making a sidelock mainspring, I wouldn't trust him with the job. L.C. Smith mainsprings are the exception because of their simplicity.

I'll note that pre-1913 ones are of higher quality than the later versions.

Top lever springs on British and European guns do break all too frequently. You'll know when it happens because the lever will flop around without tension. They are usually relatively simple V-springs, and if the pieces don't get lost, are not too difficult to make. There are a few "universal" top lever springs available and sometimes these can be modified to fit. If not, the gunsmith starts with a piece of spring stock and duplicates the original. (And by the way, a gun with a broken top lever spring is definitely unsafe to shoot. This spring maintains the tension of the locking bolt to the bite when the gun is fastened.)

I want to bring up an important point about double gun repair. There are several talented gunsmiths around the country who can duplicate virtually any mechanical part for virtually any shotgun. The trick is to have a model to duplicate. Major problems arise when the parts are lost or missing. Even if the problem parts are badly worn or broken, they give the repairman something to work from. Blindly imagining and making a part can be an exercise is futility and financial ruin. Yours or the gunsmith's.

(Several years ago I had the opportunity to buy a high-quality A&D boxlock for a couple hundred dollars. But the forend was gone, missing-in-action. Someone out there probably has it. As this was a hand-fit gun from a small Birmingham maker, long out of business, I passed on the good deal. I've often wondered how many times that gun has been sold for a bargain price without ever being fixed.)

Another problem I see cropping up has come with the popularity of shooting hammer guns. All of these guns are around 100 years old, most have Damascus barrels and few are without some need of repair. Double guns do wear out and some get so worn that they just stop working without any specific part breaking or failing. If a gun is sadly worn on the outside more often than not the mechanism is in a similar state.

One nightmare comes to mind. A fellow purchased a worn-out British double that was marginally functional but had a terrible stock. He spent the first grand for a decent, if amateur, stock job. Then he brought it to a repair gunsmith who fixed a few problems. By this time he had about $3,500 invested and it still needed a couple thousand dollars worth of work when it came into my friend's shop. That fellow now owns a completely refinished and rebuilt genuine British boxlock that might resell for $2,000. Imagine what he could have purchased with the cumulative investment.

No matter what gun you're buying for what purpose, it is wise to have it checked out before the sale is finalized. Most reputable dealers, and some who are not, allow a five-day inspection period before the sale is considered a done deal. Make an appointment with a competent gunsmith and either bring him the gun or have it sent directly. Tell the dealer what you are doing. The gunsmith can function test it and give you a really good idea if, or what, work is needed. The extra dollars spent early on could save more pain than a case of aspirin could relieve.

Anything can go wrong with any kind of gun. I've got one friend/client that has *everything* go wrong with *all* his guns. He is prone to bad luck, besides his inclination to tinker with them. I seldom have problems with my own guns which is fortunate because they might never get fixed.

An every other year strip-cleaning of your often-shot favorite will help to nip any problem in the bud.

Chapter 5

Double Triggers and Trigger Guards

From the shooter's perspective, triggers may seem small and insignificant, hidden in a colorful action mated to a walnut stock and long, blued barrels. But when one realizes they are the sole connection responsible for firing the shot, triggers take on a whole new importance. Just three quarters of an inch of finger flesh contact a narrow sliver of steel to make this complicated mechanism function. No wonder gunmakers put so much effort into getting the triggers just right.

In studying the nuances of triggers and trigger pulls, it's best to begin at the beginning-with an explanation of how triggers function.

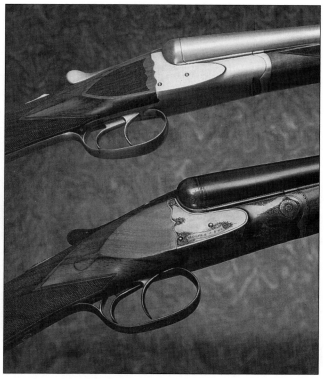

A couple of Hughes/Fox custom guns, a 20-bore above in-the-white and a finished 12-gauge below, both feature extensive metalwork. The triggers have been slimmed, refined and shaped for comfortable shooting. The trigger guards were bench-made, scaled to the action size and shaped to please and prevent recoil problems. The lower guard has a beaded edge.

While the reader studies the accompanying sketch, I'll explain what takes place when the trigger is pulled. The safety is slid forward to allow trigger movement. As the index finger pulls the pad back, the trigger rotates on the axis pin and the rear of the trigger blade raises the sear tail. As the sear tail is lifted, the sear rotates on its axis, lowering the sear nose, disengaging it from the hammer notch. The freed hammer, powered by the mainspring, swings forward to strike the cartridge.

Most doubles are cocked by opening the action and lowering the barrels which rotates the hammers rearward by one sort of mechanical arrangement or another. As the hammers approach the cocked position the curved sear face is held against the curved part of the hammer by the pressure of the sear spring on the sear bar. The sear nose slips into the hammer notch and is held there by the combined pressure of the sear spring and the mainspring. In the meantime, the trigger spring pressure lightly holds the triggers up against the sear tail.

The hammer notch and sear nose are cut at a 90-degree angle where they mate to one another. Although the engagement is very slight, the sharp faces of the hardened steel parts provide a sure grip under spring tension.

The sketch and explanation describe a boxlock gun. The parts are the same for a sidelock except for the addition of an interceptor (safety) sear and mounting them on a sideplate rather than inside the action body.

There, enough technical explanation, I'd much rather present some concepts. All this movement inside the gun takes place so quickly and smoothly that all the shooter feels is the tension of the mainsprings compressing when the gun is opened. Then we hear the *snick* of the sear noses engaging the hammer notches.

The trigger finger positions the hand on the wrist of the stock. This location helps the stockmaker determine the location of the comb where it curves down to meet the wrist. The British call this the thumbhole and it is located so many "inches from the front trigger". Of course, length of pull and the pitch of the butt are measured from the front trigger. The stockmaker lays out the buttstock's every dimension (except cast) from the center of the front trigger.

So take out your favorite double gun and let's examine the principals of trigger ergonomics.

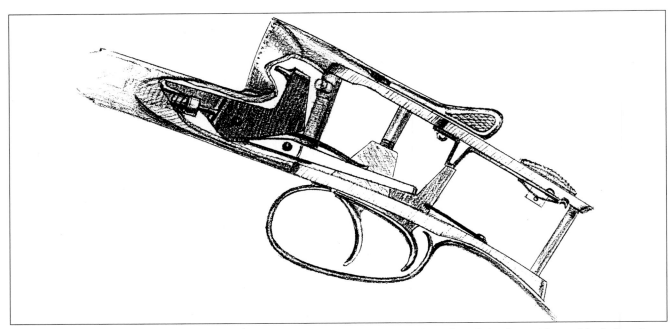

Illustrating the mechanics of trigger pull - a cutaway view of a Fox action. The safety slides forward to unblock the trigger which, when pulled, lifts the sear tail, disengaging the sear from the hammer notch, which fires the gun. Except for the coil mainspring, the Fox mechanism is very similar to an Anson & Deeley boxlock. Illustration by Thomas L. Eversman

Visually, you will first notice that the trigger pads are twisted to the right side for a right-handed shooter. (I'll discuss adaptation for lefties later.) This twist allows the trigger finger smooth access to the pad and a pull motion is more correct for the angle of the finger. The twist also makes it easier to slide the finger off the front trigger to fire the second shot. Try it, you'll see what I mean.

Good trigger positioning puts the rear trigger pad almost directly behind the front. That did sound obvious, but take a close look. The two trigger are placed in slots beside each other. If each were not bent slightly towards the center, they wouldn't line up. Both triggers are twisted and canted.

Checking a bit closer, with a small ruler you will find somewhere between 7/8 of an inch and 1 inch between the two trigger pads. Although I've never seen a standard dimension referenced, I've measured many guns to find this norm. They need to be close enough together so the front trigger isn't a reach, and far enough apart that a large finger can fit in between. The front trigger is straighter and longer than the rear and their respective placement in the guard bow is for reasons besides good looks.

The normal position for the front trigger is about mid-point front to back in the guard bow. This allows plenty of room to find the front trigger without looking. On high-quality guns the rear of the trigger guard bow will closely follow the curve of the rear trigger with not more than 1/4 of an inch between them. This dimension is especially important

on a gun that generates any appreciable amount of recoil. The closer the back of the guard is to the rear trigger, the less it will interfere with the position of the hand and the less likely you will be slammed in the second finger when the gun is fired. You might never notice this relationship unless you have a gun that bruises your middle finger. If so, the only cures that I know of are a rubber pad on the guard or a new trigger guard of better design.

Making a new trigger guard that is appropriately shaped for a particular shotgun represents a couple of long days work in my shop. Some forged

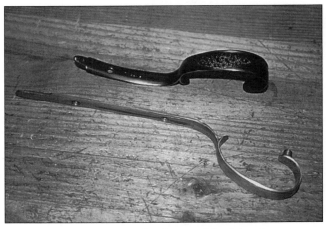

Two custom trigger guards, the rust blued version was engraved by Michael Dubber and has a beaded edge. The straight-grip guard is for a 20-gauge, single-trigger gun and is yet to be polished.

The author TIG welds the rear tang to a forged and partially shaped bow. The mounting stud was previously welded in place.

guards and a few castings are available but they never seem to have the correct shape, proportions or attaching devise for the gun I'm working on. So, I make them from scratch. When building a custom shotgun, a new trigger guard, designed for properly shaped and positioned triggers, with a sexy oval shape for the bow, adds a great deal of character to the gun.

There are several ways to make a trigger guard, but first it must be designed and drawn to scale. I know gunmakers that machine them from solid blocks of steel and I can imagine two handfuls of oily chips left in piles on the milling machine table. I employ the blacksmith's approach, fabricating the guard from three pieces of steel.

First, a 3/4-inch wide, 1/8-inch thick piece of strap steel is forged to form the bow and rear guard return (the pointed part behind the rear trigger). The forged bow is then ground and filed to create the front-to-back taper seen when looking at the bottom of the gun. A mounting stud - threaded to fit the action - is welded to the front of the bow and assembled to the gun with triggers in place to verify its form and function. To make the rear tang, a flat 1/2-inch-wide strap is bent up at one end to mate to the

rear of the bow at the appropriate angle and location. Again, this is checked in place on the gun before welding the two together. The rest of the work - filing the contour tapers and beaded edge - is done almost exclusively with hand files.

A bench-made trigger guard can have an extra long extension running well down the straight grip of the stock. It can follow the curve of a half or full pistol-grip. It can be made to mate up to a steel grip cap or it can be filed with an interesting finial on its end. If well-made and finely finished it will lend a look of harmony that is lacking in many American shotguns. (Most single-trigger doubles have guards designed for double-triggers. For example, M-21 Winchesters gave up double-triggers early in their production but the large guard bow looks like it was never redesigned for the smaller single-trigger. Note the guard I made for the M-21 shown elsewhere in this book.)

British and European triggers and guards tend to receive more attention than those found on American factory guns. On "best" grade work, the trigger guards give me the sense of a mini-sculpture because they are so pleasingly contoured and finely made. Sometimes you will find a raised bead along

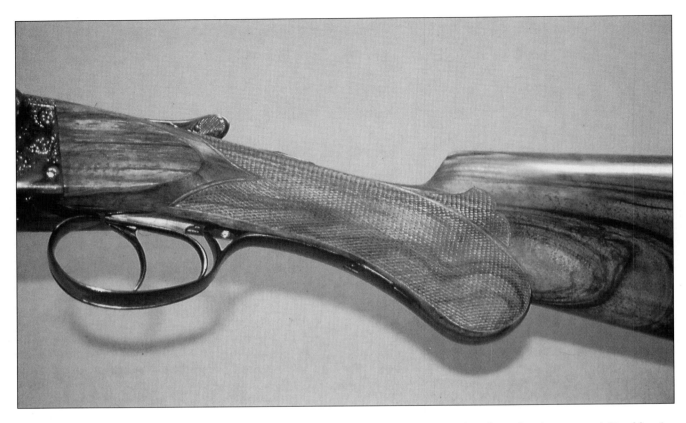

A Hughes/Fox custom 16-guage with a round knob semi pistol-grip stock sporting a bench-made trigger guard. Double triggers work well with an open pistol-grip.

their right edge, referred to as a "rolled edge" by some. This is ostensibly to provide a smooth spot to rest your finger when preparing to shoot, but I think it is done mostly to add class. I've heard it called an innovative idea and even seen it attributed to Boss Co. The fact is, I've seen many 18th Century (pre-Boss) flintlock fowlers with beaded guard bows.

Another trick item sometimes found on the upper crust of British and European shotguns is the articulated, or hinged, front trigger. The front trigger pad and blade are made as two separate parts, screwed together, with a spring-loaded hinge between them. The trigger pad only pivots forward, and the purpose is to prevent the trigger finger from being bruised by the front trigger, when firing the second trigger. They might even work with a heavy-recoiling double rifle, but I've never had this problem, even with a 6-1/2-pound 12-bore.

A fine looking trigger guard and "feel good" triggers don't mean much without proper trigger weights, or pulls. And what exactly is a proper trigger pull? I've heard and read all of the same theories as everyone else, so I'm not even going to repeat them. I've also consulted five different fellows who make their living working on double guns and they mirror my own opinion: 4 pounds for the front trigger and 4-1/2 pounds for the rear trigger is as light as they should be. Lest you think that this is an American opinion, two of my associates served apprenticeships in England.

The rear trigger pull weight is always heavier than the front for several reasons. The extra leverage afforded with a longer distance from its pivot makes it feel lighter. The rear trigger is pulled in a more upward motion which is more convenient for the finger, again making it feel lighter. I've also heard it said that the right barrel fires 70 percent of the shots over a hunting gun's lifetime. A little harder pull is insurance for the pounding the second sear takes while it remains engaged. This insurance helps to prevent the gun from doubling. Someone else told me that a harder rear trigger pull makes it less likely that you will blow the second shot on the bird that you missed with the first. Be that one as it may.

When we talk about trigger pulls there are two different items on the agenda: the "weight of pull" - measured in pounds with a gauge - and the "creep," which refers to the actual movement, or travel, of the trigger before the sear "breaks." I don't have any way of measuring the amount of creep in a trigger pull so I judge by first watching the trigger as I pull

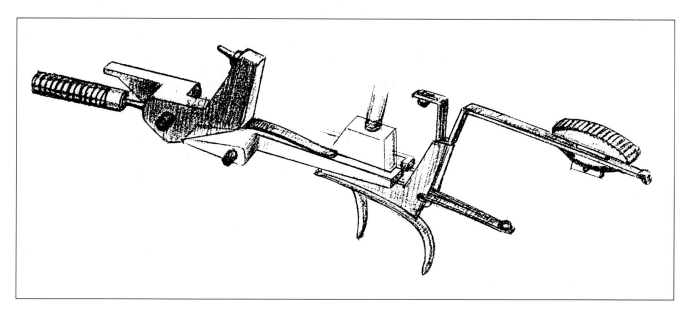

A very accurate representation of the mechanical parts of the trigger/firing system of a Fox. Illustration by Thomas L. Eversman.

it. Then I feel for movement while pulling the trigger with my eyes closed. The second method actually works better for me. (If you are going to try this, be sure that the gun is unloaded and you've got snap caps in the chambers).

Both the weight and the "crispness" (which describes a lack of creep) are equally important to a great trigger pull. A trigger that breaks at 4 pounds without creep is all that I can ask for.

There are some mechanical principals that come into play which I will briefly cover. The Fox gun in the drawing, as with all boxlocks, has long sear bars that place the lifting point of the sear well behind its axis. The mechanical advantage of leverage is tremendous and when the trigger breaks at 4 pounds of pull, there is nearer to 8 pounds present at the sear/notch engagement. The extra leverage that is great for pull weight will also proportionally magnify the amount of movement, or creep. In other words, the sear tail must be lifted about twice the distance of the actual sear nose-to-hammer notch engagement. Furthermore, because of the limited room for placing the parts in a boxlock action, the angle of the notch cannot be exactly square to the sear, or the hammer pivot points; it must be backcut slightly, which makes for a harder pull.

A sidelock, on the other hand, allows more room to perfectly position the parts for the maximum advantage of the angle of the notch. But because the lock is closer to the triggers the leverage advantage of a long sear bar is impossible. I mention all of this because some folks are sure to say, "You can always get a better pull with a sidelock."

This gets back to the workbench view my consultants and I share: If you can get a 4- to 4-1/2-pound, crisp trigger pull with either style of gun, the geometry isn't that important to the shooter.

The pull weight is mostly in the sear nose-to-notch angle. I have been avoiding the discussion of this relationship because this is the first place an amateur will want to attack with file. As Ontario, Canada gunmaker Les Paul says, "The pull can go from trying to yank a nail out of a two-by-four to closing the gun and it goes boom, boom". The weight of pull is mostly the result of this sear nose-to-notch angle.

For the perfect lock geometry, the angle of the sear nose should be the same as the angle of the hammer notch. That way they don't have to work against each other to disengage. They should contact across the entire face of each part and they should be free of any burrs or rounded edges. Both parts must be hardened equally so they don't wear on each other. For reasons of liability and because this is not a how-to piece, I'll leave it at that. Trigger pulls - and especially sears and notches - should be left to the experts.

Double triggers do malfunction and the most common problem is doubling, or both barrels firing when one trigger is pulled. Usually, the recoil from the first shot jars the second sear out of engagement. The shooter is so surprised when it happens that it feels like one blow. The extra pressure and recoil is hard on the barrel, action, stock and the shooter's body. That's not to mention how very disconcerting it is to everyone present.

Doubling is usually caused by a worn sear nose or hammer notch. Another cause can be the trigger blade being "hard-on" against the sear tail and preventing the sear nose from fully engaging the notch. There should be a "wink" of movement between the trigger blade and the sear tail which can be easily felt without disassembling the gun.

Many American guns have triggers that flop around in the trigger plate. Quite loose they are. This usually isn't a major problem, but it can effect a consistent trigger pull. They can be tightened by shimming and installing a new trigger pivot pin. You won't find that looseness in a good British gun and, if you disassemble one, you will find the triggers pivoting on a screw rather than a pin. And, although we all do it, one shouldn't test the safety by pulling on the triggers when it is engaged. The leverage exerts a tremendous strain on the pivot pin.

Another common problem that relates to these parts is the misfire. If the sear nose has been short-ened (by three successive owners of trying to improve the trigger pull), the hammer won't be fully cocked when the sear nose slips into the notch. The short sear will let the hammer pivot slightly forward, and even a small difference in the momentum of the hammer fall can lead to unsure detonation.

To include you left-handers for an ergonomically correct custom gun, the triggers can be altered to suit. By switching them side to side in the opposite slots in the trigger plate, the front trigger will be on the left side and vice versa. They might require internal fitting and will need to be bent and canted so that the pads accommodate. This also means that you will be firing the left barrel first so the barrel choking must be considered.

When building a custom double gun, I spend a great deal of time in and around the trigger mechanism. I trust that this discourse and the drawings will help you to understand some of their nuances.

Chapter 6

Single-Triggers For Doubles

During my early wingshooting career I was strictly a single-trigger man. From a single-shot Stevens to a M-12 pump to a series of over/unders, it wasn't until I was into my 30s that I switched to side-by-sides with double-triggers. Although there was some trepidation, I quickly learned to shift my finger for the second shot. Later I learned to select the tighter choke (rear trigger) when I needed it first.

I much prefer double-triggers for side-by-sides. I like the way they look and I like to have instant selection of barrel and choke. Most of all, I like my gun mechanisms simple and like taking an active part in their function.

Today, when one of my cronies insists that I try his new competition gun I inevitably find myself reaching for the nonexistent rear trigger to fire the second shot. Last fall, trying out the custom M-21 shown elsewhere, I missed the first shot on a pheasant and never got off the second as my finger searched for the other trigger. Thankfully, I now recover my senses quickly and adjust after the first mistake.

Any trigger manipulation requires some thought from the shooter. Learning to shoot a double-trigger gun is possible with a couple of rounds shooting doubles at skeet or sporting clays. It is when the shooter switches back and forth between guns that problems arise.

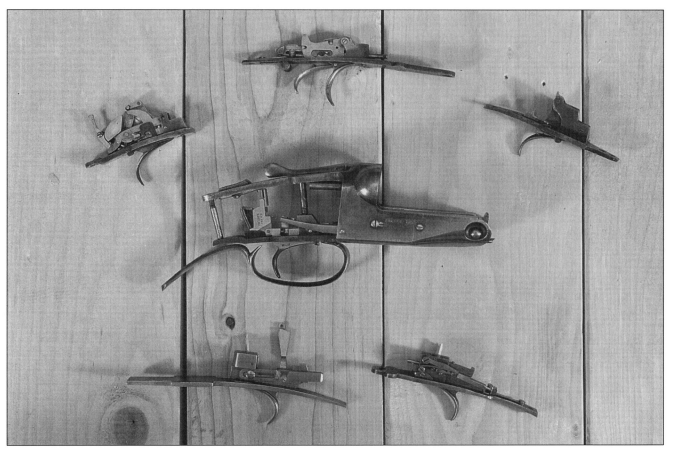

A Parker Trojan with a Miller single selective trigger surrounded by (clockwise from top left) an L.C. Smith "Hunter One" trigger, a double-trigger designed with a selector to fire either barrel, a mechanical single-trigger, an original Purdey single-trigger and a Holland & Holland-type trigger by Nick Makinson.

But even pulling single-triggers require some thought. A few months back I shot sporting clays with several guys who were mainly rifle shooters. One fellow seemed to be having difficulty with the single-trigger in his over/under gun. His second shot was delayed several times and he lost confidence in the gun and I haven't seen him back at the range.

I didn't make the connection at the time (trying to concentrate on my own mediocre shooting) but later realized that he wasn't operating the trigger properly. Being a rifle shooter he was squeezing the trigger and maintaining pressure - trying to fire the second shot without letting off. With a single-trigger one must slap the trigger then release it momentarily so the mechanism can shift to the other sear.

This may seem academic but not mentioning it will cause perfectly functional guns to be shipped to bewildered gunsmiths only to be returned with notes saying, "I can't find anything wrong with it." To test the trigger, in quick succession fire one barrel, let go of the trigger, then slap the trigger again. If the second shot doesn't fire, the problem's with the trigger. This won't work with snap caps and inertia triggers, but more on that later.

(A follow-up call confirmed that the rifle shooter's over/under worked fine when he tried this simple test with live ammunition.)

In researching this chapter I had the good fortune to stumble across H.P. "Herb" Stratemeyer, a German-trained gunsmith with more than 40 years in the double gun trade. Our interview revealed his crisp German mind for things mechanical, along with much sound advice. A good portion of his work involves competition guns firing as many as 50,000 rounds per year. Herb only works on high-grade guns and says that many of the single-trigger problems he sees are really shooter problems.

Single-triggers are a must for competition guns. There is no time for hand or finger shifting and the trigger must function every time.

"Doubling" is a common complaint with single-trigger guns. This suggests a mechanical problem, the first shot jarring off the second sear, resulting in both barrels firing. Stratemeyer says about half the time the doubling of a single-trigger gun is shooter mis-manipulation.

Consider this; if even the most experienced shooter switches gloves, hand position or adds a trigger shoe, he may unconsciously be maintaining the contact of his finger to the trigger. Herb asks them if they hear a single bellow when the gun doubles or if they hear the shot and a quick, hollow echo like slapping hands in an empty basement. If there is a fraction of a second between the shots, the gun is probably "fan firing," as in fanning a six-gun.

Fan firing is caused by the finger relaxing enough to allow the trigger to shift sears, but maintaining enough contact to jar the trigger after the first shot is fired. If you can imagine the recoil shoving the gun back, the trigger finger stays forward yet maintains enough contact that when the hand starts back in recoil it inadvertently pulls the trigger again. Stiff fingers on a cold day or even mild arthritis is enough to cause fan firing.

(I witnessed fan firing last week when an inexperienced shooter borrowed a single-trigger gun with a light pull weight. The gun doubled. I had just run a half-box of shells through it without a problem. Then another friend shot the gun several more times, no problem. It was a very chilly Montana morning.)

Of course, failure to fire at all is the number one complaint with single-triggers and this can be caused by a variety of things. The fact is, single-triggers are likely the first part, or only part, of a good gun to go out of whack. All single-triggers are complicated mechanisms, and with their many tiny springs and screws, some remind me of the imagined perpetual-motion machine: Some don't even *look* like they could work!

The tolerances between parts must be absolutely minimal and the more parts they have the more critical the tolerances become as they magnify one another. I'm not even going to begin to try to explain how they work because there are dozens of different varieties and quite frankly, I don't understand many of them myself. I will separate out the basic varieties.

First is the inertia trigger, which has a small weight - the movement of which is slowed by inertia as the gun recoils. This "inertia block," as some call it, shifts the trigger to the second sear. The Browning trigger is an inertia trigger and Stratemeyer describes it as being "ingenious, well-made and usually reliable." The inertia trigger is one of the simplest single-triggers ever invented. Anyone who has one knows that the trigger works fine if you don't get the safety/selector switch stuck trying to change barrels while you're sliding the safety off. The most common inertia triggers are selective: There is a switch, lever or button that allows the shooter to select which barrel fires first.

The major problem with inertia triggers is that if the first barrel doesn't fire there is no recoil to shift the trigger to the second sear. In this case the selector must be manually switched to fire the second barrel. The effect is the same even if the problem is a dud cartridge and not the trigger. When testing an inertia trigger with snap caps, after pulling the first time one must rap the butt of the gun on the floor to simulate recoil and let the inertia block shift positions. (Don't break the buttplate!)

As for safety/selector jamming, I've heard more profanity from Browning Superposed shooters than any others, probably because of the number of Brownings. The button is set-up in an H pattern, rear to front on either side operates the safety. Shifting from right to left sides selects the barrel to be fired first. The problem occurs mostly with older guns as the safety has worn and loosened. A right-handed shooter will inadvertently push the button a bit to the left - not even trying to switch barrels - as he pushes forward to remove the safety. It jams in the middle just long enough to miss the shot. Conscious movement returns it to normal. The sure cure is to solder or pin the safety and selector together thus eliminating barrel choice with the problem.

Mechanical triggers are just that. If the first shot doesn't go off, just pull the trigger again and it will mechanically switch to the other sear. Many mechanical triggers are selective, but many are not. Selective mechanical triggers often have the selector located down on the trigger plate or on the trigger itself. The lever or button is pushed forward, back or to one side to shift the trigger to the other sear.

Many competition shooters and virtually all pigeon shooters prefer non-selective mechanical triggers. Why? The triggers are simpler, meaning there are fewer parts to go out of adjustment and there's no recoil to rely on. These shooters don't have to worry about choosing the choke with the selector because they set-up the trigger to fire the appropriate barrel first and change the choke tubes as needed.

It is virtually impossible to buy a new over/under gun off the shelf with double-triggers. "Bespoke," or ordered guns can be had either way but unless you're spending thousands of dollars for a hunting gun, you're really better off with double-triggers, especially for side-by-sides. Many newer over/under guns were designed to work with a single-trigger that was designed to work with the gun's mechanism. Side-by-sides, however, were not. (Witness the number of patents for single-trigger mechanisms for side-bys, each adapted to a type of gun that doesn't lend itself to a single-trigger mechanism). I'm sure to catch some flack over this opinion but probably not from working gunsmiths.

If you're really looking for problems, convert a double trigger gun to a single. That's not to say that aftermarket single-trigger mechanisms don't work, but it is very likely that the trigger you use wasn't designed for whatever gun you happen to have. If you're considering such a conversion there are several things to keep in mind.

As Herb Stratemeyer says, "Building a single-trigger is such a monumental task that few gunsmiths will take on the job." They are a labor of love and many of the fellows I've talked with shy away from it unless

It's easy to see the Miller logo on this Parker shotgun fitted with a single trigger.

the customer has to have a single-trigger and is willing to spend a great deal of money for the convenience.

Be sure to ask the maker if he has built a trigger for your brand of gun before. The learning curve for adapting the trigger to another gun can be enormous. Be sure that he asks you about trigger placement in the trigger guard bow as well as desired length and weight of pull. Another major consideration is how much does the gun need to be altered to adapt the gun to the trigger. This can become a nightmare if one ever decides to convert the gun back to double-triggers.

To my knowledge, there are just a few gunsmiths offering single-trigger conversions. Probably the best known is the Miller Single Trigger Company. The Miller trigger was invented in the first part of this century by the current Mr. Miller's father. They have been installed in most every type of double gun and have a reputation for reliability among the target shooters. Remember that those fellows are requesting non-selective triggers. It comes back adjusted, with no slack or take-up in the trigger pull and set to a specific pull weight.

Miller triggers are the mechanical type and can be had either selective or non-selective. All guns will have the web between the trigger slots cutaway to fit the trigger. Some guns must have their internal parts altered quite drastically to accommodate this conversion. Also be prepared for a wide shiny trigger with "MILLER" stamped on the side.

The Griffin & Howe single-trigger has been made for more than 20 years and has a reputation for reliability. Many gun owners don't realize they have a G&H trigger because they are pleasingly shaped and hard to identify externally. This is a mechanical, non-selective trigger and it is my understanding that they are a good choice for sidelock guns. Little alteration to the gun is required, but the safety must be automatic. (If your isn't, they will convert it to this mode.) The company won't install these triggers in competition guns. G & H also converts guns *back* to double-triggers and will adjust or repair other triggers.

Gunsmith Dennis Potter occasionally makes non-selective, mechanical single-triggers for boxlock guns. One of the best features of his trigger is that it requires little or no alteration to the gun and it can be easily reconverted to double-triggers.

Gunmaker Nick Makinson offers single-trigger conversions for British "best" sidelocks, both side-by-sides and over/under guns. He builds Holland & Holland and Purdey-style triggers and will tell you which is appropriate for British guns by other makers. Both triggers are mechanical; the Purdey is non-selective and the H & H semi-selective (which he will explain). Makinson's conversions include angling the trigger for right- or left-handed shooting as well as a new trigger guard or guard bow appropriately shaped and sized for the trigger. In other words, the conversion is complete and finished-up in the best London fashion.

As for factory-installed single-triggers in older guns, I've heard just about every one of them bad-mouthed by one gunsmith or another. If yours goes on the blink, your best off finding a gunsmith experienced with that particular type of trigger. Most of the pros I know have lost their shirts learning one or more particular type of trigger to the point that they can effect a repair that you will both be satisfied with.

You will be happy to know that gunsmith Abe Chaber says many single-trigger problems he sees are actually stock problems. If the tang screw has been repeatedly over-tightened, or the stock wood oil-soaked and compressed, the trigger won't function because the tangs are not being firmly held in the wood. Often re-bedding the stock, with no adjustment to the trigger, will cure the problem - especially with L.C. Smith guns.

I've heard more bad-mouthing of the Smith Hunter-One trigger than any other. "Mousetrap" is frequently the description and "someone tried to fix it" is usually the problem. These trigger mechanisms have many small parts and springs that must be adjusted in a logical and consistent order. Each moving part influences the other parts and no matter how sharp your gunsmith is, he is smarter if he leaves the repair to someone who has already invested the time it takes to learn the proper procedure.

If your modern double has a trigger problem, contact the manufacturer's repair service or locate a gunsmith familiar with the gun.

If you must convert your fine old gun, find the right guy and pay what he asks. Most of the originals and all of the conversion triggers are made entirely by hand. The gunsmiths who fit them are specialists. Even the least complicated are very complicated and require fine adjustment. And whatever you do with your single-trigger, don't call me.

Section 3

Engraving
and
Metal Finishes

Chapter 1

Why Engrave?

It is time to tackle the delicate subject of shotgun engraving by answering the most basic question: Why?

I've studied the history of sporting firearms all the way back into the 17th Century. Through the ages, all quality sporting guns from around the world have two things in common: They all have a barrel and they all have some amount of metal embellishment in the form of engraving. Until the mid-19th Century in Europe guns were made for the wealthy, not tools so much as functional art for the few privileged landholders who had a place to hunt and shoot. But even then, most all guns had at least a bit of engraving. They didn't make the transition to tools until mass-production met the vast expanses of North America where the common man could hunt. Engraving lends a sense of respect or notion of value beyond function that has never been completely abandoned. Even today the less-expensive models often have facsimile engraving to dress-up their utilitarian selves.

At the beginning of the 20th Century all of the American double gunmakers kept this tradition alive, witnessed by the fact that even the lowest grades, the Fox Sterlingworth, VH Parker and Field Grade L.C. Smith had rudimentary embellishment. And all of these makers offered a laundry list of grades, each increasing in desirability and sophistication with the amount of engraving and special features. So today, when we think about a custom, bespoke or collectible shotgun, we simply can't leave it naked.

In my custom gunmaking business I have two kinds of clients who have two entirely different attitudes towards having their projects engraved. One fellow, for whom I have built a series of single-shot target rifles, takes a very pragmatic approach to firearms embellishment. He wants the caliber engraved on the barrel, the sight plane matted, if appropriate, and just a modicum of border work to break-up the gun's metal surfaces. Each time I'm finishing a target rifle for this fellow I have to talk him into adding a bit to the engraving so he will have what I consider a complete project (as I know these guns will endure into the future). In retrospect, he has always been happy with the extra embellishment. But a best-quality rifle barrel and custom chambering reamer are vastly more important to him.

Another client starts thinking about suitable scroll styles and designs before we have chosen a stock blank for the project. In the early 1960s he bought a brand-new Winchester lever-action and sent if off to the legendary Arnold Griebel for full-coverage engraving in a Western theme. This fellow actually discovered custom gunmaking through his appreciation of firearms engraving.

When a fellow is having his first custom gun built he may start the project saying, "This is going to be a hunting gun so it won't need much engraving." Often, by the time the project nears completion, he will be excited and want to highly embellish the piece. I warn my new clients at the get-go, if they're serious about hunting with the gun not to get caught up in making a museum piece.

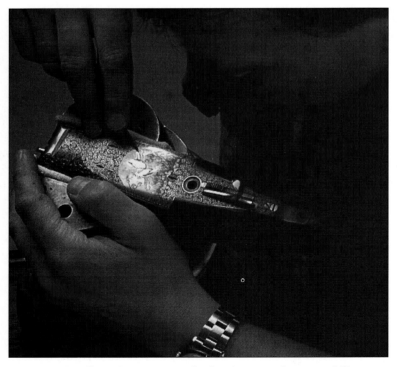

Engraver Geoffroy Gournet puts the finishing touches on a full-coverage Parker project. Note the loop pinched in his eyebrow and the padded ball vise. Geoffroy Gournet Photo.

Eric Gold's engraving on this Krieghoff shows deeply cut and backgrounded Germanic scroll with elaborate borders, lettering and a sporting vignette with a personal portrait. It has it all. The German gunmaker was reluctant to let the gun out of the factory unengraved because they didn't think anyone could match their own work.

Many of the highest-grade and most expensive shotguns made today fit the museum piece category. You may have seen Italian guns with nudes, London guns with dinosaur or Hollywood themes or American guns with game scenes inlaid extensively with gold. How many of these guns ever see a few raindrops? I've built a few of these in my time, have shot them all, and enjoy that kind of project. But working for a serious shooter gives me a different kind of satisfaction.

The fact is, engraving adds little to the function of a custom gun. Beyond the aforementioned caliber designation, sight plane treatment and perhaps the makers mark, engraving could be considered worthless. A waste of money. The flip side is the enormous potential for the enjoyment of an art form that is as technically difficult, demanding in medium and conservative in subject as any in the history of applied decoration. (Besides that, can you imagine what that Griebel job is worth today? It cost but $310 in 1965.)

In my experience, the fellows that say, "I don't want any engraving, I want a hunting gun," are often looking for a bargain or are simply inexperienced. The avid shooters that I've worked with want a custom gun that is as esthetically pleasing as it is func-

tional, and as I mentioned before, sometimes I have to put a cap on their enthusiasm. So please realize that I'm not an advocate of either extreme, but I do think that an expensive gun *should* be engraved.

Engraving is an applied art. Prior to the widespread use of photography in periodical reproduction, engraving could have been considered either a pure art form or a semi-professional trade. Working in steel or copper, engravers were tradesmen who made mirror images for illustration used in the printing process. (Bank notes or stocks and bonds are well-remembered examples.) Today, except for a few craftsmen who inscribe precious metal jewelry, most engravers work on firearms and custom knives. (Most jewelry store engraving of today is machine-cut with a pantograph.)

So the answer to the question "Why engrave?" is quite simple: It is a personal thing; and if you have to ask, you're probably not going to make a very good client for the engraver.

If embellishment is something you're interested in, the next most obvious question is; What engraving is appropriate for my shotgun? Several themes and subjects go all the way back to the beginning of firearms decoration. During the 18th Century, one of the brightest eras of firearms devel-

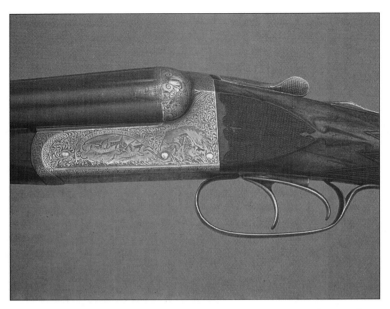

Remington Model 1894, Grade EEO Trap Gun manufactured in 1899. The turn-of-the-century engraving is comparable to the finest work done today. Although the animals are a bit comic in rendition, they are vastly more lifelike and show more character than most contemporary scenes. The small, backgrounded scroll, borders, lettering and layout are exemplary. Charles Semmer Photos

opment, there was a tremendous resurgence of rococo and baroque themes in the art of the Western world. Baroque foliate forms and the rounded, rococo scroll can be found ornamenting buildings, furniture, china, tapestry and nearly every surface deemed acceptable to applied art. All but the most utilitarian, or military, firearms of that period have some degree of metal engraving and most follow a baroque or rococo theme.

The same basic scrollwork is found in contemporary engraving. Each great era of sporting firearms development has added depth and vitality to the engraver's art. Easy to remember examples include: 18th Century Louis XIV gold-encrusted flintlock fowlers, late-19th Century lever-action rifles and Parker shotguns from the 1920s and 1930s in this century. Fortunately for all of us, we are today in the midst of another "golden age" of sporting firearms.

I have often said artisans today have very distinct advantages over earlier craftsmen: the printed page and the electric light. Illustration allows us to study preceding work and the electric light allows us to stay up late looking at photos and practicing our techniques.

Besides scroll there is one other theme in firearms decoration that has transcended the ages; depictions of the hunt. The pursuit of the quarry or more simply put for shotguns; dogs and birds are the theme. These animals or vignette scenes vary enormously in style, quality and design.

Recently I saw an early-20th Century double rifle with caricatures of a tiger and another beast I guessed to be a blackbuck. The fine rifle was obviously built for use in India. It was also quite obvious that the engraver had never seen his subjects and, I imagine, neither had the engraver illustrating the book they were copied from. American shotguns from the vintage years have similar comic renditions of wildfowl. Although they could be considered quite primitive, I prefer to think of them as quaint, even when I can't identify the fowl in question.

A working American engraver told me one of his greatest fears is that his birds will look like the stiff dead chickens of earlier work. They don't. Look at the renditions of deer, dogs and birds on the Remington gun shown here. Although slightly humorous, they display anatomy, character and action beyond most of the contemporary vignettes.

But before we pick a theme or subject for embellishing our beloved shotgun, let's take a moment

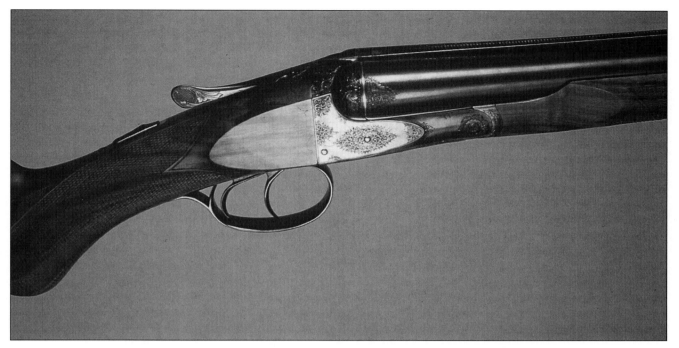

Michael Dubber engraved this Hughes/Fox with backgrounded small English rose and scroll with a negative space layout. The unengraved steel is an important design element.

to think about choosing an engraver and learning to work with him. The artist should have an enormous influence on the choice of theme, the overall design and the execution. Chances are he knows more than you do about the subjects.

I've worked with perhaps a dozen different firearms engravers over the years and have had only one bad experience. That was the first experience and the whole problem stemmed from choosing the wrong guy for the job. I chose him because the price was right, which is not to say that in itself was the mistake. He did not understand the subtleties of the 1860-era percussion derringer I was restoring and although my efforts saved a badly damaged pistol, his $35 worth turned out to be an embarrassment. He didn't want to replicate the gun's original engraving and unfortunately chose to do his own thing.

The other side of the C-note is a class of engravers whose patrons have supreme sophistication and the silk purses necessary to commission the art. These engravers are not only expensive but often booked a couple of years ahead with involved projects. They only finish a few commissions per year, and their work enters the realm of the patently exclusive. These guys are the trend setters and those whose work will be appreciated by all, increase in value and transcend the ages.

So when I tell you the best criterion for picking an engraver for your project is simply your enjoyment of his work, realize the engraver himself may have his own criteria for accepting a project. Everyone I know would love to have Winston Churchill (or Robert Swartley, Ron Smith, Eric Gold or Lynton McKenzie) engrave a shotgun. Few do.

In between there are many craftsmen of different levels of talent, experience and skill. It is not hard to find a fellow who will polish your pump gun, chisel some large elaborate scrolls on the flats and re-blue it for you. If this will make you happy, do it! There are some mighty nice guns done in just such a manner. But think twice before you ask him to do a portrait of your setter. Comic figures have fallen from favor. Bulino can be a yardstick away from pleasing scroll.

It is wise to chose an engraver who has experience with the type of gun you have. Obviously, the layout for that pump gun will be quite different from a sidelock because of the vastly different contours and surfaces. This concern presents a different dilemma that I recently experienced.

I had a rifle project that needed some border engraving with a bit of scrollwork and some lettering. Exhausting my regular engravers who were busy, I asked a few custom gunmakers friends for a referral. One name came up twice as an advanced professional who might be between commissions. He did a fine job on the small project and helped me meet a deadline. I was very pleased.

I mentioned an upcoming sidelock gun and he was enthused enough to send me his complete portfolio. Unfortunately, there wasn't a single photo of a shotgun let alone a sidelock. As this was my client's first custom gun I didn't think it fair to send him photos of bolt-action and single-shot rifles for him to visualize sidelock engraving. I believed the engraver could do a fine job and told him so, but he got very upset with me for not sending the photos to the client.

It's the old conundrum: You need a union card to get the job but have to have the job to get the card. I've been there many times and can empathize, but ultimately I chose not to confuse the client.

The next best piece of advice I can give is to chose a professional - one who has devoted his career to the art form. There are many part-time craftsmen who do fine work but they may not be as devoted to delivery deadlines or learning to properly reassemble firearms mechanisms.

The Firearms Engravers Guild of America is a good place to start looking for a craftsman. The organization acknowledges a "Professional" category of membership and publishes a directory with photos and background material pertaining to each member's work. Or you can personally visit the Custom Gun Show (Currently held each January in Reno) to see a multitude of engraved custom firearms in the flesh, so to speak.

Please do enough study and research that when you start contacting craftsmen you don't have to completely rely on their work-time for an education. (Time *is* money, after all.) Probably the best initial investment you can make is to purchase a few books. *Understanding and Drawing Scroll Designs*, by Ron Smith - a long-time, full-time professional engraver - was written for craftsmen but conveys a world of information to any student of the art. Another is *The Art of Engraving*, by James B. Meek.

There are many other books that show hundreds of pictures of ornately engraved guns, but these two volumes offer insight into the craftsman's approach. It is much easier to study scroll design, coverage concentration and basic themes when not looking at stunning photos of unobtainable pieces of art.

Coverage is the term used to denote the actual amount of engraving applied to the firearm. Generally the reference is to one-quarter, half, three-quarters or full-coverage. These are relatively meaningless terms for custom work ordered from craftsmen. They do suit the photo captions that accompany brochures detailing factory engraving that offers standardized designs. I always want to ask "which quarter?"

The amount of engraving you would like is important but equally so is the amount you can afford and the amount necessary to present a pleasingly balanced example. I like to have most all of the parts of a fine gun touched by the engraver, which can get very expensive if one does not plan the balancing act.

When a minimum of engraving is desired, I design what stockmaker James Tucker quaintly refers to as a "trim job." As an example, one could have all the screw heads engraved with a petal motif, simple or elaborate borders surrounding the action sides, top and bottom, the serial numbers cut in the trigger guard tang and SAFE gold inlaid on the top tang. Additional borders on the forend latch and guard tang along with cut checkering for the top lever and safety button would dress it up a bit more. Add small gold bands at the barrel breeches, small scroll clusters in the corners... you get the picture. This is design by the addition method. A bit later I'll tell you about designing engraving by the subtraction method.

Often engravers approach the quandary of "How much coverage?" with the question, "How much can you afford?" This is not their attempt to get their hand into your pocket but a measure of judgment, or scale if you will, of how to design a balanced layout and give you the particulars you desire without breaking the bank.

A couple of years back I commissioned an engraving job for a client, set a price limit, decided on a scroll style and necessary details, and left the rest up to the artist. He made an error in judgment by starting with the buttplate which he ornamented lavishly. By the time he finished the requested details and got to the action sides he was way over his head for bench hours. I wound up having to ask the client for more money which still didn't pay for the extra scroll needed to balance the action coverage with the buttplate. In the end everyone was quite pleased, except the engraver, who couldn't cover his butt with the bucks. I think he learned a valuable (or costly) lesson with that job. Any successful artist who accepts commissions must balance time and money with his personal creative drive in order to avoid these situations.

There is one more point to bring up regarding engraving coverage. There are two shortcuts to full-coverage: more scroll or larger scroll. The British tend towards more while the American work has larger scrolls. I'm sure that you can visualize those early Winchesters with about three individual scrolls, with many smaller tendrils, covering the whole side of a large lever-action. (Some of the same historically acclaimed engravers did extraordinarily fine scroll work and elaborate vignettes.) By contrast, the English and the folks who copy them, lay tiny scrolls next to tiny scrolls beyond count until all of the surface is scrolls. (Again, there was also advanced work by the same tradesmen.) Although there are many who like these styles, personally, I don't care for either approach. You can't see the forest for the trees.

When full-coverage is the desired effect, often the quality of the cut of the individual scroll, or the quality of the design, is sacrificed. Much full-coverage English scroll, when viewed under magnification, is just singular scrolls laid next to one another. There is seldom a main stem that the individual scrolls emanate from and rarely any backgrounding to distinguish the scrolls from the surface metal. (To judge the quality of full-coverage small scroll look at how well matched the scrolls are side-to-side off the center-line of the action bottom. Does the third scroll out from the middle on the left match its counterpoint on the right?)

Large scroll, full-coverage jobs leave me with the impression that the engraver's challenge was to get as much fly line or lasso in the air as possible, for it's own sake. Sometimes the background is stamped with a "dot punch" to fill in the blank spaces. I prefer my engraving as flowing cuts with recognizable scrolls and few punch marks.

(Have you ever heard that full-coverage engraving is meant to hold oil on the surface of a gun to prevent corrosion? That's a bunch of hooey! Another one of those romantic notions dreamed up by a gun writer to explain or justify something gunmakers do traditionally.)

And while I'm at it I'll risk aggravating you by laying into your favorite factory gun. Chances are, your engraving wasn't engraved.

All true engraving is cut from the base metal with gravers or tiny chisels. One cut at a time, just as a wood carver would cut wood with chisels and gouges. When it comes to modern factory "engraving," most is actually applied with a roll die or photo etched. The first process involves making a die similar to a narrow rolling pin and pressing it, with great force, against the shotgun action. Because only one part of the die is in contact with the metal at any given time, a roll die can impress quite deeply. You can often feel the sharp edges where the metal has been displaced.

Photo etching involves coating the metal with a "resist" that masks off everything except the pattern, then covering the action surface with an acid that etches or eats away the metal. Unfortunately it is difficult to align a roll die or photo template close to an edge so rarely do you get definitive border work to richly enhance the overall lines of the gun. Usually they apply a central theme that does little but take up space in the middle of a slab-sided action, the lines of the gun go unnoticed.

Take some time with a magnifying glass, looking at the trees of your engraving. Imagine a tiny chisel in the hands of an artisan making each individual cutline. Look a bit closer. Can you separate the shading cuts from the deeper work? Look a bit closer...then step back and look at the forest.

Chapter 2

Stylishly Scrolled

In the last chapter I left you with a magnifying glass. What did you see, with magnifier in hand, peering at the cut lines on your shotgun? Did it confound, please or confuse you? Believe me, I've been looking closely at firearms engraving for a couple of decades and frequently have all these feelings.

I suggested that you peer into your own engraving example because I'm about to start separating the wheat from the chaff so you can understand design and engraving styles. Each varies enormously depending upon when, where and who cut the lines in the metal. If you took the time and had the patience to view engraving under magnification, you understand explicitly, rather than conceptually, that for each engraved line on your shotgun, a chip of steel landed on the floor.

I don't like to judge the hand engraving of a fine shotgun, new or old. (I don't relish jury duty either.) Nearly all of it can be criticized. If pressed, I'll point out herky-jerky scrolls, uneven border lines or what I consider poor design or layout. At least two of these are a dead give-away of amateur or inexpensive work. Any engraving example is the cumulative product of the craftsman's experience, artistic talent and the time allotted for the job. Few engravers have unlimited resources in all three categories.

In the same vein, all engravers where not created equal and there is no Colt revolver nor magic potion to bring them up to par. Every engraving project I've commissioned for clients could stand criticism, and I've worked with some high-powered names. I've seen shotgun tangs bent, the edges of bench-made trigger guards

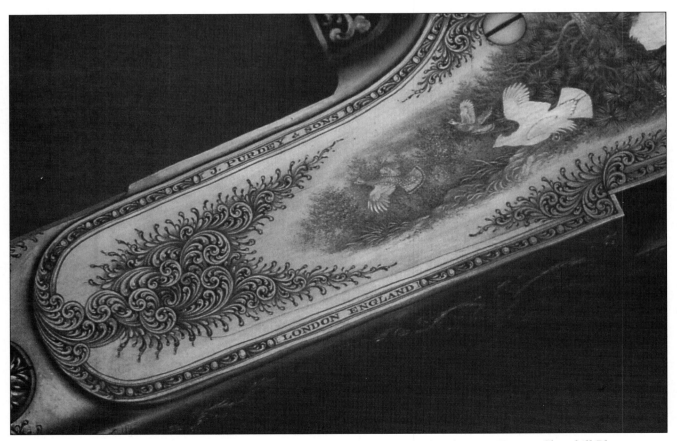

The Purdey project is in progress by Winston Churchill. The work is described in the text. Winston Churchill Photo.

marred and had to hassle with engravers who didn't want to see color case hardening camouflage their art.

Presented here, because few could find fault with it, is a photo of work in progress by Winston Churchill. At first glance it is clear to see that the craftsman didn't lack skill, talent or time. The work, as a whole, is honest and vibrant, but it is the many individual elements that make it so. Viewing the extraordinary work is worthwhile as it pertains to what we can comprehend and adapt for our own enjoyment. Separating this engraving example into its elements and explaining how they work individually and collectively, presents the avenue towards understanding the art.

Most all engraving has some aspect of a negative space[1] design simply because the variety of surfaces - fences, action panels, top lever and so on - prevent the entire surface from being engraved. Churchill's Purdey exhibits the three best examples of the use of negative space. Border work - in this case tasty ball and scroll boxed in with five individual lines - delineates the shape of the metal edges and captures the interior space. The lettering is conspicuous but delightfully integrated. Second, the major scroll clusters float inside the borders yet are attached at their various points of origin. This grounded effect ties the work together yet the floating arrangement distinguishes the scroll from the remaining engraving. And third, the shape of each scroll mass sets up the remaining open space for the central vignette.

For a better understanding of artistic layout, it is helpful to break these forms down one at a time.

I suggest an interactive exercise that can be done with most firearms engraving to help see the elements and examine them individually. Cut a small scrap of paper that will just cover the central vignette and no more, and lay it on the photo. If you could draw a series of scrolls to correspond with this shape you would have a fine example of English negative space layout. A central element of scroll, or better yet rose and scroll, instead of the vignette would look nearly as good. The English, to the best of my knowledge, pioneered this use of negative space themes in firearms engraving. Tracing the history of firearms embellishment otherwise most often turns up the French as the originators.

When the central picture or scroll is eliminated with the white paper, doesn't the remaining scroll and border work hold up as a lovely piece of firearms decoration?

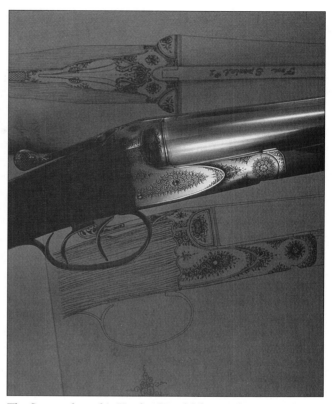

The fine work on this Hughes/Fox 20-bore is by engraver Eric Gold as are the design drawings. The negative space layout forms a secondary pattern with the absence of engraving.

Now, with more white paper, block out the front bottom and top scroll masses, leaving just the first scroll that is attached to the border. Does this not also remain a simple but finely designed embellishment?

Simplified one step further with the removal of the ball and scroll border cuts, one is left with basic thick and thin border lines and highlight scrolls, well-drawn and executed. This is the beginning of most any gun engraving, outlining and defining the existing shapes.

Now let's look at the elements in the opposite direction. Can you see how crisp, unwavering and true to form the basic border lines are? See how each border scroll and ball displaces the same space, has an equal amount of "fish-hook" and how each is lightly shaded to encourage the look of dimension?

At the front of the pattern, the larger scrolls mature in size and grow directly from the repetitive border work. Each larger hook is formed from and with the tiny scrolls until it grows to the major fron-

---

[1] Negative space design incorporates the use of two visual images. When closely viewed, the scroll embellishment appears to be the theme. When one steps back a few paces to view the work, another design, formed by the scroll masses and unengraved portions create a separate design the compliments the gun's shapes and contours. Often the negative space presents geometric forms, ribbons, circles or ovals.

A sampler of four scroll styles by engraver Eric Gold. (1) Small English (2) Floral (3) Vine and (4) German scroll.

tal element. A definitive core, like the eye of a tornado, is the central emanation of each scroll mass. The scrolls hook over, around and through one another creating movement and energy. Tiny tendrils burst out from the edges, yet all is cohesive and follows the form of the gun's shape.

Similarly, minute shading cuts begin the edges of the game scene. They take form as rocks, bushes and clouds. Individual blades of grass, pine needles, branches and bark become larger and clearer towards the center of the story.

The inlayed gold grouse are treated in a like manner, with the smaller, less-distinct birds at the edges defining the sense of perspective. As pictured here, in this stage of the engraving the largest grouse has yet to be detailed. But a close look at the dropped leg shows the individual toes and the spur shaded to appear life-like. Each separate primary feather is a singular slice of gold separated by the base metal. Churchill has begun to delineate the rump and wing of the bird and anyone who has held a grouse in hand will believe his anatomy.

So the collective elements of the gun's contours, the negative space, central scrolls, landscape vignette and gold inlay all paint the picture. Subtracting any element in order of sophistication does nothing to diminish the beauty and grace of the art.

When deciding on the engraving for my own Fox gun I commissioned the engraver to design and draw a scheme with elaborate coverage. I then photocopied his art and used white-out to test his layout. Individual elements were eliminated until I found what pleased me and what I could afford. (A look at the gun, shown elsewhere, will give you the picture.)

For someone interested in firearms engraving as art, it is money well spent to pay for sketches and drawings. All of the engravers I have worked with

have been quite agreeable to this design stage as long as money wasn't in short supply. If your wallet is thinner, the best approach is to pick from photos or smoke-pulls of their existing work and trust that the artist can combine your chosen elements in a pleasing manner. A "smoke-pull" is created by using the finished engraving as a plate, smoke or ink is applied to "pull" a print directly from the finished work. This provides an honest reproduction and will show fine quality as well as tiny flaws.

Less than reputable individuals have conned engravers into providing a free drawing and then shopped it around for the lowest bidder. Besides the fact that the result usually appears as a comic rendition of the original design, I think the perpetrators should be skinned with a 1mm graver. At a recent show, engraver Eric Gold saw his scroll sampler diagram (shown here) reproduced and displayed as another engraver's practice plate. While only marginally ethical, the lack of originality was duly noted.

With various scroll forms, it would be nice to believe there are standard artistic terms to identify each of the styles, but damned if I can get two engraves to agree on such. So all I can offer is a scroll design sampler, provided by Eric Gold, to pique your imagination and help to interpret my words.

In size, engravers speak of large, medium or small scrolls. Churchill's example shows some of each and is an excellent example of how the sizes can be blended. "Large scroll" could be any with individual spirals of a 5/8 inches or greater. Small scroll might measure a quarter of an inch or tinier. Large scroll will combine small and medium scrolls as Churchill's example shows, although it is difficult to use the term when only one scroll of the engraving could be seen as large.

Large scroll is often associated with the more coarse examples of early American shotguns. But some of the finest doubles in the world sport the big spirals. A typical engraving design I'm sure you can find a photo of is the large scroll that is almost the standard form found on Holland & Holland "Royal" guns. Uniformly large spirals ornament the fences, sideplates and bottom of the action. It is interesting to note the number of London guns that *do not* have "small English scroll" engraving.

For scroll design and layout comparison I can recommend a couple of books: *Il Grande Libro Delle Incisioni, "The Modern Engravings Real Book"* for exquisite Italian engraving and *Modern Sporting Guns* for English engraving. For American engraving I suggested a few titles in the last chapter. Each text provides a perspective of the different sizes and styles of firearms decoration in their own context. *Il Grande Libro* shows the extraordinary capability of the Italians to duplicate other engraving styles or create their own unique engraving, and the text is in both English and Italian. (You *will* enjoy the fantasy scenes of nudes with jungle cats, reptiles or birds of prey, I guarantee it!)

Venturing beyond scroll size, one starts to recognize the style or flavor of the nautilus - that fully organic spiral. It is first important to identify the way in which the scroll is actually cut with the chisel. Is each scroll a singular cut or two chisel channels are used to outline each edge of each scroll?

The first case is most often seen in "small English scroll." In size, these are uniform and small to minute. In design they are often used as a mass of "full-coverage." In execution small English scroll may be the easiest to accomplish although extensive coverage takes a lot of time and lends an elaborate air to the work. High-grade Parker guns are the American doubles most often cut with small, single-line scroll with interior shading.

Any scroll gains depth and character when "backgrounded." When each side of each scroll represents a separate chisel cut, the area between the scrolls must be removed to distinguish them from one another: backgrounding.

Removing the metal between the scrolls varies from shallow, uniform cross-hatching - like stock checkering - to deep chisel work, typified by the Germanic styles which exhibit boldness and a distinct third-dimension relief. Regardless of the depth, the background must have some type of texturing or matting, to appropriately display the scroll. The finest and most complex small English scroll will also be backgrounded.

Relief chisel work is the sculpture of engraving and is often reserved for the more substantial parts of the gun such as the fences and top lever. With the extra metal available it is possible to overlap, intertwine and model the work much like wood carving.

The baroque forms of scroll interplay foliate design with the basic spiral - leaves and scroll with the Greek acanthus leaf as the origin. This is commonly called floral scroll and the amount of foliage varies considerably. Some has just parts of leaves developing from the scroll stems. The more elaborate floral work all but eliminates the spirals except as a way to twist and tangle the leaves. Floral scroll should not be confused with "rose and scroll" which is a form of English scroll incorporating clusters, or bouquets of roses. Nor is it similar to "oak leaf" which is Germanic and very graphically named.

"Vine scroll" is another common form that relies on vegetative forms. In this case thin vines, like grape or honeysuckle, form the spirals with the use of leaves to give the work greater body and substance. This style is seldom backgrounded and because of the remaining large areas of negative space vine scroll can cover a lot of surface without a great deal of metal cutting. When executed in deep relief or as gold sheet and wire inlay, vine scroll can be quite striking. These more sophisticated forms of vine scroll, when executed with an exotic flair, are sometimes called Arabesque.

"American scroll" is a term that covers so many different styles that it is difficult for me to define. Essentially it is a larger, open scroll with larger leaves and more background space between the spirals. Although it is seen on some American doubles, the most recognizable firearms are turn of the century revolvers and lever-action rifles. I don't consider American scroll particularly appropriate for fine shotguns. Quite frankly, it looks better on silver belt buckles with tooled leather holsters for Colts and Winchesters.

"German scroll" is another term that I find very difficult to define or describe because of the great number of interpretations. As done in this country, it is often a bold, leafy style with open scrolls and heavy backgrounding. The use of long stems with tight spirals at the ends is characteristic of the design. German scroll is typically presented in perfectly symmetric panels designed outward from the center-lines of the gun.

As for Churchill's scroll, it is just that - his own. By the time an engraver attains a profound degree of accomplishment he has also developed a unique style that warrants his name. In my opinion, at this level the work should be appreciated as a form of fine art as valid as oil painting or sculpture.

Chapter 3

More Than Meets The Eye

In the first two chapters of this section I wrote about engraving design, scroll styles and the men who chisel the steel. Now, I'll discuss some of the various methods and techniques employed to decorate and embellish shotgun metal.

As I've stated before, firearms engraving is similar to wood carving. The major differences are the hardness of the material and the size of the tools and subjects. As steel is so much harder and tougher than any wood it is easy to understand why engraving rarely exhibits the depth or dimension of wood carving. And because of the size of the various shotgun parts and the fact that what is inside them must function, engraved decoration is usually limited to applied art on the external surfaces.

The chisels, or gravers, are miniature carving tools with flat, square, diamond or triangular faces that cut the steel. Few gouges or round grooving tools are used in hand engraving. Hard steel dictates that the gravers be forcefully pushed by hand with a wood-handled tool or struck with a small hammer.

Chiseling steel with a hammer is called "chasing" so the tool is called a chasing hammer. It has a round face about 1-1/8 inches across with a smooth, flat striking surface and a ball peen on the opposite end of the head. The shape of the handle is as important as the head. It has a long, narrow shank and an oval shaped bulb on the far end that serves as a counter-balance. The handle is held between the thumb and forefinger and as

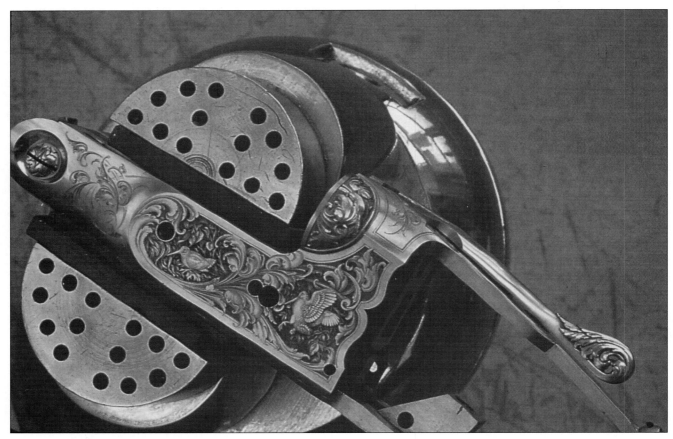

A Parker 28-gauge action sitting in the engraving vise in the studio of Winston Churchill. The gun exhibits a variety of engraving techniques and visual impressions from the pierced and deeply chiseled top lever to the light and airy vine scroll. Winston Churchill Photo

the blows are struck with a see-saw motion, the bulb bounces off the palm of the hand. Hickory wood makes the handle light and springy and the tapping motion must be short and quick strokes with uniform impact to achieve a consistently smooth, even cut.

James B. Meek in his book *The Art of Engraving*, talks about "strokes per minute" and shows three identically sized small scrolls to illustrate chasing technique. A deeply cut scroll took about 60 heavy strokes to cut. A smoother, lighter scroll took about 700 strokes and the lightest and smoothest took about 1,200 strokes. With this number of strokes for a small, simple scroll, I can imagine how many hammer strokes are required for a complete engraving job. Mind boggling.

In these modern times an air-driven mini-jackhammer is often the motivating force. Imagine the machine that tears up the side-walk reduced to the size of a fat fountain pen and you've a good idea of the tool used by many modern engravers. Although not as quaint or traditional as a graver pushed by hand or tapped with a delicate hammer, the pneumatic power tool makes chasing a one-handed operation. The length and impact of each stroke from the machine is infinitely variable so the craftsman can chisel in deep relief or shade a finely detailed vignette. The primary advantages of the pneumatic tool are the consistency of the stroke and the absence of fatigue because the tool does the work rather than the hand and wrist. Power engravers don't make instant artists and most of the accomplished engravers I know first mastered the chisel and hammer.

The gravers are either hand-held or slip fit into the head of the air-powered tool and they come in multitudes of sizes and shapes. When I speak of a square or diamond-shaped graver that is the shape you would see if looking down the "muzzle," so to speak. One pointed corner of the square or the long point of the diamond actually does the cutting while tipping the tool sideways varies the width and shape of the cut.

These tools are supplied as blanks and each craftsman must grind and sharpen the cutting surface at an angle appropriate to the line to be cut and the angle the tool is presented to the metal surface. Most engravers use a rotating circular stone that looks like a very small record player. The tool is held in an adjustable fixture to maintain a consistent grinding angle. As with stockmaking, learning the proper techniques for sharpening the tools is a prerequisite to performing any quality work. A correctly sharpened graver will turn up a fine curl of metal as it cuts, just as a sharp plane turns up a curl of wood.

In most cases the steel the graver is made from must be harder that the steel to be engraved. When working on a soft shotgun action the graver may only need to be sharpened every two or three days. American engravers frequently bitch about particularly "hard" actions such as the Ruger #1 because they may have to sharpen the tool every 45 minutes. A tedious, but necessary task for the artist.

Carbide tools are often used on the hardest metal and they are sharpened with a ceramic wheel and polished with a diamond dust compound. With an appropriately ground face, correct angle of attack, lubricating oil and the right amount of force applied to the cutter, cobalt alloy tools will chisel metal harder than they are, but don't ask me why.

If one is to pound on a piece of steel with a chisel, how one holds that gun part is critical. Most engravers use a ball vise which is a precision clamp with a ball-shaped bottom. The vise must weight at least 25 pounds to steady the work and it sits in a doughnut of leather or a small garden tractor tire.

When using a hand-held graver the ball vise can be swiveled with the left hand as the right holds the cutting tool. The leather or rubber base absorbs shock and allows the vise to swivel when cutting the arc of the scroll, yet there is enough friction to prevent the ball from swinging freely. If you look closely at the photo of engraver Geoffroy Gournet, the vise, ball and doughnut are evident.

Early European ball vises were sometimes made from iron cannon balls and some modern ones use bowling balls. Each seems a bit odd, but fully practical.

The vise jaws that hold the gun part are padded with a host of different materials. Some engravers use soft pine blocks, or leather or sheet lead. Odd-shaped parts are often attached to a block of wood with screws or epoxy which is then chucked in the vise. The traditional method is to sink the part into a "pitch block" of melted pine tar which cools and solidifies to secure the metal.

Optics are an essential part of fine engraving particularly for individuals whose focal length is stretching. Some engravers use a simple visor-type magnifier with quality optics, often with a higher-powered loupe that can be swung out of the way. Some use a monocular loupe squinted between the eyebrow and cheek. The current high-tech solution is a binocular microscope that zooms from 3 to 20 power. Just as a brain surgeon would, the engraver peers through the lenses to perform finer work than the naked eye can see. And that is the point of magnification: the engraver can see and cut finer lines than you, to present an image that is more than what first meets the eye.

Light is also essential to good vision. Contrary to my thoughts, some engravers use florescent light rather than the good, old Edison light bulb. They don't want the surface to look yellow or cast too

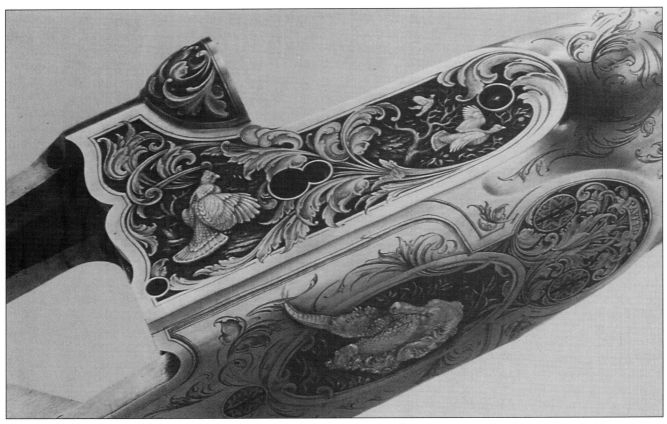

Although this engraving is considered fine art at its highest state, Churchill doesn't lose sight of the canvas. It is easy to see the design is dictated by the gun's contours and surfaces which are accented and enhanced by the embellishment. Winston Churchill Photo.

much glare back at them. A whole lot more diffused fluorescent wattage will light up the subject without blinding the artist in the reflection. It is hard to imagine British engravers from early in this century using a single gas light or imagine their predecessors using candles or whale oil lamps.

The last, and maybe most important, tool of the professional engraver is the printed page. Between 1650 and 1683 a number of books of engraving designs were published in France that had a profound impact on firearms engraving. Much of what we see today is based on these texts. When *Master French Gunsmith Designs* by Stephen V. Grancsay was reprinted by Winchester Press in the 1970s I missed getting a copy and am still looking.

I've already mentioned a few engraving books. Beyond these, every practitioner I know has files of photographs of other firearms engraving. They also file a horde of subjects, from photos of animals to potential border designs, or renditions of fine art that may be applicable as subjects, themes or inspirations.

Throwing all the high-tech stuff aside, modern firearms craftsmen have two huge advantages over our predecessors: the electric light and the accumulated printed page.

There is one more prerequisite to high-quality firearms engraving: metal preparation. Hand-polishing is absolutely the best treatment for gun metal. All of the flats, curves and contours must remain true with crisp edges. There are a very few craftsmen in this country who can successfully machine-polish gun metal. The vast majority of buffed guns show dished screw holes, rounded edges and much too high a polish for the traditional metal finishes such as color case hardening and rust bluing.

Starting with 150-grit cloth backed with a file, block or other stiff surface, each bit of the metal is hand-sanded to blend the curves, true the flats and sharpen the edges. Most engravers prefer a 400-grit finish. This degree of polish leaves the metal scratch-free and bright without a mirror-shiny surface. It is easily touched up and won't shine light back into the engraver's eyes.

The actual engraving design must now be transferred to the metal for the gravers to cut. There are many different ways to layout the images onto the steel but most engravers start by coating the metal with blue or white layout fluid that dries and dulls the surface.

Some engravers start with a pencil or fine scribe and simply draw the design right onto the surface. Others use a photographic process and actually develop a film image onto the metal. Another process entails transferring a photo-static copier image with acetone. There is a mechanical technique using a pantograph or duplicating machine that will scale down a drawing as it is transferred to the gun metal. Some are transferred by coating the back of a drawing with graphite and pencil tracing it onto the metal. Finally, some engravers layout out their original sketches on a grid, shrink the grid to the actual size of the engraving and, after transferring the grid to the metal, they connect the dots from square to square to sketch the design onto the gun's surfaces. Regardless of the technique, it must incorporate the use of a mirror image if one side of the gun's engraving is to match the other.

With the action hand-polished, the design transferred and the works chucked in the ball vise it's *lights-camera-action*: We are ready for the gravers.

Like all experienced craftsmen, each engraver has developed his own routine and approach to starting the metal cutting. From here on out the process entails choosing the appropriate graver and chiseling a line either by tapping the tool with a hammer or using the air-powered device. A good place to start is with the border lines. No matter the sophistication, single lines or elaborate ball-and-bar, the border lines must closely follow the lines of the metal. Chiseling a straight, clean cut of uniform depth is much more difficult than you might imagine (and it is quite easy to see if they're off).

The main stems of each major scroll and vine are then outlined with the graver. Most scroll work involves a cut on the outside of each scroll to distinguish it from what will become the background. The engraver must anticipate the overlapping elements and stop the cut to start again on the other side of the overlap. After the major components are cut in place all the little leaves, scrolls and tendrils are added to the design to form the inside of the scroll. (A close look at most engraving will reveal the outside line of each fish-hook scroll is usually a single, arching line while the inside cut has the small complicated elements.)

Cutting down the background around each scroll in effect raises the engraving and gives it depth and relief. The background is first cut with a series of chiseled lines that remove some portion of the metal. Particular attention is needed in the minute corners where elements start, end or come together. The graver is held at a steep angle to the work and the cuts must be sharp and deep, like the sides of a grave. Care must be taken so that the heel of the tool doesn't damage the raised scroll.

The background is then matted, usually with a tiny pointed or cupped-end punch so it is uniform

and the individual punch marks are indistinguishable to the naked eye. This is called stippling and levels the surface and adds texture. Another type of backgrounding seen on some Parker engraving uses finely cut lines all in the same direction. Regardless of the method, the desired result is that the matting or texture of the background will absorb light and appear darker and therefor deeper than the actual cut depth, This visually raises the scroll.

If the upper surface of the scroll is to be modeled (as a carved wood leaf is), to give the scroll a mid-depth sense of relief, now is the time. Modeling an engraved leaf is the technique used to make them look like they twist and turn over themselves. Each lobe is cut with ridges, valleys and folded points.

Tiny cuts of fine-line shading are the final step to detailing the engraving. The best shading is cut with an extraordinarily fine single-point tool. Each of the multitude of cuts being individually incised to converge on the main stem. Skilled line shading can enhance the work's visual depth and darken the deepest parts of the modeling.

Less detailed engraving and production work employs the use of a multi-line shading tool that lays in a series of shading lines with one cut. By tipping the tool the shading cuts can be stretched out to follow the curves of the scrolls and to prevent them from ending at the same place.

Voila! All that is left is to clean up any small blemishes and remove the burrs at the edges of the cuts. A straightforward job may have taken a day or two and elaborate artistic renditions may consume many months.

Whether it is the maker's name, "SAFE," or an animal in a vignette, gold inlay is quite popular for shotgun engraving. It is good to remember that annealed 24-karat (pure) gold is wonderfully soft and can be easily worked to shape and form by a skilled craftsman. (Raised gold inlay is frequently done with less-than-pure gold which is harder and less likely to wear or abrade.)

There are two basic methods of gold inlay. When applying lettering - raised or flush - each letter is cut into the metal as a single trough with square sides. The groove is then undercut, like a dovetail, along the bottom corner of each side of the cut. Gold wire, usually round in form, is lightly tapped into the groove with a rough-face punch or a hammer that will lightly grip the gold.

For larger inlays such as full-figure birds or animals, the single-wire method is sometimes used except that several gold bands are laid next to one another within the drawn perimeter of the figure. This method typically is used for raised gold inlays and each gold wire is left proud of (above) the surface then peened and burnished together, blending the edges so they become a single piece of gold.

The metal surface must be immaculately clean so that no dirt will be trapped in the joints to discolor the inlay. The outer surface is then modeled and engraved to distinguish the features, musculature and hide or feathers of the subject.

The second method of gold inlay is usually employed as flush inlay - flat with the surface of the steel. After the outline of the subject is carefully drawn on the metal it is outlined by cutting in with a graver. As with backgrounding, the inner metal is removed with cutters by chiseling back and forth in a diminishing grid pattern. The edge is under-cut and tiny barbs (or teeth) are cast-up throughout the middle of the recess. These will help lock the gold in place.

The form is sawn from sheet gold to match the recessed area exactly. The sheet gold is then peened into the recess with particular attention to anchoring the metal by forcing it into the undercut edges. When all is perfected and secure, the gold inlay is dressed flush with files and polishing cloth.

The gold inlay is then engraved to represent the character of the subject. The use of bulino or bank-note engraving can turn a flat piece of gold into an almost living, breathing being. Bulino is an Italian term for the finest of fine-line engraving usually used to depict a portrait-like subject or scene. If you use magnification to look at a black and white photograph printed in this book you will see that it has been reduced to a series of tiny dots. The density of these dots form a gray scale that depicts the lighter and darker shades of black to present an image to the eye. If you look at a $5 bill under the same magnifier you will see the portrait of Lincoln rendered in tiny dots and lines that shade his brow, project his nose and form the weave of his coat.

The gray scale formed by the minute lines and dots is the essence of bank note or bulino engraving. Each line that hollows Abe's stupendous ear was cut with a graver by a skilled artisan. The Italians have perfected the art and have been very instrumental in developing the techniques used by talented engravers worldwide. The best bulino engraving truly expresses the cliche' "more than meets the eye."

With a basic understanding of how engraving is designed and executed, taking a close look at the photos of Winston Churchill's ornamentation of a 28-gauge Parker is in order.

First, I will dissect the engraving on the woodcock-side of the action. Note that the borders are very

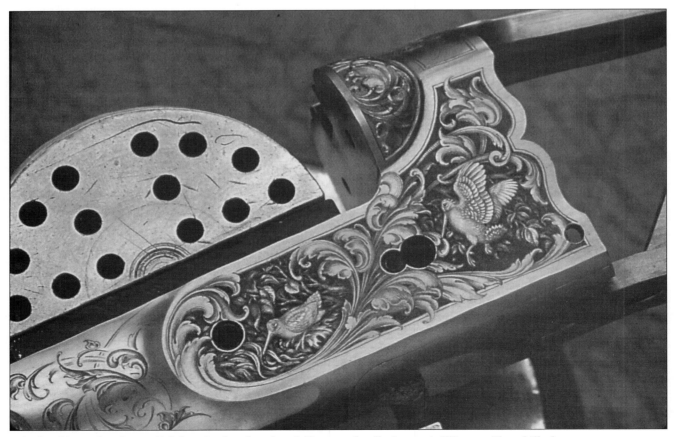

Inlaid gold woodcock are slightly raised and sculpted. The text details the work. Winston Churchill photo

finely cut single lines - as fine as any of the cuts and they simply outline the contours of the action.

The overall scroll style is decidedly floral, consisting of stylized shoots, vines and leaves. There is only one true scroll at the rear-center of the side. In this case the origin of the design - or eye of the hurricane - is imagined at the lower front, just below the standing woodcock. The border lines begin here, as does the forward scroll cluster, the central floral work and the leaves and vines above the flushing woodcock. The most basic element of the design is a long, lazy S lying on its back. I imagine that Churchill began his composition by simply drawing an organ S on the action side.

Although this engraving is deeply cut, it is the heavily matted background that raises the scroll and accentuates the borders of the layout. Each of these elements - border lines, scroll and backgrounding serve to enhance the basic design as well as complement and accentuate each other and the gun's form.

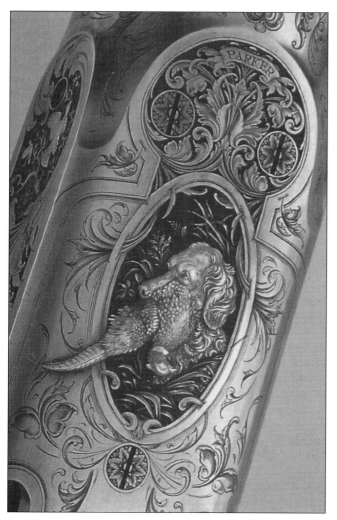

As described in the text, the bottom of the Parker is a study in design and engraving technique. Winston Churchill Photo.

Change your focus for a minute to the action fences. In contrast to the other engraving, they are very deeply chiseled and do not rely on backgrounding to simulate relief. The gun's metal is much heavier here, enough so you can see four different levels of relief above the background. The motif is again floral, but the extra depth is cut so the leaves and vines overlap, twist and fold over themselves. The leaves are deeply modeled so you can see each lobe, the ridges separating them and the rounded stems and leaf tips.

Looking back at the side of the action, note how Churchill has used delicate shading cuts to achieve the *look* of the modeling without deeply cutting the steel. Focus on the forward leaves for a moment. With the use of shading cuts, the leaves emanate from - and delineate - the borders which follow and enhance the shape of the raised metal of the action panel. Shading down the center of the largest leaf separates the engraving into four distinctly different levels of depth. The lines of shiny untouched metal are the surface of the action. Shading lines cut on the lower leaf edges give the appearance of undercutting (level one). The center of the leaf is shaded to give depth (level two) and show a ridge down the middle (level three) and the deep black line next to the white metal (level four) looks to be nearly as deep as the background.

The appearance is as if we are looking down into the work, but in truth the deepest cuts on the action side aren't as deep as the mid-level modeling of the fences. Add in the top surface and the bottom of the background for six different visual depths. On the chiseled fences, the same six levels could be measured with a depth micrometer.

Note the style and sophistication of the central leaves on the action side. They twist and turn over at the edges, the vines disappear and reappear with grace and fluid movement and the main stem continues back to burst into leaves in the upper-rear corner. You can see the main stem through the curl of the single true scroll. Pleasingly spaced around the sides of the action, floral work pierces the borders, spilling slightly over them, as if on top of the gun metal. Also note, they don't interrupt the rear border at the scalloping because this presents a major architectural element of the gun that shouldn't be softened. Even the screw recesses have borders pierced by engraving. These circles are the only pure geometric form dictated by the gun's mechanics, but don't seem to disturb the flow of the engraving.

Although it may be difficult to see in the photos, the inlayed gold woodcock are slightly raised and sculpted in relief. It is easy to distinguish - and count - the primary, secondary and wing cover feathers of the flushing timberdoodle. Her eyes almost sparkle and, if you look very closely, you can see some of the bird's toenails - the tiniest slivers of gold. The leafy brush around the woodcock lends another bit of dimension which is appropriate for the vignette and strengthens the floral engraving.

Switching the focus to the photo of the action bottom, you must shift gears to appreciate a very different presentation. The forward scroll cluster has all the visual and technical elements of the other engraving, yet the design is much tighter, in mirror image and accentuates the Parker's distinguishing contours. Notice the lower foliate blades piercing and overlapping the oval, tying them together.

An oval - much like a 19th Century mirror or picture frame - borders the sculpted gold setter and pheasant vignette. There is a great deal of relief in this game scene, but this time the gold is raised above the gun metal and deeply sculpted as are the leaves and bushes above the background. The pheasant tail spills over the oval frame and ends in a flush inlay overlapped by a scroll.

The scroll outside the oval is the same design as the rest, yet it has a light, airiness because it is cut into the surface rather than backgrounded. Again, ribbons pierce and capture the bottom of the oval, tying the whole together.

It amazes me how Churchill uses the same scroll style in three distinctly different modes on the same gun; Deeply chiseled on the fences, cutaway and backgrounded on the sides and the breezy vine scroll on the bottom of the action. A perfect example of how different metal cutting techniques lend an entirely different look using the same scroll. Can we call it 21st Century Baroque?

I am immensely proud for the opportunity to present and describe this work.

Looking at any hand-engraved guns with a glass or loupe will show each of the individual cuts, processes and techniques I have described. Several American engravers are pushing the envelope of the art and they need fine guns to embellish. I know Holland & Holland has sent at least five sidelocks guns to American engravers in recent years. Projects as shown above and other work coming from the small American shops will set the stage for a new generation of firearms engravers. I am thankful for the patrons of fine gunmaking and engraving who provide the canvases for the art.

The Rest of The Parker Story

It's delightful to have such pretty pictures of Winston Churchill's stunning engraving, but I thought you might like to know the rest of the story of this Parker 28-gauge gun. It started life as a VHE pistol-grip gun and evolved much like my Fox project detailed in the next section.

Preeminent "gun mechanic" Jerry Fisher created the custom shotgun. Fisher is widely considered the dean of custom gun craftsmen and no doubt the perfect partner for Churchill on this project. Starting with the metalwork, Fisher sawed off the guard tang, welded a long, straight grip tang in place and file-shaped it. All surfaces of the action were filed up to remove the original engraving and to perfect the surfaces and contours. The back of the action was scalloped by hand-filing and frame rebates were added at the rear of the

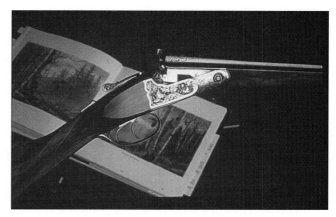

Jerry Fisher was responsible for creating the custom Parker for Churchill to engrave. Tim Rice Photo

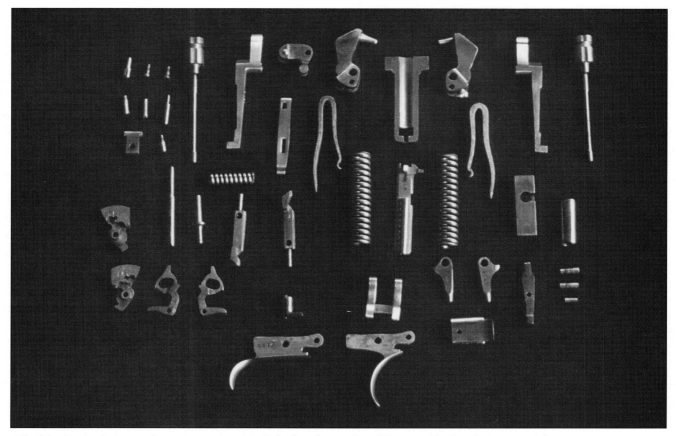

All of the Parker's internal parts were hand-polished and stoned and later, gold-plated. Tim Rice Photo.

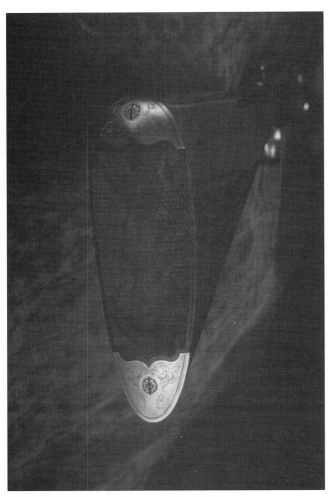

trigger plate. The barrels were hand-struck and polished. Fisher made wart-hog ivory (doesn't yellow) front and middle beads for the barrels. The triggers and all the internal parts were hand-polished, stoned and gold-plated. A new tool steel hinge pin was made and installed. All new screws, 10 in all, were lathe-turned and hand fit to the various parts of the gun.

The Parker was stocked in a dark and lovely stick of English walnut. The stock has a straight-grip and splinter forend and sports bench-made heel and toe clips. Carved drop points follow the oval stock panels. It is checkered 28 lines per inch on the grip, forend and back of the butt. Long diamonds and mullered borders accentuate the grip.

Fisher rust blued the barrels and nitre blued the screws and pins and a gold monogram plate was made and installed in the bottom of the buttstock.

Isn't it good to see the gun-art as a complete shotgun? Isn't it good to know it looks great on the inside? I think you will enjoy this as much as I do.

Fisher made heel and toe clips for the Parker and checkered the butt 28 lines per inch. Tim Rice Photo.

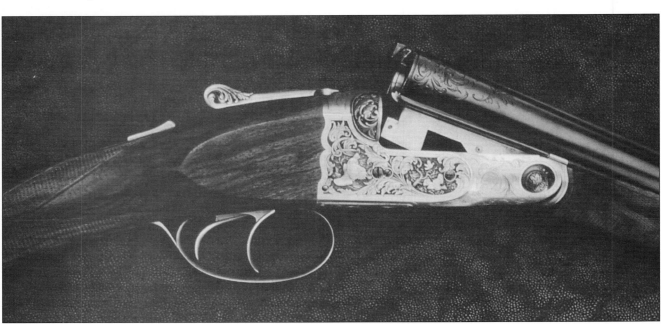

Up close the detailing of the Fisher/Churchill Parker are obvious and lovely.

Chapter 4

Brown, Black and Blue

Color is not usually what makes the first impression with fine firearms. But just the other day I showed a recently completed project to an oil painter friend and she said, "Wow, the colors are gorgeous!"

Janie paints flower gardens and landscapes and is full of color but knows little of guns. The freshly finished piece sports multi-hued case-colors on the action, subtle blue/black barrels, brilliant cobalt-blue screws and the rich yellow-orange-brown-black tones

A custom Winchester M-21, 16-gauge shows rust bluing on all of the metal except the nitre blued screws and pins. The gun has been completely remodeled by removing the action panels, shortening and rounding the frame, reshaping the lever and safety and a new trigger guard.

of English walnut. Small inlays of shiny 24-karat gold add sparkling highlights to the rest of the rainbow.

Janie commented on the complimentary colors - blue and orange, purple and yellow; opposites on the color wheel. The mottled case-colors intrigued her, and I was delighted with the compliment. It is easy to recognize a finely finished gun but not so obvious are the individual colors and how they come about.

I've been studying metal finishes for two decades. Creating muzzleloading guns gave me an appreciation for them and forced me to learn to duplicate and impart a variety of finishing colors to custom guns. A brass-mounted, maple-stocked fowling piece with a browned barrel, fire-blued screws and a case-colored flintlock is about as flamboyantly colorful as a firearm can be.

On the other side of the spectrum is the "brown" gun - I'm sure you've seen them. In a three-gun buy, I recently purchased a Model 1889 Remington hammer double made in 1895. The heavy 10-gauge gun had Damascus barrels and the whole gun - wood and metal - was a uniform deep brown color, but it appeared to be untouched except for a shortened buttstock.

Not having much experience with American guns of this era, and even less with Remingtons, I wondered what the original metal finishes had been. I really didn't want to spend much time with the gun but my curiosity got the better of me and I decided to do a bit of archeological exploration.

Removing the forend revealed the attractively contrasting twist barrel finish. Where the barrels had been protected by the forend they were black and white striped which looked to be close to the factory finish. The forend iron showed a good bit of case colors and under the wood it showed nearly new. The screws that held it in place, and had been protected by the barrels, had strong nitre bluing colors. A nice touch.

The action, locks and other exposed metal had a pale yellow tone over the brown and I suspected someone had varnished over the entire gun. Removing the barrels presented faint, but distinct case colors on the action flats. Cocking the hammers revealed case colors in the protected areas behind them. Except for the nitre blued screws there had been no surprises so far and I had guessed the metal finishes accurately. I would have guessed the trigger guard had been originally blued but couldn't detect even a dab of color showing because of all the gunk between the spur and guard tang were I usually look.

There wasn't a trace of color on the guard screws, even after removing them and inspecting the underside. Because the slots hadn't been marred, I suspected they had been case hardened. Touching the back side of the heads with a needle file - which slid right off instead of cutting metal - I confirmed the hardness of the surface skin. Wiggling the guard to loosen it, I removed it to find traces of case colors underneath. This was a surprise.

There is no mystery about Parker, Fox or Smith metal finishes. And virtually all British guns from the turn of the last century were finished in a predictable manner. Metal finishes on guns from earlier eras are not always so readily known and disassembly and careful examination is how the professionals find out. If I wanted to restore the Remington to its original factory freshness, I now have a good idea how it looked when new.

What I enjoy most about the tones and hues of newly finished gun metal is their naturalness - earth tones if you will. Most are imparted by archaic methods with age-old formulas that reek of the "art and mystery" of gunmaking. No pigment stains or dyes are used as metal finishes and the abundant colors are the results of sophisticated small-shop processes.

In this chapter I'll present the various blue tones and some explanation of the techniques used to render them. The following chapter will discuss two types of color case-hardening and the so-called French Gray finishes as well as a bit on metal preparation.

Gun bluing is done with purpose, to protect the metal from rusting. The earliest firearms were left "in the white" as polished iron. Of course the metal tarnished or, more realistically, it rusted, even when oiled and cared for. The brown patina seen on the oldest guns was not put there by the maker but by time and use. One would like to imagine that some ancient gunmaker discovered that once this patina developed it actually aided in preventing further rusting of the metal.

So before there was blue, there was brown.

All gun blues are oxides of one form or another. Red rust is ferrous oxide, and when applied as numerous fine coats with each rubbed off before pitting occurs, one has a "browned" finish that will protect the metal very well. Thus we conjecture that controlled browning was developed as a process of accelerating the patina on iron and steel. Gun barrels have been purposely browned for more than two centuries.

The pinnacle of rust browning came during the days when the Damascus barrel was king. The elaborate patterns of forged steel and iron became works of art as gunmakers perfected this metal finish. Numerous fine coats of rusting and aggressive rubbing or "carding" leave the figure of the Damascus swirls a deep brown while the adjacent metal is almost white. An artfully browned Damascus barrel leaves one with the impression that they are looking down into the depths of the metal.

Many early fluid steel shotgun barrels were also browned. In fact, if you came across a mint condition pre-1900 London gun there's a very good chance the barrels would be brown. In 1881 Greener (in *The Gun*) mentions "black-brown" as an alternate finish. (This is the beginning of rust bluing or blacking.) Because the British are so adept at "re-doing" guns, few non-Damascus brown barrels remain. We will discuss this "black-brown" a bit later.

The first gun blue is know by many names: fire blue, temper blue or nitre blue. They all describe the same basic process. Anyone who has seen the translucent blue of a finely tempered gun-spring or even an old-style blue spring-binder clip recognizes the color.

When drawing the temper by heating polished tool or spring steel, it will change colors in a predictable sequence. At about 400 degrees a faint straw will appear. As the temperature increases the color changes

The author swabs a coat of rust bluing solution onto these nearly finished barrels. The damp box is to the left, with a light bulb and pan of water for heat and humidity. The stainless steel boiling tank is to the lower right.

to a deep straw then into purple and then into blue. At about 600 degrees the steel becomes a wonderful royal blue more jewel-like than metal should be. This is also the correct temperature for drawing spring steel.

Some shotgun sidelocks will show the tumbler protruding as a straw color while the screws, or pins will show the fire blue. Although these colors are the true temper colors of the part and denote proper heat treatment, they have become equally important as a cosmetic feature.

This color can be easily created by simply heating a polished part with a propane torch. To achieve a true temper and a lasting color one must immerse the steel in a bath held at the appropriate temperature out of the atmosphere. Early 'smiths blued their barrels in a container of sand brought to temperature over a forge. Somewhere along the line it was discovered that saltpeter, or nitre, melted at about the perfect temperature and is clear as water, so the color changes can be seen. Hence the term nitre blue.

(I have to a **MAJOR SAFETY WARNING** here: I heard a story the other day about a nitre bluing pot erupting as it was coming up to temperature. Moments before, the gunsmith had left the room which was splattered floor to ceiling with hot bluing salts. He has no idea how it happened, but I know that even one drop one of water in the tank, be it from condensation or any other source, will cause the salts to explode. This is an extremely dangerous undertaking as the nitre melts around 600 degrees and can cause third-degree burns and start fires. Don't try this at home!)

I use a commercial bluing compound that melts at a slightly lower temperature. With a gas burner and a thermometer I can hold the bath at exactly 610 degrees and "soak" the gun part for a deep, rich and lasting blue. Unfortunately I have to admit that while startling in color, nitre blue doesn't hold up all that well, so I coat the blued parts with a touch of lacquer for color longevity. Your hand sweat will wear it off the trigger guard screws, but the color of untouched parts will remain indefinitely.

The color of temper blue is easy to recognize but the darker blues used as classic shotgun finishes can be more difficult to identify. All of the pre-war double guns had their barrels rust blued because the process requires minimal heat and won't melt the solder that holds them together.

Rust bluing doesn't appear on firearms with any regularity before about 1850. It is hard to imagine that rust blue wasn't used in the 18th Century or earlier because the process is almost identical to rust browning except that after each rusting the barrels are boiled in water. The boiling converts the red ferrous oxide to blue/black ferro-ferric oxide as if by magic.

Here is an explanation of the process as I do it. With the barrels completely polished they are thoroughly degreased. One must be very thorough with old doubles because of the accumulation of grease and oil in all of the hollows, dips and voids between and under the ribs, barrels and extractor. If oil leaks out at any stage of the work the blue will

From the shop of Doug Turnbull, rust blued barrels, charcoal blued top lever and guard with nitre blued screws.

be streaked or altogether absent in spots and the water tank will be contaminated.

First I like to swab the bores with varnish to protect them from rusting, then plug the barrels with hardwood dowels to use as handles and seal them from the corrosive effects of the solution. The bluing solution is swabbed on in long even strokes and the barrels are placed in a "damp box" which is controlled for humidity and temperature. About 80 percent humidity and 80 degrees is needed for the best results.

A few hours later a fine "bloom" of red rust has formed on the metal. Wearing sterile cotton gloves throughout the process, I remove the wood plugs from the bores and replace them with rubber ones to seal the bores. The barrels are immersed in a tank of water at a rolling boil. In just a few minute they turn blue/black although I always boil a bit longer.

Out of the tank, the barrels are hung to dry and cool and the rubber plugs swapped for the wood handles. The surfaces are coated with a very fine black oxide dust that must be carded or scratched off. This is done with a wheel that has rows of extremely fine wires, just .003 inches in diameter. All traces of the powdery dust are removed by the revolving brush and the barrels re-coated with the bluing solution and placed in the damp box for the next rusting.

I consider six cycles to be a minimum and sometimes as many as 10 are required to achieve the desired finish. The depth and appearance of the bluing can be altered by a number of variables. If, for example, a shiny surface is the goal, the barrels spend less time in the damp box between coats and the RPM of the carding wheel are increased. A deeper etch with a more grainy surface can be had by lengthening the rusting process. Different solutions will result in different hues and texture variations as well.

After the final carding the varnish is cleaned from the bores. The muzzles, water table and breech face are polished to remove the bluing and all is given a coat of oil and left to cure overnight. The next day the barrels receive a light coat of wax which removes any trace of oxide and brings up an attractive shine.

(My explanation of the process is somewhat shallow and lacking the hours of phone conversations with other gunsmiths and 15 years of experience with rust bluing. There are so many variables and techniques for different parts, it would take pages to relate them all. This is a process that could be done on small gun parts at home, but the difference between turning a part blue and getting a fine finish is well beyond the experimenting stage.)

Rust bluing is a procedure well-suited for small shop. Individual hand-polishing, preparation and handling during the bluing is critical to obtain quality results. To quote Greener it, "It is a dirty, a long, and a tiresome process." So I only blue the guns I build. There are several firms that offer rust bluing and there is a bit more you should know when talking to them.

Rust bluing is perhaps the most durable firearms finish with only the very best caustic bluing rivaling it for wear and rust-resistance. When properly performed it gives a beautiful semi-gloss surface and a color achieved by no other method. But there are two different processes and one should know the differences between them.

What I've described is called slow rust bluing. The second method is known as express, hot or fast rust bluing. Instead of rusting the parts in a damp box, the barrels are lightly but uniformly heated and the solution swabbed on while the metal is hot. It dries instantly on the surface and the oxidation takes place immediately. The barrels are then boiled, carded and reheated for several cycles.

Because the rusting happens so quickly each coat is but a very light etch. With this method it is possible to achieve the smooth shiny finish found on the barrels of London guns. The down side is that it is not nearly as durable a finish as the slow rust process. I've used both methods depending upon the results I'm looking for, but vastly prefer the slow rust process for its wear-resistance and semi-gloss sheen. It is possible to achieve a deep, shiny blacking with the slow process but few gunsmiths have mastered it.

Fox Sterlingworth barrels (the working man's variety) will exhibit a slight graininess and a rich black color with blue highlights. Pre-war Purdey barrels, when viewed in strong sunlight, will show a deep shiny blue with almost maroon undertones. Although the process for finishing each of them was very similar, the metal preparation and the formula of the solution was quite different. It is matching these subtleties that make things difficult for modern practitioners but also distinguishes the highest quality restoration from mere refinishing.

Charcoal bluing is another finishing method that was used extensively for shotgun parts. The earliest usage I have seen is on late-English flintlock guns from the beginning of the 19th Century. The most prolific usage is with American firearms - both Colt and Smith & Wesson revolvers and pre-war Winchesters were charcoal or carbonia blued. Although very different in appearance, both the deep dark blue/black of S&W and the translucent blue of Colt guns were achieved by similar processes.

In *The Gun* Greener writes of the charcoal bluing process for it was in common usage by this time. (The British refer to both this process and rust bluing as "blacking"). Most trigger guards and iron buttplates from the period 1850 to 1940, both in Europe and America, were charcoal blued. The appearance of the parts is characterized by the depth and darkness of the color and the shiny surface of the metal. Some of this effect is in the metal preparation and Greener mentions "burnishing" after polishing with abrasive grit. Burnishing will flatten the minute burrs raised on the surface by the cutting action of abrasive polishing bringing the parts to a higher state of shine.

Charcoal bluing is done by placing the parts in a vessel filled with charcoal and heating them to about 600 degrees. The exactly controlled temperature, the contact of the charcoal with the metal and the smoke given off during the process all combine to oxidize the steel. It is interesting to note that restoration wizard Daniel Cullity believes that both the charcoal and rust bluing processes came into widespread usage during the machine age. He figures that the advent of steam power endowed firearms makers with a surplus of controlled heat and humidity. Applying these to finishing the metal parts of the guns they manufactured was a by-product of the ingenuity and necessity of the era.

The modern "caustic" or "hot-dip" bluing is the bane of older double barrels. This is the shiny black finish seen on most all modern American guns. The steel is quickly oxidized by boiling in a tank of commercial bluing "salts." Although this can be a very durable, and to some an attractive metal finish, it can be death to soft-soldered double-barrels. The caustic effect of the salts attack and weaken the solder that holds the ribs and barrels together.

A dead give-away to hot-dipped doubles is the super-shiny black surface. Usually a closer look will reveal that the lettering or numbering will have a washed-out or dished look. For many years in this country the popular refinishing technique employed the use of a high-speed buffing wheel and a caustic bluing. (A few months ago I saw a shotgun recently imported from England that sure looked buffed and hot-dipped blued to me. The barrels had a dull rattle when struck with a brass rod which is a good indication of loose ribs).

Caustic bluing is fine for modern imported doubles that have brazed barrels and ribs. (I believe most contemporary Spanish and many Italian doubles are hot-dip blued.) The salts will not deteriorate the high-temperature alloy. But the finish looks like hell to me - and to a friend who wants me to rust blue the barrels of his Browning sidelock.

Just as in the ages before, today's finely finished firearms sport a full spectrum of color. The British maintained this tradition throughout their long history of fine gunmaking. America lost many of these processes because our guns were initially developed for mass manufacturing, which sadly has put speed and shine before tradition and durability.

Our current infatuation with quality firearms has been the inspiration for re-developing many lost or forgotten techniques. America's custom gunmakers and restoration specialists are striving not only to recreate the past but to add quality and an abundance of color to their work.

Chapter 5

Only Skin Deep

Color case-hardening is largely recognized as a cosmetic finish for modern shotguns. The lively interplay of blues, yellows, reds, grays and even greens is lovely to look at. Case-hardening is the expected finish for the world's finest shotguns dating back more than two centuries. But in reality the colors were not always so important and when they are, the beauty is only skin deep.

To fully understand case-hardening one must first understand the difference between iron and steel. Iron is a metallic element (Fe) and steel is a compound of iron and carbon. Alloy steel is iron mixed with carbon and other minerals to give it a variety of different properties.

Carbon is added to iron so that the metal can be hardened to a greater degree. If carbon steel is heated to cherry-red (the "critical temperature") and quenched (rapidly cooled) in water (or oil depending on the alloy), it is rendered glass-hard and nearly as fragile. Drop hardened tool steel on a concrete floor and it can shatter. If the hardened steel is tempered with heat, it will progressively soften as the temperature is raised. Heated to about 400 degrees, it will remain hard enough for chisels and edge tools. If tempered to about 600 degrees, steel springs will flex and return to shape without bending or breaking. These are wonderful properties that don't exist with iron.

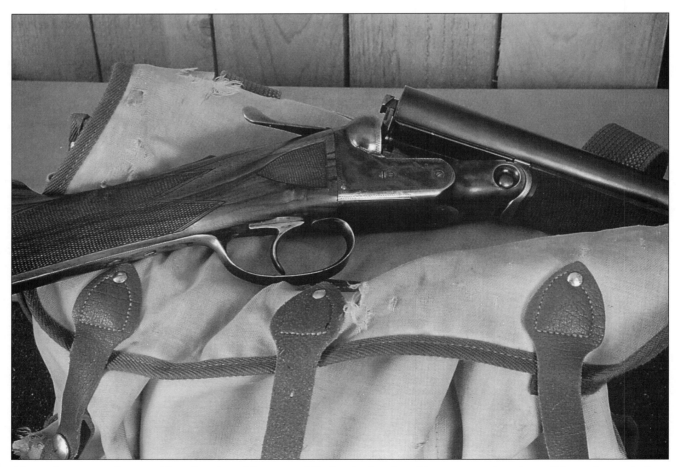

After a few years of competition shooting, this restored Parker is showing shiny spots at the edges of the action and along the trigger guard. Both case colors and rust bluing will wear quickly when handled extensively.

Hardened steel, when again heated cherry-red and left to cool slowly, will be changed to it's softest state (annealed). The study of the development of iron and steel is so thoroughly intertwined with the development of blades, armor and guns that to study one is to learn about the other.

Case-hardening is the earliest and crudest method of melding carbon and iron. A short explanation of the process follows: The iron is packed in charcoal (carbon), heated to the critical temperature, soaked at that temperature, removed and quickly dumped into water. The carbon bonds to the metal during the soak and is fixed in the quench. The iron is surface-hardened by the addition of carbon but the core of the metal remains soft.

Iron takes on several beneficial properties when case-hardened. These become evident when considering the various parts of a flintlock, the grand-daddy of today's sidelock. In the 18th Century the steel needed to make gun springs was rare and expensive, so iron was used to make all of the other lock parts. Sometimes the lockplate would warp with the shock of quenching but because of the soft core it could easily be flattened with a hammer and anvil. The shallow penetration of case-hardening is particularly important to such parts as the tumbler and sear. The working surfaces of the tumbler axle and notches and the sear tip are equally hardened to prevent wear. The surface penetration is only a few thousandths of an inch thick, with the core of these fragile areas remaining soft so they are less likely to break.

The glass-hard skin on the moving parts would resist wearing, binding or galling. In fact, case-hardened iron is slicker than tempered steel and is the perfect frictionless surface for the interior of a lockplate. Imparting surface carbon also added resistance to corrosion and rust. If traces of rust form on a gun, it is less likely on the case-hardened action body, especially it seems, after the colors are gone.

Perhaps the most important use of case-hardening was for the frizzen of a flintlock. As the flint rotates downward it strikes the hardened frizzen, ripping off tiny slivers of metal turned white-hot by friction. The sparks tumble downward causing the "flash-in-the-pan" that ignites the charge. Flintlocks simply did not work without a case-hardened frizzen.

Interestingly, the furthest thing from the mind of the early gunsmith was the cosmetic "case colors". Rare is the original flintlock that was left externally colored after the hardening process. I've examined many original flintlocks that have traces of the case colors on the back side, but were intentionally polished bright on the outside. It wasn't until the late-flint/early-percussion period that coloring was an intentional byproduct of the hardening process.

Let's have a look at my favorite gunmaking text (*Espingarda Perfecta, or The Perfect Gun*, published in Portugal in 1718) to see how they accomplished the process.

In order to temper iron, however soft it may be, so that it may become as hard as steel itself, the most common and easy secret that there is, is to roast some ox-hooves on the fire.... and when they are cold to hammer them, and add to them as much salt, and one part chimney soot. All must be well crushed and put together in any vessel, and then on this is poured enough urine in order to incorporate all of it. And let this advise be taken, that the older this mixture be the greater is its force and activity. And then on to a steel plate are placed the pieces which are to be tempered....and under it a layer and over it another layer of the aforesaid mixture, in such a manner that such pieces be well covered. Then they are put on the fire covered with coal, using the bellows until the fire be strong, and then the fan be used for about a quarter hour, heating this material until it be burnt..... When it is thus burnt, the pieces shall be put into water, and they will be as hard as steel. Let warning be taken that this semblance, and hardness which the iron attains, does not enter inside it, but is only given to its exterior, entering only to a certain limit, which does not happen with steel, which totally, both outside and inside, remains hard. And in the same way shall be tempered the frizzens of the locks, without these remaining so long in the fire, so that they be not to hard to be incapable of executing their function, nor too soft...that they catch the flint-stone and have no effect.

Please notice that there is no mention of case colors anywhere in this text!

W.W. Greener describes the process in his 1881 volume *The Gun,* in a similar manner:

The body, fore-end, hammers, lock-plates, bridles, triggers, escutcheons, and all the screws are hardened, and also the lever...The work to be hardened is placed in a cast iron pot along with charcoal (made by parching bone dust) which must entirely cover the work. The pot is then placed in a bright coal fire, where it remains until the whole is of a worm red. The fire must be a slow one, and the work will require to remain in from one to one and a half hours, according to the body of material to be hardened. When taken out of the fire, the work is plunged into cold water. The iron when at a red heat absorbs the car-

bon, which causes the surface to become perfectly hard after being suddenly cooled, and also gives a nice mottled colour to the iron. ....Some work is case-hardened by plunging when at red heat into a solution of prussiate of potash, but the work so hardened will be found of a dead grey hue, and wanting the fine mottled colours so much admired."

Greener verifies that by 1881 there was case-hardening, and there was *color* case-hardening, with much importance attached to the colors.

(When we describe this process all of these names are somewhat interchangeable: color case-hardening, case-hardening, case-coloring, pack-hardening, bone charcoal case-coloring etc.)

To quote Major Sir Gerald Burrard in his 1931 text *The Modern Shotgun*, "It is not difficult to get a good color: nor is it particularly difficult to obtain the correct degree of hardness; but it is a matter of considerable difficulty to get a combination of beautiful color and proper hardness."

So when one looks at the color case-hardening of a fine shotgun it should be remembered that all gunmaking processes are a product of function and that case colors are just a by-product of the hardening process.

Modern methods have changed just a bit since 1718. Charred ox-hooves - the carbon - is now in the form of cleansed bone charcoal. The parts are packed in a sheet steel box with a lid and handles to grab with tongs. Today's "fire" is a thermostatically controlled furnace and all of the practitioners that I know have eliminated the urine.

There is still a bit of mystery involved even though our modern specialists have made the process more of a science. And color case-hardening is still a bit of a crap shoot because no one knows exactly how the colors are going to turn out. Besides, dumping a red-hot piece of complicated gun metal into a vat of water will always invite warping.

On the other hand I must admit that I've only seen two instances of warping in the dozen-plus actions sent out for case-hardening. The first required straightening of a shotgun top tang. I had purposefully bent the tang upward during the gunmaking process and the metal appar-

ently tried to return to its original form. Because the core of the metal remained soft, re-bending was a simple, if touchy, job. The other warped action was a single-shot rifle that required three hours of hassle, curses and worry before I got it tweaked and lapped back to functioning condition.

When an action is returned after color-hardening, prior to reassembling the mechanism, I first try to install the action to the stock. Because I know it fit perfectly before heat treatment, if it doesn't slip right back into place, I know adjustments must be made. During the mechanical re-assembly I am acutely aware that the action had seen intense heat and quenching. I pay careful attention to how the parts fit back together.

Partially because of the possibility of warping, there are some differences of opinion about case-hardening actions solely to renew the colors. Case colors just don't last if a gun is used. They begin to rub off after a few seasons afield, especially at crisp edges, around the engraving and anywhere there is direct hand contact. I've heard it said that sunlight will fade the colors but can't verify that one.

But do remember, the hardness and corrosion-resistance doesn't fade with the colors. The surface metal stays just as hard as when freshly finished.

Most of the older doubles that look like they have a "coin" finish will show faint case colors on the water-table, bottom of the forend iron of some protected place under the wood. Personally, I find

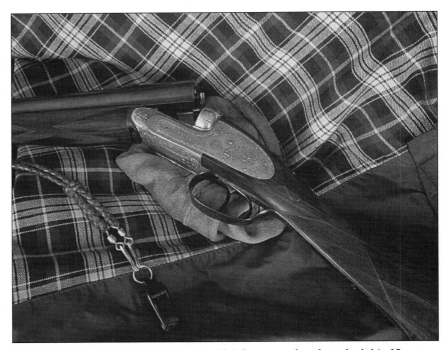

Although gunsmith Dennis Potter completely restored and stocked this 12-gauge Purdey, he choose not to re-color the action, preferring the bright coin finish look of polished case-hardening.

this look quite pleasing and when renewing an older gun I might refinish the stock, black the barrels and leave the action alone.

My friend Ross called last week to talk about re-coloring a London hammer gun he had recently purchased. I asked if he was unhappy with the bright metal look. He said the stock had been nicely redone and he imagined the metal with the same sort of renewal. I told him if he was going to shoot the gun regularly he would have to go through all the stages of fading and color loss until the gun again looked as good as it does today.

Another consideration is the hinge pin. It is my understanding that London "best" guns are hardened with the pin removed and the action "blocked" at the knuckle to prevent warping. On the other hand, many American doubles have semi-permanent (not easily removable) hinge pins and were originally case-hardened with the pin in place. How is your gun to be treated during a re-coloring?

The crux of the difference lies in another metallurgical principal: When two metal parts work against one another they should be of like hardness. We know that the barrel lumps - and therefore the hook - can't be hardened because the heat would cause the soft-soldered barrels to fall apart in the process.

So the question is: Will the hardened face of the pin cause undo wear on the barrel hook? In my opinion the slippery surface of the hardened pin shouldn't cause undo wear on the polished hook. But, my approach is to avoid re-coloring/re-hardening a shotgun action unless one has a very good reason to do so. Of course my custom projects that have all of the case-hardened skin and all of the engraving removed, must be re-colored as well as hardened. A complete restoration of a shotgun requires the process as well. But for a shooter, do remember that those colors are going to disappear all too rapidly.

So how do we preserve that fresh rainbow of rich hues and tones? In a word: varnish. As engraver Lynton McKenzie, told me many years ago, "Case colors are only as good as the varnish put over them."

Again from Burrard, "This varnish soon wears off, seldom lasting more than a season. For this reason I have made it a practice with one gun of mine which has exceptionally beautiful coloring to have the sideplates re-varnished at the end of each season." He goes on to write, "The color is as good as ever, although other guns made at the same time have lost theirs."

I use a "thin varnish" just as Burrard suggests. The varnish, and then the colors, do wear off, but I think it looks fine. (I can imagine how fine my Fox will look if I shoot it enough - and live long enough - to see a shiny silver action. Can you imagine the memories I'll have?) There is a commercial "baking lacquer" available that I'm sure will outlast my finish. Unfortunately the stuff is so hard that if one has to remove it lacquer thinner won't do. The finish may have to be sanded off.

The alternative form of color case-hardening is done in a bath of cyanide. The colors are quite different than the pack-hardening process. I don't think them unsightly. When appropriately done they are quite attractive. But I can tell the difference between pack-hardened and cyanide colors at a glance. This method was used extensively in America by A.H. Fox in the later years, and by Stevens. The striped case colors on Stevens single-shot rifles are singular to the maker and the process.

Unfortunately this method is only done by commercial heat-treaters who are not necessarily experienced with firearms. It is a worthy, if dangerous, color-hardening process. In my experience, cyanide colors wear very well, lasting at least twice as long as pack-hardening colors.

Somewhere around the shop I have a muzzle-loader tang casting that was cyanide-cased by a very experienced backyard gunsmith. Although done more than 15 years ago it has beautiful colors and not a trace of rust. The fellow gave up the process because of the danger and difficulty of disposing of the chemicals.

Resistance to wear and corrosion bring up the question of the so-called "French gray" finish. My objection to this term, and to the finish, is that no two people agree on a common process and few of the methods I'm aware of offer little, if any protection from corrosion. I've never French grayed a gun but I have lacquered over polished steel at the insistence of a very talented and expensive engraver.

You will find French gray the preferred finish of engravers simply because it shows their work at its best. When a gun owner spends as much, or more money on the engraving as he did on the gun, it makes sense to show off the work.

The most common French gray process involves lightly etching the metal. My notes from gunsmithing school relate the Browning repair shop method of baking the parts with a coating of navel jelly. Others use a diluted acid in one form or another. The result is a slightly frosted appearance to the bare metal. It sure shows the engraving well but doesn't make much of a rainy-day gun. Matter of fact, I think the rougher surface of the etching might promote corrosion.

The method I would use would be to first color case-harden the action - with the cyanide process if possible - then remove the colors. If removed with Scotch Brite pad (a considerably finer grade than used in the kitchen) some of the colors will be left in the bottom of the engraving cuts which could be quite attractive. The other method would be a bath in a very mild acid solution. Just enough to remove the colors but not etch the surface. In either case the point is to have some genuine surface carburizing (hardness) then remove the colors and not the hard skin. So we are right back were we started: that beautiful look of a case-hardened shotgun with all of the colors worn off.

I don't know much about the so called "coin finishes" used on imported guns today. I suspect that in earlier times this was a nitriding process, not unlike case-hardening. The modern Spanish and Italian guns look nickel-plated to me. I'm sure open to any information if any of you know better.

A few years back an ingenious engraver started very lightly bead blasting his metal and then nickel plating it. This makes a lot of sense to me as it offers a good-looking flat finish and great protection from corrosion. I don't know anyone currently offering the finish to the trade.

All of the metal finishes described in this and the previous chapter require advanced metal preparation. I only hand-polish my guns. As I've said before, it is a dirty, gritty job and the best reason I know of to have an apprentice. (Thankfully, I've found Thomas Harms who is diligent and enjoys the work.) If one is starting with a previously case-hardened action it is even more of a chore because the hard skin must be broken through first. I find abrasives are the best way for an amateur to accomplish this, although I surface anneal, which can be risky.

Patience and diligence are the primary prerequisites to achieving a good hand-polish on gun metal. And one of the flaws I find hardest to forgive is seeing scratches or dings beneath the surface of newly blued or case-colored steel.

Section 4

A Hughes/Fox Custom Shotgun In The Making

Full Circle Fox

In January 1991 I had the good fortune to meet Michael McIntosh in Reno, Nevada. As we sat at the Lion-Fish Bar in the Nugget Casino, my friend and client Jim Flack posed a question that proved fortuitous for my career.

"What American double shotgun would you chose as the basis for a high-grade custom project?"

Without hesitation McIntosh replied, "If it were mine, it would be a Fox."

While we consumed the next couple of rounds of drinks I listened while Mike and Jim discussed the concept and I started to develop the gun I wanted for myself. I agreed with the notion of starting with a Fox, as they have the best proportion of gauge to action size of any American double. With lightweight barrels a 12-bore Fox has a reasonable beginning weight. The mechanism is uncomplicated and reliable, the barrels are made from highly regarded "Chromox" steel and we all agreed that the action is trim and attractive.

As these knowledgeable gentlemen conversed, I imagined what modifications would mimic the balance and handling qualities of a fine British double. As I visually blended the stylistic features of a London "best" boxlock action with the utility of the American gun and mentally stocked in with a choice stick of English walnut and the concept materialized.

To throw gasoline on the fire, none of us could recollect anyone having done up a Fox like this.

There are several qualities inherent to a British game gun which are seldom found in a mass-produced American double. Balancing on, or near, the hinge pin distributes the weight so that 50 percent is between the hands, a quarter forward and a quarter in the butt. Often described as "dynamic handling" the gun is neither butt heavy nor muzzle light. The mass pivots around the center in the hands.

So balanced, a 6-3/4-pound 12-bore feels like a 6-pounder and a lighter, small-bore gun swings like it weighs a half-pound more than its weight. (With

As purchased, the Fox Sterlingworth 12-gauge had a good action and barrels but a poorly refinished stock.

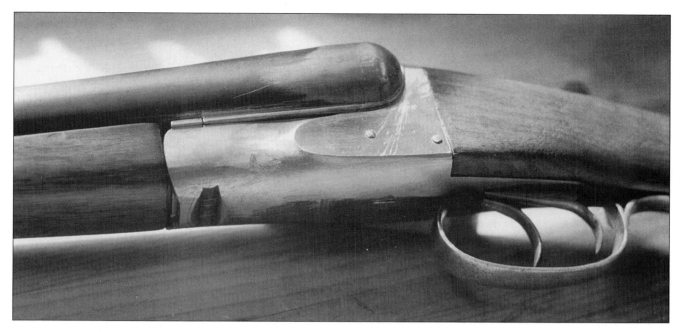

Early metal shaping included rounding the forend iron where it joins the wood and filing the action panels to an oval shape. Installing the original wood helps show the alterations.

the exception of some 16- and 20-gauge Foxes and No. O frame, 16-bore Parkers, you don't often find this balance in an American double.)

Because American guns were designed to last like farm machinery and handle any sort of long-range goose load, the barrel walls, and therefore the weight, is greater than a British gun. And typically the longer the barrels the heavier the wall thickness. Fox guns were offered with four different barrel weights so a 28-inch #3-weight set of barrels approximates the reasonable blend of weight and length found on English guns.

Even though Fox actions are trim by American standards there is enough mass to reshape the action, top lever, safety, triggers and guard to provide a sleeker look and remove excess weight at the same time. I perceived this metalwork as if the factory parts were rough forgings given to a British action filer.

Dynamic handling, reasonably long barrels and light weight could be had while transforming the look and charisma towards the British character. In the mean time I could lavish the hands-on detailing of London craftsmen to a machine-made American gun and blend in the superior woodwork of an American custom gunmaker. It all seemed a worthy goal.

Actually crafting my dreams sometimes makes me feel like Lewis and Clark embarking on a cross-continental wilderness journey. The reality is that a custom shotgun takes a year to create and the cost can easily run into five figures.

It all began with planning, sketches and acquiring the proper project gun. Then came 200 bench hours of hand work spread over 12 months, sending the barrels out for specialty work, a couple of months for the engraver and another few weeks of finish time. Before starting any particular custom project I try to avoid thinking about all that is entailed. Instead, I use the enthusiasm of the dream to launch the endeavor.

I've never given birth, but I have seen enough long-term projects from conception to completion to have an inkling of what it must be like. To give you an idea, I documented and recorded details for this photo odyssey of creating a custom Fox shotgun.

Because this is my own work on my own gun I'll stay away from judgments of aesthetics. Suffice it to say that I built this gun for myself and had no one to impress or to please except my own notions of what I wanted. Actually, the possibilities, styles and configurations are limitless, but I'll stick to the more universal techniques and experiences.

As purchased, the Fox was a Sterlingworth 12-guage with 28-inch #3-weight barrels choked full and fuller. The stock was absolutely trashed by amateur refinishing but the barrels and action were excellent.

METALSMITHING

Every firearm has its assembly and disassembly idiosyncrasies. Fox doubles employ a small coil spring (top-lever latch spring) under the bottom plate screw that is easily lost. The sear spring tension must be relaxed and the sears removed before the buttstock comes off. And the sear pin cannot be driven out until the tiny lock screw is removed. Other lock screws cap-

Various hand files were used to remove the rudimentary engraving and shape the action panels.

ture the hammer pin and top-lever nut. Before removing the ejector trip rods, special shop-made tools, must be lathe-turned. Each of these items must be addressed before the gun is disassembled the first time.

After stripping the gun to its component parts, the action was surface-annealed to soften the metal. Then I had right at it with coarse files. I like to take on the things that scare me most right off the bat, so I reshaped the action panels to an oval form. This was the first, and perhaps most drastic, alteration to the Fox character and the beginning of "Anglicizing" an American gun.

The initial file work included removing all the rudimentary engraving and the deeply stamped "Sterlingworth" on each side of the action. Metal chips piled up under my bench vise as ounces peeled away from the overbuilt frame.

Then, when there was no turning back, I sketched a full-scale profile of the metalwork on the drawing table to determine the lines of the new stock. For a higher comb without a ski-slope comb nose, it was immediately apparent that the tangs must be raised. The sketches helped to determine the amount needed. After carefully measuring the distance between them, I heated the top tang cherry red and bent it upward. A second heating and a few swats with a hammer on the anvil, flattened the tang's curve.

It is relatively easy to snap the tang off at the major screw hole but, with careful thought and judi-cious work, all went well. I reassembled the bottom plate and lower tang and repeated the operation on the bottom tang. Then came some minor tweaking to refit the major screw which, when completed, showed the tangs had been properly realigned.

With the action held firmly in the vise, a chisel and hammer were used to form raised beads around the fences. They are refined with rifflers and needle files prior to polishing.

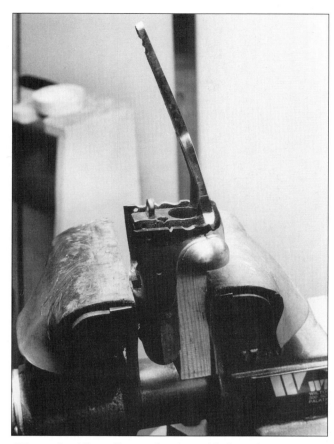

"Fancy Back" scalloping has been filed on the far side of the action. After making a template to ensure proper location, the first file cuts were done on the near side.

The rear tang screw (or hand pin) was another matter. Farthest from the bend, the top and bottom holes where completely out of alignment. So I used a hack-saw to cut off the last half-inch of the lower tang and gas-welded a new blank extension in place. (I chose to alter the lower tang to stay away from the safety divots in the top tang. Besides, if the weld didn't turn out cosmetically perfect, it would be covered by the trigger guard.)

I cleaned the heat scale off both tangs and re-shaped the lower one to match the original contours. The hole location in the lower tang was calculated, drilled and counter-bored for the screw head. Then I made a new tang screw and all was back to normal.

While I had the gun apart I removed, finish filed and polished each of the internal parts. The sears, hammers, top lever and inside of the action body were slicked with a number four Swiss-cut file and given a thorough refining with grit cloth. I was careful not to remove metal where it was likely to change the tolerances of the moving parts and inhibit the function.

Next, the triggers and safety had to be refit. So I thinned, lightened and reshaped the trigger pads. After being completely reassembled, the trigger and safety were brought back into the correct relationship with each other and with the sear bars. I even soldered tabs on each trigger to thicken the metal for a closer, rattle-free fit in each of their slots. With these operations complete, I prepared myself for the task of shaping ball and bead fences from the existing metal.

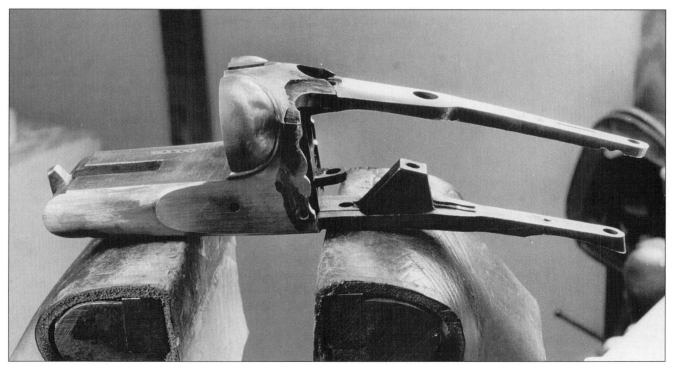

At this stage the rough action shaping is nearly completed, including the rebates where the upper tang meets the action body.

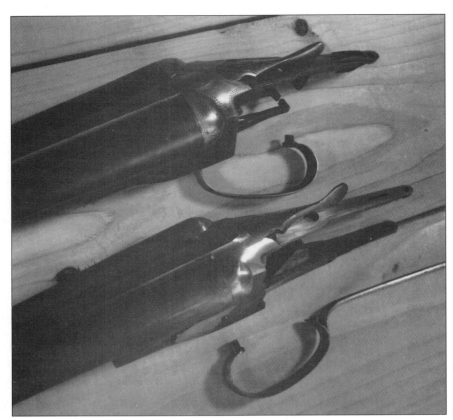

Reshaped top lever, action panels, scalloping, ball and bead fences and new trigger guard are all obvious when compared to an unaltered Fox action (above).

The completed barreled action and trigger guard with the metal polished to 320-grit sits atop a stick of California English walnut prior to stockmaking.

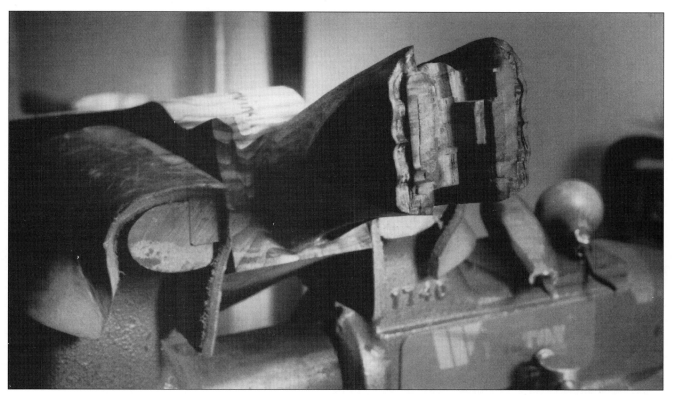

The head of this stock has more internal wood than any factory Fox. Blocks of wood that enter the back of the action also serve to support the delicate scalloping. Looking closely, one can see how well the wood contacts the metal.

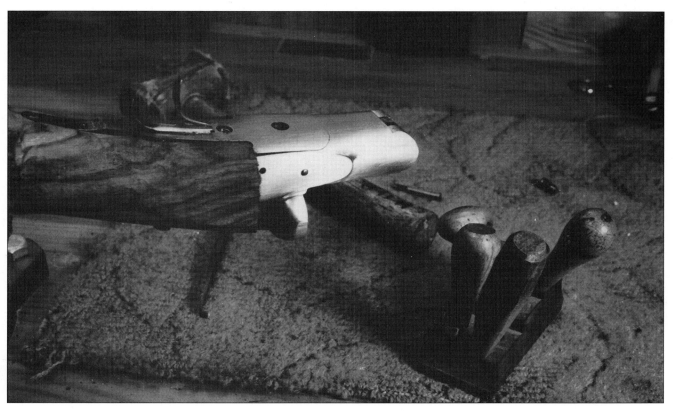

After the action is married to the stock, the bottom plate is inlet downward. The block in the foreground holds tiny bench-made chisels employed in the task.

The author presses the bottom plate into place before rapping it with a mallet to seat it.

Original Fox actions are nearly flat across the top from the height of the fences to the rib. I wanted to shape the fences to dip down next to the rib and follow the contours of the barrel breeches. In this small space I had to find room to fit the ends of the fence beads and create a raised oval surrounding the barrel extension.

With the barrels locked onto the action, I began to whittle away the excess metal with a safe-edged square-file. Then, as I neared the barrel contours, my trusty die sinkers chisel came out of the tool box along with an 8-ounce brass hammer.

I pen-sketched the bead from the bottom of the fence at the barrel bar, around to terminate at the lowest point next to the rib. Solidly held in the bench vise, I literally carved the outline of the bead around one of the fences with chisel and hammer. (The old forged iron is quite malleable once the case-hardened skin is removed and the work is great fun once the initial blows are struck.) With the right side roughly outlined, I mathematically and visually laid out the other fence bead and really enjoyed sculpting that side.

The rest of the form was raised and rounded with smaller chisels, three-cornered files and die-sinkers rifflers, which are small and oddly shaped needle files. The better part of a day and a half, less

time than I would have imagined, was consumed by forming and refining the ball and bead fences. The toughest part is matching the beads from side to side. I used all the layout lines I could and then worked by eye to perfect their appearance.

The top of the action was shaped to blend with the new contours and an oval panel was raised, by lowering the rest of the metal, around the rib/barrel extension. Half-round "rebates" were filed at the junction of the upper and lower tangs and the action body. (These look snazzy and serve to lock the head of the stock into the action, lessening the wedging affect of recoil on the stock.)

The rear of the action was then scalloped in the traditional manner that is found on a few high-grade Fox guns. (This is called a "fancy back" in the British vernacular.) I placed the center of the pattern a touch high to keep it away from the lower pin hole and to put it closer to the true center of the side of the stock. (This would improve the lines when it came time to shape the stock panels.) One side of the scalloping was done entirely with tiny needle-files then a brass template was made to match. The off-side was carefully laid out and both sides were filed with a slight inward bevel for good wood-to-metal fit. Four and a half hours were consumed by the fancy-back filing.

The new trigger guard is surrounded by the materials it was made from. Clockwise from the bottom: tang bar stock, rough-forged bow, bow metal cut to length and an original Fox guard.

The heel and toe plates were drawn on paper which was pasted to sheet steel, then cut and filed to shape.

As the heel and toe plate are installed the screw must be angled to pull the plates towards the scalloping to ensure a close fit. Note that the butt is slightly concave.

Unlike the original Fox guns, I like to have fingers of wood entering the back sides of the action to strengthen the stock. These fingers also support the fragile edges of the scalloped wood. In order to accomplish this I had to grind down the backs of the hammers so the wood had some place to fit. The lighter hammers will speed the lock time. The cosmetic scalloping turned out to have an all-around beneficial improvement on the guns integrity and performance.

(These cosmetic alterations are not without precedent. The A.H. Fox company had the so-called "Special" guns altered with these same features. The exception being the oval action panels I chose. Fox guns had pointed or arrowhead-shaped panels. I'm relatively sure the Burt Becker custom Fox guns, the first "Specials," were hand-shaped employing the same methods I used. Scalloping, tang juncture rebates and beaded fences are each seen on the Becker guns and the later, presumably, "in-house" Specials.)

To complete the action shaping, I rounded the upper and lower tangs for a more pleasing wrist and shaped the forend iron by rounding it to match the action knuckle. The half-round shape vastly improves the look of the forend wood-to-iron juncture.

In all, almost a half a pound of metal was removed. I even scalloped the inside, center section of the forend iron of this extractor gun to eliminate a couple more ounces.

All metal parts have been fit to the stock blank, which has been cut with a band-saw to profile and had layout lines for contour shaping drawn on it.

The surrounding hardware was next. After studying dozens of photos of top levers, I settled on a design and filed the Fox's to suit, removing the coarse checkering as well. My top lever is much more British-looking and further disguises the gun's origin. The safety was whittled down to a button with a checkered pad, more like a Holland & Holland than a Fox.

This left me to face the trigger guard. I just chucked the original guard into the scrap bin and set out to make a new one. (Four years later I had a fellow offer me $50 for a factory guard.) The new one started with drawings. Then I forged the basic oval of the bow from 1/8-inch by 3/4-inch strap steel. After grinding and filing a taper to each side and the rudimentary shaping of the bow, the rear tang and threaded mounting stud were welded in place.

I left the tang to shape later to suit the stock. Although the bow had about the same dimensions as the original, there is more open space in front of the triggers and less behind. The spur follows closely behind the rear trigger to prevent a sore knuckle on the shooting hand. The guard was filed to its final form with a raised bead along the right edge in the style of British guns that goes back to the flintlock era. The triggers were shaped and bent to blend and mate with the guard. It took a whole day to make the trigger guard.

The final parts to manufacture before stockmaking were the heel and toe clips. They were designed, drawn and the drawings pasted to sheet steel. I used a hack-saw to cut the rough form and filed the contours and the scalloping in a scaled-down version that matches the action. Each is mounted with an old-style full-threaded gun screw.

The barreled action was sent to Dennis Potter for barrel bore work. He lengthened the chambers to 2-3/4 inches, reamed the chokes to Skeet II and Improved/Modified and mirror-polished the bores. Starting with a Full/Fuller choked gun allows any possible choke combination. I like the idea of having an open and a tight choke to take full advantage of having two barrels and two triggers.

STOCKMAKING

Many contemporary stockmakers have adapted the use of a precision pantograph, or duplicate-carving machine, to lessen the drudgery and repetition of certain phases of their work. I like to think of this dupli-

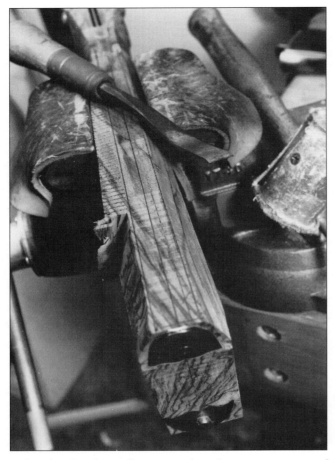

A flat chisel and a mallet are used on the square corners of the blank during the initial contouring stages. Note that the left side is being chiseled away from the prevailing grain flow to prevent splitting the wood.

graph - just like the one used in a certain London maker's factory. The stock blank (a juicy stick of California English walnut) was machined for the inletting, stock panels and first three inches of the wrist. The inletting was left .020 inches oversize and the outside a full .125 inches, or an eighth of inch. The rest of the blank remained square, to be shaped as I pleased.

The action doesn't slip right onto the machined wood and, to "head-up" the stock, about a paper-match thickness of wood must by removed from all surfaces. The traditional chisels and scrapers were used for this work, which, according to my log book, took 4-3/4 hours of fitting the action to the stock. (In the photo of the stock head you will notice a darkening of the wood where it meets the metal. This is the transfer of inletting blue traditionally used to achieve a near-perfect wood-to-metal fit. Non-drying "Prussian Blue" is painted on the metal surfaces with an old toothbrush. The action is slipped into the head of the stock and seated with a swat from a rawhide mallet. A spot of blue remains on the wood wherever the metal contacts it. Then a chisel or scraper can surgi-

cating machine as my apprentice - one who lessens the burden but leaves the precise and artistic work for me.

Knowing I would be building more than one 12-bore Fox stock, I started by making a pattern stock so that the major inletting of the action could be repeated by machine.

Starting with a machined stock from a commercial supplier, I built up the interior wood at the action so there would be more material than any factory Fox stock ever had under the metal.

The action was then hand-fit to the pattern stock and epoxy-bedded to achieve a perfect fit. I now had what you might call a precision casting of the stock head with just enough wood removed to allow the moving parts to function.

Some may find this non-traditional approach disillusioning; but after 15 years of hand-inletting virtually every type of gun metal into solid blocks of walnut, I call it smart. There would be more than enough hand work later on.

The stock pattern was then machine duplicated on a $15,000 American-made single-spindle panto-

Almost 8 ounces of wood were removed from the butt by boring two holes and chiseling the web between them. The sawn-off butt scrap is being fitted as a plug.

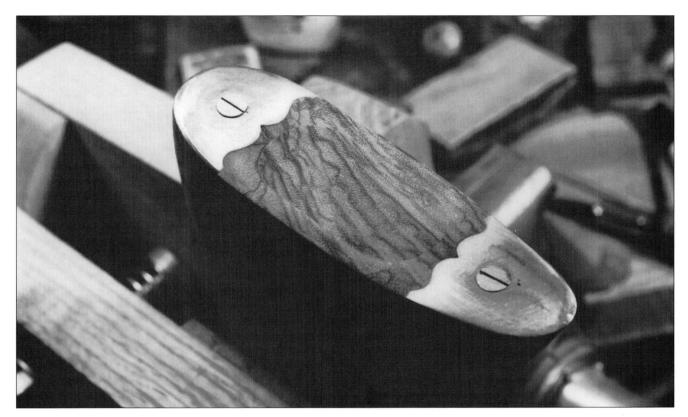

Only careful inspection will reveal the plug in the hollow butt.

The guard tang has been inlet and the screws installed with careful attention to preserving the toe line of the stock. (Engraving design sketches form the background of the photo.)

The author saved most of the scrap wood sawn, chiseled and rasped away during the stock-making process. It makes quite a pile.

cally remove the slivers until near 90 percent or better contact in achieved.)

Installing the tapered tang screw draws the metal back onto the stock the final few thousandths and seats the tangs into their inlet. When all was tightly seated, I removed the tang screw, held the works upside down and rapped on the side of the stock. This is to make sure that the wood and metal will stay together by the tight fitting alone. It is the very test they are reported to do in London.

Employing another non-traditional method, I wet all of the inletting at the head of the stock and dried it quickly to raise the grain and open the pores. Then I prepared a thin mix of epoxy and lightly brushed it onto the inletting. The metal, coated with a release agent, is socked up tight and all left to dry. The epoxy sealer is my guarantee that gun oil migration won't turn the head of the stock punky. The wood-to-metal fit is so close before the epoxy is applied there is not a trace showing on the finished gunstock.

Publicly revealing these non-traditional methods leaves me open for criticism or congratulations. Regardless of judgments, I try to make the best and longest-lasting gun I know how.

The forend wood was treated in a similar manner. After the iron was inlet and installed, the wood was closely fitted to the barrels. The wood under the barrels was not epoxy-sealed, as I prefer to finish it with the same process as the outside of the stock.

After years of building stocks for other folks, I have a pretty good idea what I want for stock dimensions, but rarely the opportunity to apply them. Now is the time to draw them on the side of the square blanks attached to the action and barrels.

It is amazing how fast the basic profile shape is achieved from this point. First the comb nose and then the length of pull are located on the stock. The drop at the comb and heel are measured down from the rib and marked on the wood. The height of the butt is marked then drawn at the appropriate pitch angle.

After that, it was a matter of connecting the dots to complete the pencil profile on the side of the blank. A straight line connects the comb to the heel. The curved line of the butt runs from the heel down to the toe. A sweeping, slightly concave line connects the toe to the lower tang. And, back up on top, the tang line rose to form the comb nose, or thumbhole, of the stock.

Detail stock shaping includes hand-carved drop points and forend beading where the iron meets the wood.

No matter the number of stocks I have made, nor the number I've yet to make, I always pause before I turn on the bandsaw. There is no backing up so I re-check all the measurements and set the gun up on the wall to visually check the lines and flow of the stock profile felt-tipped on the lovely walnut.

Next, the comb nose was sawed, then the top line of the wrist. Off came the slab on top of the comb and finally, the toe line was cut from lower tang to toe. Only the butt end was left uncut.

Centerlines were established all the way around the stock. Top tang back to heel and bottom tang to toe. The cast at the heel and toe were marked and the cast centerlines added. Having both sets of centerlines on the stock gives me the chance to visually compare the amount of cast and twist (if the stock is cast more at heel or toe) with the true center.

I squared a line across the top of the butt from the cast-off centerline. The bandsaw table was tilted to match the angle so the butt was sawed square with the cast and not with the action.

(I was sure to pick up this last scrap of wood from the floor so my springer, Lilly didn't carry it off. One sliver of walnut in my coffee ruins the cup, but she seems to enjoy the flavor. As we shall see, this is a very important piece of walnut.)

With the blank profiled I was left with the laborious task of contouring the stock. There are a few more things that can be done to aid this process. In this case, I inlet the toe and heel plates on center, into the back end of the blank. These will help to show me the shape and also start serving their intended purpose of protecting the fragile edges. If this were to be a checkered butt, the butt shape would be drawn on the end of the stock.

Inletting the heel and toe plates was not exactly a walk in the park. The proper curve of the butt had to be maintained, which means the angle of the screws was critical. They must draw the plates down tightly and up against the scalloped inlet at the same time. A couple of hours were spent inletting each of the plates and properly installing the deep threaded gun-screws.

The heel and toe plates establish the finished thickness of the butt and I can usually band saw a slab off each side from the butt end down to the wrist thickness. Any time wood can be removed with machines I take advantage of it, but fine quality handwork will never be replaced by machines.

Then it was time to get serious.

If one is to shape a stock from a blank, at some time in the process, the wood must literally be attacked to achieve the bulk of the contour shaping. I'm not Sam Maloof and don't try to use a bandsaw to cut the corners off the blank. Nor do I use the Alvin Linden hatchet method, nor even a draw-knife in this case.

When looking straight on to the butt end, quarter-sawn wood will have grain running across the

The forend is shown with its hardware removed. The forend tip was forged from steel as was the oval escutcheon. The iron itself has been skeletonized to remove weight.

thickness of the blank. Slab-sawn wood will have the grain running from heel to toe. You'll notice in the photos this particular stock blank is nearly quarter-sawn from the head through the wrist, but the grain takes a major twist starting around the comb nose. It winds up being perfectly slab-sawn at the butt. That's a 180-degree turn in about 8 inches.

The grain twist paints a pretty picture on the sides of the stock but makes it dangerous to shape with edge tools. They want to dig in and split the grain rather than cut along it. This is one of the reasons that for centuries stockmakers have preferred quarter-sawn wood. The quadrants can be peeled off relatively easily with edge tools. Sometimes the wood is removed from wrist to toe and sometimes from the opposite direction.

I laid out each corner quadrant with lines running front to back. For twisted or contrary grain flow I used a fine saw to cut across the corners and I chipped out the pieces of wood with a 1-inch flat chisel and a rawhide mallet. All of the various methods, except the bandsaw, are very laborious, but with this one I can remove a bunch of wood in a hurry, without too much worry about splitting or digging into the grain.

With this particular stock I decided to hollow the butt about half-way through the quadrant shaping. The wood was extremely dense and heavy so I

knew a major cavity would be needed. Normally I would have the stock shaping nearly finished and would hollow the butt as needed to balance the gun's weight. When left thick and square, the stock is easier to hold securely and is stronger so I could really clamp it down in the vise without fear of crushing the wood. A firm hold is needed to bore and chisel a cavity this large.

I laid out the approximate size of the cavity on both sides and the back end of the butt. I planned to hollow the stock 1-1/16 inches X 2-1/2 inches X 4 inches deep. A couple of 1-1/16-inch holes were bored to nearly full depth. The upper hole follows the comb line whereas the lower hole is angled slightly upward at the angle of the toe line. (When I figured it correctly, the holes met edge to edge down in the bottom of the cavity making it easier to chisel out the web between the holes, 4 inches down in there. The angled holes also maintain the best structural integrity.) Almost 8 ounces of wood were removed.

After chiseling out the center, the very outboard edge of the cavity was tapered slightly to accept the plug. I retrieved the sawn-off butt end and spent way too much time matching the end grain before cutting out the plug. It was fit very closely until there was a full 3/8 inches of wood plugging the finished butt. The plug was set aside until the stock was nearly finished in case I had to remove more wood to achieve

A couple of passes with an electric checkering tool precede the work with hand tools. (This is a 20-gauge Fox with checkered stock panels.)

the perfect balance. (Typically, when a butt is finished and checkered, it is virtually impossible to detect the plug. That's part of the reason I like to shoot a photo of the stock boring process - because some people can't believe it.)

All four quadrants of the stock were sawn and chiseled to round off the edges (which removes a great deal of wood.) A 3/4-inch gouge and a mallet were needed to peel some of the excess wood to form the comb taper above the wrist. After that I used a pattern-maker's rasp for most of the shaping.

Each side of the stock was reduced in thickness to a flat from the butt to the wrist. Layout lines on the top, bottom and sides of the blank set the maximum amount of wood to be removed. There had to be a uniform taper from the wrist to the butt; the toe line had to be well-rounded and the comb had to have something of a compound taper (with the angle increasing towards the comb) and be well-defined within the wrist of the stock.

The majority of this work was done by hand with a rasp. Sweat formed on my brow and my breathing got ragged while I was bearing down with

the tool. Piles of sawdust accumulated on the floor and the blunt-cornered blank started to take the form of a gunstock.

The rough shaping was completed with layout lines on the stock: A V-line on the top of the comb, a 1/2-inch-wide flat the length of the toe line, and a flat defining the highlights from the wrist center towards the heel and toe on each side.

Next it was time to install the trigger guard and inlet its tang. (I'd left the guard tang as a rectangular blank a full 6 inches long. A long guard tang looks especially good to me.)

First, the finial at the far end was filed to shape. It was stepped down, with shoulders leading to a 1-inch-long tapered section ending in a gently rounded point. The edges were filed with a slight bevel so they wedge down into the wood. This is called an inletting bevel and helps in fitting the guard by taking up gaps between the wood and metal as it is installed.

The tang was inlet to just past half depth, with extra care to maintain the slightly concave toe line of the stock. (If the line from the back of the guard to the toe were ruler straight, it would look full and heavy.)

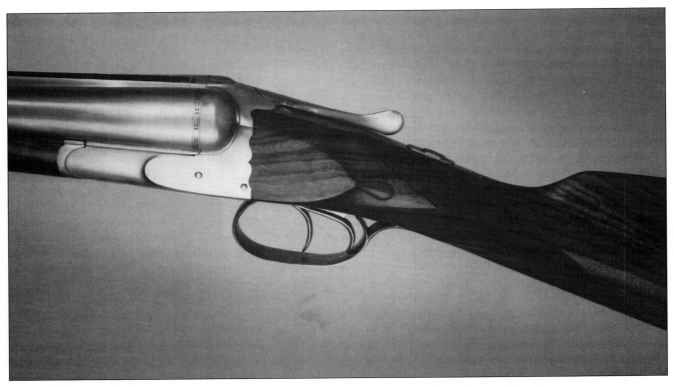

The grip is checkered with 26 lines per inch in a long point pattern with mullered, or grooved, borders.

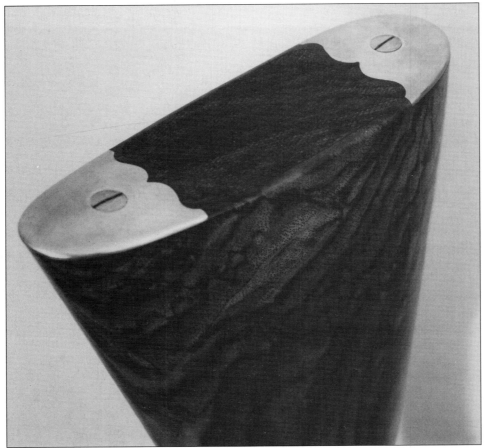

After checkering, all traces of the wood plugged butt disappear. Can you find it?

The forend checkering is completed in a point pattern with a small border around the oval escutcheon.

I wanted a very slim wrist for this gun, so the distance between the top and bottom of the wrist-and therefore the toe line and guard-tang inlet-was extremely critical. Although a straight-grip shotgun stock looks to be one of the simplest designs, deviating as little as 1/16 of an inch in any of the lines will alter the form, character and handling of the gun.)

The object was to make the gun look slim-waisted without looking skinny or slab-sided through the wrist. It is my experience that a stock will feel much as it looks; slim is great but skinny or slab-sided feels awkward.

The tang was inlet by tracing its outline on the cast off center-line, stabbing in with a flat chisel along each side and then gently lifting out the chips down the middle. It took me two hours to inlet the tang and install the screws.

Next, the toe line shaping was completed with the guard tang in place on the stock. I had to be careful not to drag metal chips into the wood as the final rounded form of the toe line was filed to shape.

My stock pattern had oversize stock panels behind the action so the machine had roughly pre-shaped these. The fun part was detailing the shaping of all of the stock subtleties. To get the British appearance I was after I wanted oval-shaped panels with drop points, an un-fluted comb nose tapering to a point and something of a diamond grip as shaped in the cross section. Although I used basic layout lines for this shaping, so much was done by eye and by feel that is extremely difficult to describe. Looking at the lines and subtle character of the finished stock says more than I can on paper.

There is a purpose for drop points besides the decorative affect. When looking down at the top of the wrist it is necessary to make a clean transition from the width of the action to the width of the wrist. There is nearly an inch of difference on this Fox gun.

I began by gently tapering the flats of the panels towards the butt. Changing to the profile view, the panels were shaped to a point at the rear with a ridge running down into the center of the wrist. (All original Fox guns and many other double-guns have these pointed stock panels. I shape them all this way and sand the stock as if it were completed.)

Drop points were then drawn on the stock along with the rear oval of the panels. I then carved the shape of the drop points with tiny chisels and a carving knife. The tops were precisely rounded and blended until I had the look I wanted. (By shaping them from the existing wood, they look like what they are - part of the stock rather that dollops of wood pasted on.)

When viewed from above or below, this created a flowing transition from the panels to the slim wrist, without a hard line or ridge characteristic of some other styles. Some stockmakers tell me they leave extra wood to shape the drop points but I just can't imagine how they do this without them looking like extra wood.

There is no great trick to shaping the forend except figuring out how to hold it in the vise. I have some simple fixtures that I use to clamp it solidly for shaping.

My forend is fuller in both width and thickness than the factory Fox splinter. Again, the shape is an interpretation of British form. (Note that the fence beads actually begin at the borders of the checkering

As received from the engraver, the metal-work has been transformed. A light ink wash in the cuts helps show the details.

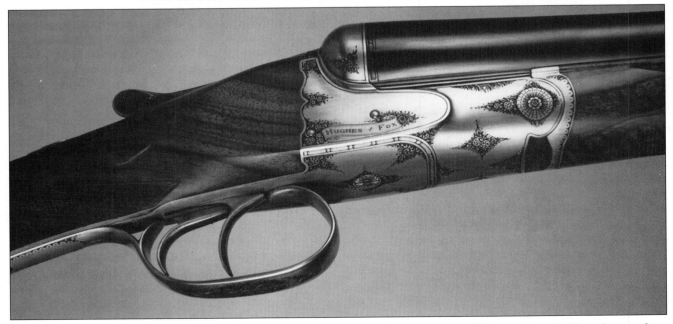

As mentioned in the text, the engraving seems to shrink and tighten the appearance of the metalwork. (Note the wood-to-metal fit.)

The negative space of the engraving design forms its own statement. Note the ball & bar border around the bottom plate that is repeated on the barrel breeches. Nick & dot borders meet the forearm and grip.

as relief-carved details. These details follow into the forend iron and barrel bar and mate to the fence beads themselves.) A steel forend tip was forged and fit along with an oval anchor/escutcheon that attaches the iron with a through-bolt.

THE FINAL TOUCHES

My custom Fox was complete except for checkering, engraving and wood and metal finishing. Although I had a cohesive, shootable gun, the checkering and finishing would account for almost 40 percent of the entire project. Up to this point I had invested some 120 bench hours on the gun. The finished project would ultimately involve more than 200 hours, not counting the engraving.

My bank account was diminishing rapidly and it was good to approach the part of the job (waiting for the engraving) that would allow me to work on paying projects.

From there on it was mostly nit-picking work and the intensity of checkering. But the sanding, polishing, checkering and finishing techniques separate the merely good work from the very best projects and are absolutely essential to fine gunmaking.

American stockmakers are fanatical about stock finishes. The first step to a good finish is wood preparation. Starting with 100-grit paper, I hand-sanded the stock progressively with 120-, 150-, 180- and 220-grit paper. The paper was backed at all times with a rubber block, an eraser or motorcycle gas-line tubing depending on the contour being sanded. (Each backing material somewhat conforms to the stock curves yet is hard enough to keep the edges true and sharp.) The stock was "whiskered" by wetting it with water and rapidly drying it between each sanding. If this process is ignored the first time the gun sees a serious rain-wetting the grain will rise right up through the finish.

All metal parts were left in place during sanding, and the wood was left the slightest bit high above the metal to accommodate future refinishing.

After the final sanding all of the metal was removed from the wood. The grain was again raised to open the wood's pours and clean out the sanding dust to accept the sealant. A water-thin stock sealant was used to saturate all bare wood surfaces inside and out until the wood could drink no more. This was especially important at the end grain of the butt. On all stocks the area thirsts for moisture and soaks up, literally, coat after coat of sealant.

Sealing the wood is an important part of protecting against shrinking and swelling with seasonal variations in moisture. Contrary to popular belief, linseed oil will pass water like a sock and, in my opinion, is perhaps the worst stock finish around. I'm sure to catch some flak here but, though I can't deny

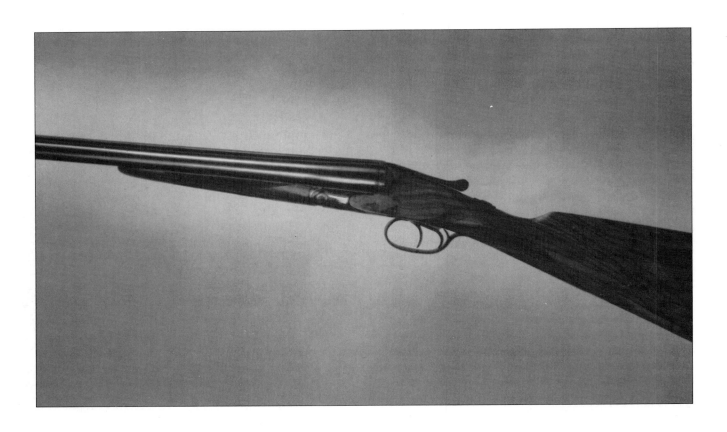

It is difficult to recognize the origin of the gun by look or feel. It no longer has any of the characteristic Fox features, weighs a pound less and is well-balanced.

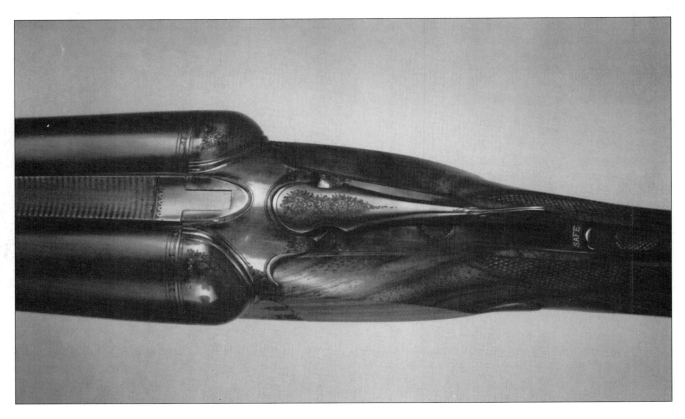

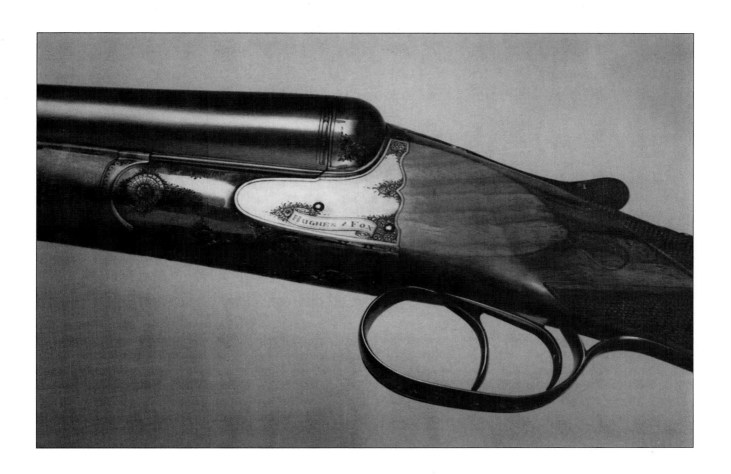

Metal finishes include color case-hardened action; rust blued barrels, guard and top lever and nitre blued triggers, pins and screws. Equal attention to detail throughout the process makes for a truly unique custom shotgun.

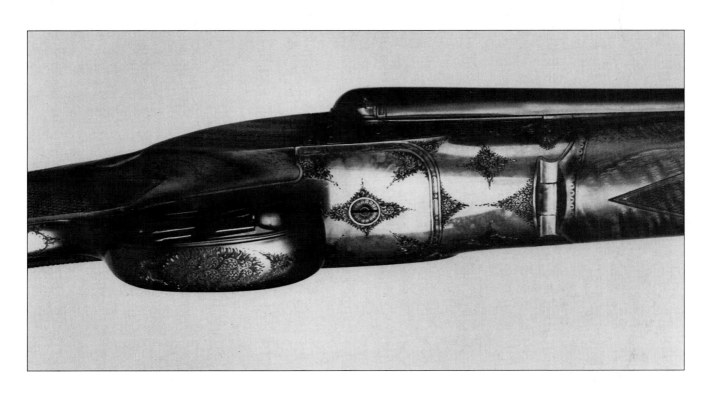

The Fox looks clean, sleek and slim in profile. All of the lines seem to thrust forward.

linseed oil is the best looking finish, it won't hold up to moisture or rough use like the modern concoctions. In fact, many older guns that you might think are oil-finished actually have a spar varnish (as in sailing ships) that is top-coated with oil in the form of a French polish.

I test my stock finishes on kitchen knife handles, my backyard bird feeder and most recently, the maple threshold at my shop door. Monitoring this extremely rough use gives me a good idea of how a finish will hold-up. I use a tung-oil modified with urethane that gives a hard, moisture-resistant surface with the look of oil.

After a second coat of sealant, the stock was wet-sanded with 320-grit wet and dry paper. A couple more coats of sealant followed as did another wet-sanding with 320. I repeated this process until the grain pores were filled level with the stock surface.

The checkering was then laid out, spaced and cut nearly full depth. The first two passes, which represent about 40 percent of the work, were cut with a hand-held electric checkering tool. The remainder was all done with hand tools. The complete checkering job took about 30 hours.

As my goal was to "Anglicize" this American gun, I cut 26 lines-per-inch checkering in a traditional point pattern found on British work. The borders were cut in a fashion known as "mullered" with unbroken lines on either side of a concave groove. The forend, grip and the wood between the heel and toe plates were checkered alike. The butt checkering completely camouflaged any trace of the plug in the back of the stock.

After the checkering was cut and the borders added, I wet sanded again with 400-, 600- and 1,200-grit paper. This gives a mellow sheen and almost soft surface to the wood. Final rubbing with linseed oil

and rottenstone top-coated the finish for the best appearance. Three or four passes with hand tools were then required to point up the checkering.

While I was waiting for the stock finish to dry, I hand polished the metalwork. The barrels were "struck" or draw-filed to clean up the surfaces and remove any irregularities or tiny pits. Each and every bit of the metal was hand-polished with 150-, 180-, 240- and 320-grit cloth. All was then gone over with a blending pad to even the polish. The last step was to again hand polish with 400-grit prior to engraving.

Hand-striking and polishing the barrels consumed a day and a half of tedious work by itself. It is a hard, gritty and dirty job. It is also the best reason to have an apprentice. I believe that preserving the details of finely shaped metal and wood work is absolutely vital to fine gunmaking and that hand-sanding and polishing are the only way to accomplish this.

Years ago I decided that all my custom projects should be hallmarked in 24-karat gold. The stamp I use is a 1/8-inch x 1/4-inch oval, with a raised "SDH" in the center. A heavy brass hammer was used to strike the stamp and make the inlay from sheet gold, which was then cut with a jeweler's-saw and inlaid into the lower tang at the rear of the guard bow. I call this my tombstone, and it is the only headstone I'll ever need. (If you look closely at the photos, you'll see this sparkle of precious metal.)

At this point I essentially had a completed gun ready for test-firing. I knew the piece was going to function because I had been testing it all along with snap caps, but a few heavy loads confirmed that the stock was properly bedded and wasn't going to set back and split. Patterning with target loads showed the gun shot to point of aim and close to the desired pattern percentages.

All that was left was the applied art of the engraver and protective finishes for the metal.

I got to know engraver Eric Gold when I was asked to photograph work he had done on the American Custom Gunmakers Guild's #9 raffle gun, a .22 bolt-action. The engraving took my breath away as it was done in a tiny and precise form of English scroll with gold bouquets throughout.

It is easy to remember looking at the scroll with a 10X loupe and thinking how appropriate it would be on a British side-by-side. It presented the notion that artistic simplicity and attention to detail are the basis for elegance.

Although I feel that all fine guns should be engraved - and the vast majority of my custom work is - few of my personal guns have more than a bit of scroll work, simple borders and hand-cut serial numbers. But with the enormous investment of my time in this Fox project, I knew it deserved more than a modicum of applied art. Fortunately, Eric could use my photography skills and was excited about the gun so we struck a deal that would work for both of us.

Months before, I had commissioned Gold to design an engraving layout for my Fox project. I wanted something that would show-case the possibilities to my clients. Gold supplied me with a lovely pen and ink rendition of our combined notions of how the gun could be elaborately embellished. The engraving that ended up on this gun is something of a simplification of Gold's original design. In fact, I took white-out to a photocopy of the original art to come up with the final design.

Over the next couple of months, I would talk with Gold and he would somewhat shyly admit he was pleased with his progress on the Fox. I am familiar with this situation. One wants to convey the delight of artistic accomplishment but also feels uncomfortable praising one's own work. This is especially true if you know that the client has a good deal of experience and high expectations.

Needless to say, I was very excited when a small but heavy package with a Flagstaff return address arrived at my door. I cleared my work bench, slit the tape and carefully unwrapped each piece. My finely polished Fox metalwork had returned looking like it has shrunk a third in size. (The first look at engraved parts often conveys this illusion because one is used to seeing the expanse of unengraved metal.)

The fluid lines of the metal had been pulled together by the engraving and a black-ink wash in the cuts brilliantly displayed the work. What had been a mass of oddly shaped, bare and bright steel surfaces had been fit together like the beginning of a jigsaw puzzle. It was all I could do to photograph the parts before assembling the rest of the pieces into a shotgun.

Like my spaniel, I nearly wet myself with excitement. I called Eric, and he got the picture even though for once I was at a loss for words.

Another roll of film documented the assembled gun before I reluctantly disassembled it for the hundredth time to send parts out for color case-hardening. The action and forend iron were packed and labeled "Doug Turnbull Restoration" and shipped the next day. Gold had previously engraved the barrels and returned them so they could be rust blued with another batch. I could also rust blue the lever, guard, forend parts and heel and toe plates.

Rust bluing is a four- or five-day operation. After degreasing, the parts are hung on wires and coated with my "secret formula" rusting solution. All are placed in a "sweat box" that is simply but efficiently controlled for temperature and humidity. An hour later a "bloom" of orange begins to appear and the metal is re-coated to catch any bare spots. A couple more hours of 90 degrees and 90 percent humidity produces a very fine surface rust all over the parts.

The water tank is set to boil and when rolling along, individual wires hang the gun parts in the caldron. In 10 minutes the red oxide is magically converted to a black dust finer than talc. The parts have to be handled with white cotton gloves, as any oil would spot the finish.

They are "carded" with a rotating wire brush having rows of steel bristles just .003 inches in diameter. The carding gently removes the surface oxide leaving the metal a dark gray.

The parts are re-coated, rusted, boiled and carded another 10 cycles to produces the fine-grain blue-black sheen that is found protecting the metalwork of the world's finest firearms.

While waiting for the rust to bloom, I fired up the nitre tank. At room temperature, the tank is filled with a solid block of what looks like frozen milk but, at 600 degrees Fahrenheit, the nitre is clear as water. Each of the screws and the two triggers were individually immersed, and I watched for the color changes as the parts hung in the tank. First a light straw which became a darker yellow and then started to change into a deep maroon. As the red color slipped out of the metal, they turned a brilliant cobalt blue. This is what I'd been watching for.

Depending on the mass of steel, the parts take from three to ten minutes to come to temperature and complete the color change. If left even a minute too long they would have turned a lighter blue and I would have had to re-polish and re-color them. I used long tweezers to grab the parts from the tank and quenched them in warm water. This quenching removes the melted nitre and freezes the colors.

Both rust and nitre blued metal must be cured in light oil for a day or two, replacing the oil removed by degreasing and heating. All rust-blued parts are then lightly coated with a high-grade wax. When hand-buffed with a cotton cloth any remaining rust residue is removed and a low gloss highlights the deep blue-black.

With perfect timing, the action and forend iron arrived from the New York. Turnbull gave me a fair price, great turn-around and lovely subtle colors reminiscent of original Fox guns. All that remained was to lacquer the case colors and nitre bluing, cure the lacquer and assemble the gun. As a final touch I installed an elephant ivory bead at the muzzles.

As finished, my Fox weighs 6 pounds, 10 ounces and balances smack dab on the hinge pin. It handles like a British gun of similar gauge and weight. With twin triggers, the open/tight choke combination and medium barrel length it has worked well for me from south Texas bobwhites to late-season Montana sharptails. I've hunted grouse in Oregon with the gun so drenched it couldn't have been any wetter if I had thrown it in a lake. On a chukar hunt in Idaho the guides had a wager, betting that I wouldn't take it up into the scree slopes and rock out-croppings. They lost.

Writing about this project has brought the experience full circle. In the past four years I have shot a few thousand rounds through my Fox, shown it at the Custom Gun Show and seen some pretty

AUTHOR'S NOTE:

This is not meant to be a how-to article. Dozens of the small tasks and special methods have been left out for brevity. I hope that other gunmakers will learn from this essay, but that no one will try these techniques without proper training and experience. Specific mechanical operations were skipped over for these reasons, but rest assured the inside of the gun got equal attention.

SDH

pictures in several magazines. I have taken seven species of upland birds and a 20-pound gobbler while hunting five Western states with the gun.

Almost seven years have passed since my good friends Michael McIntosh and Jim Flack conceived the project as I sipped amber liquid an listened. As I now look at the Fox the case-colors are mostly gone from the action bottom as is the bluing from the guard tang. Assorted small dents in the stock remind my of shots and hunts and special friends.

What is most important is that I know how the gun shoots, how it functions and how it is going to hold up to heavy use. Of course I'm proud of my work, but there is a pleasure that transcends that pride. Simply put, it is great to have a gun that shoots good and fits perfectly. It's also a good feeling knowing that it will be in my hands for years to come.

Glossary

GUN METAL AND GUNMAKING TERMS

ACTION BODY: Or frame, is the forged iron mass that encloses the gun's mechanism with the knuckle at the front and the tangs to the rear.

ACTION FACE: The flat vertical part of the action at the breech of the barrels, perpendicular to the watertable that the firing pins or striker project through.

ACTION FLATS: Also known as the watertable, where the barrel flats mate to the action.

ANNEALING: The process of heating steel and letting it cool slowly to produce its softest state.

ARTICULATED TRIGGER: Some double trigger guns have the front trigger hinged to swing forward so when firing the second barrel, the trigger finger is not jarred in recoil by the back of the front trigger.

BARREL EXTENSION: Protrudes from between the barrels at the breech end and fits into a recess in the top of the action. Some are used to engage a rotary or cross bolt and some, known as a "doll's head" are shaped to support the barrel breech during recoil.

BARREL FLATS: The bottom of the barrels that mate to the action flats.

BARREL BAR: On the outboard side of the barrel flats, the bar is usually a half-round or angular ridge of metal.

BARREL WALL THICKNESS: The thickness of the thinnest point of a shotgun barrel wall as measured with a special wall thickness gauge. This measurement cannot be determined by subtracting the inner diameter from the outer because wall thickness varies considerably.

BENT: See notch.

BITE: A slot in the barrel lump that is engaged by the locking bolt which locks the barrels to the action.

BOX LOCK: A shotgun action with the moving parts enclosed inside the frame. The Anson & Deeley is the original British boxlock. M-21, Fox and Parker guns are some American boxlocks.

BROWNING: Red rust, or ferrous oxide, when applied as numerous fine coats with each rubbed off before pitting occurs, one has a "browned" finish that will protect the metal very well. Commonly used to color and protect muzzleloading and Damascus gun barrels.

CARDING: Numerous fine coats of rusting and aggressive rubbing or "carding" leave the figure of the Damascus swirls a deep brown while the adjacent metal is almost white. Rust bluing is carded between coats.

CASE HARDENING: A surface hardening process that bonds carbon to the metal by heating in a charcoal pack, or cyanide bath, and fixes the carbon by quenching in water. Beautifully mottled colors are a by-product of the process. This colorful metal finish is traditional for double shotguns.

CAUSTIC BLUING: Also known as hot-dip bluing. Developed during WWII as a means to quickly finish huge quantities of gun parts. Hot-dip bluing is the most frequent method used on modern firearms. The parts are immersed in a tank of liquid bluing salts that form an oxide on the metal. These salts will corrode the soft-solder that hold many double barrels together.

CHAMBER: A reamed recess where the cartridge is inserted in the breech end of the barrel.

CHAMBER LENGTH: Measuring chamber length of a shotgun barrel is easy - with the right tools. Early American shotguns had chambers of 2-1/2" or 2-5/8" depending on the gauge. Pre-WWII British and Continental game guns were most often chambered for 2-1/2" shells. Pigeon and waterfowl guns often had 2-3/4" chambers, and there are a smattering of 2" chambered guns around. Todays American standard is 2-3/4" for all gauges with 3" chamber available in many guns.

CHARCOAL BLUING: Also known as blacking or carbonia bluing. Applied by heating gun parts in a vessel filled with charcoal. Appears as a deep blue-black with a shiny, almost translucent look. Commonly seen on trigger guards, buttplates and small parts of guns from the 1850-1940 period.

CHOKE: The amount of constriction in a shotguns muzzle to hold the shot pattern together longer. Common chokes are called: Cylinder (no choke), Skeet, Improved cylinder, Modified, Improved/Modified and Full Choke. In England: Cylinder, 1/4, 1/2, 3/4 and Full. Choke constriction has little to do with the actual choke measurement. It has everything to do with the difference between the choke and bore dimensions. You must measure the bore and measure the choke, then subtract the difference.

CHOPPER LUMP: A barrel forged with an integral lump. Two chopper lump barrels are brazed together at the breech for the highest quality double barrels. Identified by a faint line down the center/bottom of the lumps. The term is graphic as the barrel and lump look like a hatchet, or chopper.

COCKING INDICATORS: On sidelocks the protruding end of the tumbler shaft has a gold inlaid, or raised metal line that indicates if the lock is cocked. When the line is in a horizontal position, the lock is not cocked. When it appears at 45 degrees, the tumbler is cocked. Some boxlocks have small pins protruding from the top of the action as cocking indicators.

CREEP: The amount of trigger movement before the gun fires.

CROSS BOLT: Usually a third locking mechanism that passes horizontally through the fences to engage a barrel extension.

DAMASCUS BARRELS: An archaic method of manufacturing barrels by forging ribbons of iron around a mandril. The plainer variety are called "twist" steel, the more elaborate have beautiful patterns welded into the barrels. Once considered unsafe to shoot, some Damascus-barreled guns are being proofed for low pressure, or blackpowder cartridges.

DOUBLING: When both barrels fire when one trigger is pulled.

DOVETAILED BARRELS: When the lumps are formed as a separate piece then dovetailed and brazed to the barrels.

ESCUTCHEON: Either an oval or diamond shaped metal anchor for the forend iron installed in the bottom of the forend, or a gold or silver oval set in the toe line of the stock for a monogram.

EJECTORS: A mechanism inside the forend, attached to the forend iron that selectively throw a fired shell from the gun when it is opened. There are many different types of ejector mechanisms.

EXTRACTOR: Does the primary lifting of an unfired cartridge in an ejector gun or does the only lifting in an extractor gun. Ejector guns have twin extractors while non-ejector guns have a solid extractor.

FENCES: The ball shaped bolsters of the action at the back of the barrels. Fences often have decorative beads surrounding them which may be singular or multiple, flat or half-round.

FLUID STEEL BARRELS: Modern manufacturing method where the barrels are forged and bored from a single piece of steel.

FORCING CONE: The part of the barrel bore that makes the transition from the chamber to the bore diameter. Long forcing cones are currently in vogue.

FOREND: The stock in front of the action which includes the forend iron, forend latch and possibly a forend tip. The size and shape of the forend determines its name as in; splinter, semi-beavertail and beavertail forends.

FOREND IRON: The metal part of the forend that contacts the action knuckle and houses the ejectors. The wood forend is attached to the forend iron.

FOREND LATCH: Attaches the forend to the loop on the barrels. There are four basic types: the Anson sliding snap bolt; the Deeley and Edge pull-down lever; various rotating latches; and the pull-off, or spring-tension, forend.

FOREND LOOP: Usually an L shaped metal bar projecting below the barrels that the forend attaches to.

FRENCH GRAY: A metal finish commonly used on actions that is a soft gray in color. Achieved by a variety of methods, this finish shows engraving at its best.

FURNITURE: The various small metal parts of the gun such as the trigger guard, buttplate, triggers

HAND POLISHING: The best kind of metal polishing for fine firearms. All surfaces are polished with grit cloth backed by a hard or semi-hard tool maintaining true flats and contours with crisp edges. Although once perfected, machine polishing with grit charged wheels is a lost technique. Most modern machine polishing causes dips, dished screw holes and rounded edges.

HARDENED STEEL: Carbon alloy steel in its hardest state achieved by heating to the critical temperature and quenching in water or oil. Once hardened, steel may be softened for better working properties by heating. This process is known as drawing, or tempering. When heated to the critical temperature and left to cool slowly the steel in returned to its softest state called annealed.

HEAD OF THE STOCK: The wood at the front of the buttstock that mates to the back of the action body. Fitting the action to the stock is called "heading-up".

HEAL AND TOE PLATES: Also called clips, these two pieces of steel are installed on the top and bottom of the sole of the butt to prevent the stock from chipping at the fragile edges.

HINGE PIN: A large pin through the front of the action at the knuckle that the barrels rotate on. Some are removable and some are semi-permanently fitted.

HOOK: The semi-circular cut in the forward lump that engages the hinge pin.

INLETTING: Any part of the stock that has been carefully chiseled out to accommodate a metal part, or the act of doing this.

IN PROOF: A gun is said to be in proof when the barrels - and their fit to the action - have not been altered by wear or gunsmithing after being tested at the proof house. There is no proof house in America so this term does not apply to American guns.

IN-THE-WHITE: Steel polished bright and left that way, usually prior to engraving.

KITCHEN SINK: This one's for Tim, who says I ought to include it as the place I wash the nitre off gun parts after bluing.

KNUCKLE: The semi-circular front of the action that contains the hinge pin, where the forend iron meets the action.

LEVER: Use to open the action and drop the barrels. There are top-, side- and bottom-lever double shotguns.

LOCKING MECHANISM: Also called the bolt. Locks the barrels to the action. Fox and L.C. Smith guns have a "rotary bolt" that locks a barrel extension slotted into the breech of the action. Most of the rest have some type of underbolt (under the barrels) that engages the "bite" or notch on the barrel lump. The most popular British locking mechanism is the Purdey double underbolt that engages two lumps. Locking bolts are usually tapered to compensate for wear. O/U guns sometimes have a slide on top of the barrel breeches or pins projecting from the standing breech into recesses in the barrels.

LUMP: Protruding below the barrel flats on the bottom of the breech end, the lump engages the hinge pin with a "hook" and has a "bite" where the locking bolt engages it. Many American guns have a single lump while most British guns have two lumps and twin bites.

MAINSPRING: The primary spring that powers the hammer to fire the gun. Most British and European guns have V shaped mainsprings while many American guns have coil mainsprings.

NOTCH: Also called the "bent," is a notch in the tumbler or hammer that the sear nose engages when the action is cocked.

NITRE BLUE: Fire blue or temper blue all describe the same basic process. Anyone who has seen the translucent blue of a finely tempered gun-spring of even an old-style blue-spring binder clip recognizes the color which is a wonderful royal blue more jewel-like than metal should be. Applied by heating the metal to about 600 degrees, sometimes in a bath of nitre. Commonly see on gun screws and small parts.

OFF THE FACE: Means that the barrel breeches don't fully contact the standing breech of the action which is the face that the firing pins protrude through. This is usually caused by a worn hinge pin or "hook" (the hooked shaped part of the lump that contacts the hinge pin). When a gun is off the face it is "re-jointed" to reestablish the relationship between the hinge pin, standing breech and the barrels.

POINTS OF CHOKE: The amount of choke constriction, as the English express it, meaning thousandths on an inch. That is: 40 points of choke equals .040" which is expressed as forty thousandths of an inch.

REBATED FRAME: I've never approved of this term because I don't think it of gunmaking origin but, for lack of better: these are half-round file cuts, usually where the tangs join the action body, that help lock the wood at the head of the stock to the metal to lessen the chance of the tangs wedging and splitting the wood under recoil.

RIBS: Side-by-sides typically have a top rib running down the length of and between the barrels that fills the gap between them and provides a sighting plane. There are many different styles of top ribs. The bottom rib fills the void between the bottom barrels. Over/under guns often have side ribs and a top rib which provides the sighting plane. Some guns have ventilated ribs which are slotted to dissipate heat.

RUST BLUING: Also called blacking. The process used to blue soft-soldered double barrels. The process involves rusting the metal, boiling it in water which turns the red-rust a black color, and then carding off the residue. Several cycles are needed to achieve a dark, uniform finish.

SAFETY: Usually a sliding pad on the top tang that blocks the triggers to prevent the gun from firing. Greener safeties are mounted on the left side of the stock and rotate forward and backward to block the triggers. High grade guns often have a gold inlaid S or SAFE that is exposed by the button when in the safe position.

SEAR: Engages the hammer notch, or bent, to hold the hammer cocked. Pulling the trigger lifts the rear of the sear (sear tail) to disengage the sear nose from the notch to fire the gun. Usually pivots on the rear pin hole seen on the side of many boxlock actions. A sear spring provides tension to move the sear. Many sidelock guns have an interceptor, or secondary sear, to catch a secondary hammer notch to prevent the gun from firing if the sear fails.

SCALLOPING: Also called a "fancy-back" action, is decorative file work, usually in the form of a center point with arching curves above and below, on the back-side of the action body. Looks like the mathematical symbol known as a "braces" (used to confine a column of figures).

SIDE CLIPS: Ears or wings of metal protruding forward from the sides of the fences that mate with cuts on the outboard edges of the barrel breeches. Prevent lateral movement of the barrels.

SIDELOCK: A shotgun that has the lock parts mounted on sideplates behind the action body.

SIDEPLATES: Refers to the plates that hold the working parts of a sidelock or plates fitted to a boxlock to make it look like a sidelock.

SINGLE TRIGGER: Referring to a double barrel gun with a single trigger. The two most common types are inertia and mechanical triggers, some are selective to fire either barrel first, and some are non-selective.

SLEEVING: Or retubing, is the process of cutting off ruined barrels and fitting new tubes. Many modern shotguns have sleeved tubes into a mono-block action.

SNAP CAPS: Dummy cartridges with spring loaded cups to protect the firing pins when dry firing to test the gun's function or trigger pulls.

STANDING BREECH: Also known as the "break-off". Is the face that the firing pins protrude through, perpendicular to the watertable.

STRIKERS: Firing pins.

STRIKING: Filing and polishing the barrels lengthwise to remove ripples.

TANGS: Double shotguns invariably have upper

and lower tangs projecting rearward from the action. Long tang actions are usually held to the stock with two tangs screws, or pins. The top lever screw (under the lever) is tapered to snug the stock to the metal and threaded into the trigger box, which is also tapered, to pull the action back into the stock-head. The rear screw, or hand pin, is inserted underneath the trigger guard tang to threaded into the upper tang at the hand of the stock. Short tang action are typified my many modern O/U guns that are held to the stock with a through-bolt from under the buttplate to the back of the action.

TRIGGER GUARD: Surrounds the trigger and helps prevent accidental discharge. The bow is the oval shaped portion which mounts to the trigger plate by means of a threaded or slotted stud. The spur hooks back around the rear trigger and the guard tang, or strap, is in-let into the wrist of the stock.

TRIGGER PLATE: The metal plate on the bottom of the action that the triggers are mated to. Also includes the lower tang.

TRIGGER PULLS: The amount of weight it takes to pull the trigger and fire the gun expressed in pound and ounces. The rear trigger pull is a bit heavier to prevent the recoil of firing the first barrel from jarring the second sear.

TRY-GUN: Used for stock fitting with a buttstock adjustable for drop, length and cast.

TUMBLER: Also called the hammer in a boxlock. In a sidelock, the tumbler hits the striker to fire the gun. Powered by the mainspring.

UNDERBOLT: A locking bolt that engages the bite of the lumps when mounted under the barrels.

WATERTABLE: The flat of the action that the barrel flat sits against when the gun is locked. The watertable is pierced with slots for the lumps.

GUNSTOCK AND WOOD TERMS

BUMP: Slightly rounded hump at the heel of a wood butt.

CAST: The amount a buttstock is bent away from the center line of the stock when viewed from the butt forward. Cast-off is away from a right-handed shooter and cast-on (appropriate for left-handers) is bent towards the shooter. A stock can be made with cast or sometimes heated and bent later. Cast is measured at the toe and heel of the stock in fractions of an inch. If there is more cast at one location the stock is said to have a twist.

CHECKERED WOOD BUTT: When the butt end of the stock is left as wood and checkered to secure it to the shoulder when shooting.

CHECKERING: Cross hatched, incised lines at the wrist and forend of the stock to aid in firmly grasping the gun. Checkering is raised, pointed diamonds. The fineness is referred to as "lines per inch" (LPI) with 20-26 lpi being the norm.

COMB: The top of the buttstock where the cheek rests. Usually a straight line from the comb nose to the heel.

COMB NOSE: The part of the buttstock that rises up from the top of the wrist to the comb.

DROP AT COMB: A stock dimension measured from the plane of the top rib, extended over the butt, down to the comb nose. The drop at comb and drop at heel are called "bend" in the British vernacular.

DROP AT HEEL: A stock dimension measured from the plane of the top rib, extended over the butt, down to the heel.

DROP POINTS: Decorative petals relief carved at the rear of the stock panels to help step down the thickness of the stock to the thinner grip.

FIGURE: Describes the luminescent cross-grain in wood most commonly seen as fiddleback or feather-crotch. One look at the back of a violin is all that is needed to recognize the cross-grain stripes of fiddleback. Feather-crotch grain has a similar luminescence as fiddleback and appears in the tree where a large limb or root joins the main trunk. The "feather" radiates through the wood like a plume.

FILL-IN PATTERN: A checkering term describing a pattern with the entire border is cut in first, the master lines laid out in the middle, and the checkering cut to fill in the center. These are known as "borderless" patterns because the diamonds run right up to the edge, with no borders outside them. Often Fluer-de-lis or other motifs are used in conjunction.

FLAT-TOPPED CHECKERING: Checkering with unpointed diamonds - is often found on field grade American guns as well as older London "best" guns. On the economy models, the maker simply quit checkering with the V shaped tool before any of the diamonds were pointed. By contrast, early English flat-topped checkering was cut with a parallel sided tool much like a small back-saw.

FLUER-DE-LIS: (flower of the lily) A checkering term describing a three petal design commonly done as a borderless fill-in pattern.

HEEL: The upper, rear part of the buttstock, top of the buttplate.

LENGTH OF PULL: The length of the stock as measured from the front trigger to the center of the height of the buttplate.

MASTER LINES: Are the first two actual checkering lines cut in the pattern. Each forms one angle of the diamonds. All of the other checkering lines are cut by spacing off of these master lines.

MULLERED BORDERS: Describes concave U-shaped borders cut at the edges of a checkering pattern.

PITCH: The angle of the butt end of the stock in correlation to the top rib or sighting plane. Pitch is measured in three ways: 1. The competition, or included angle method, referred to as "degrees of pitch" as in zero degrees of pitch would have the butt 90 degrees from the sighting plane. 2. The American method referring to inches of pitch, as measured by elevating the muzzles until the butt end is perpendicular with a flat surface. 3. The British method using two length of pull measurements from the trigger to the heel and to the toe.

POINT PATTERN: Checkering term for patterns that end in a V with the checkering lines forming the edges of the pattern.

STOCK BLANK: The raw wood block that stockmakers start with. Typically 2-1/4" to 2-3/4" thick and in the form of an irregular rectangle or triangle. Supplied as a "sporter" blank, long enough to build a bolt-action rifle stock or a "two piece" blank with butt and forend pieces.

STOCK FINGERS: The four parts of a sidelock stock that surround the lockplate and mate to the back of the action at the head of the stock.

STOCK PANELS: The flat stock surfaces immediately behind the action of a boxlock or along the sides and back of a sidelock. These are often terminated with drop points which look like carved tear drops behind the stock panels.

THUMBHOLE: Where the top of the grip of the stock rises to form the comb nose. A British term to describe where the thumb of the trigger hand rests over the grip.

TOE: The lower rear pointed part of the buttstock or bottom of the buttplate.

TOE LINE: The bottom line of the buttstock, usually a straight line from the back of the pistol grip, or trigger guard, to the toe.

WALNUT: The most common wood for gunstocks. *Juglans regia*, commonly called; English or French walnut may be referred to by where it was grown: California, Moroccan, Turkish, etc. *Juglans nigra*, black walnut is native to North America and is the most frequently used wood for factory gunstocks. *Juglans Hindsii*, Claro walnut is native to California and is increasingly popular for higher grade factory gunstocks. Bastogne walnut is a hybrid of English and Claro trees.

WRIST: Also known as the grip or hand of the stock. The area immediately behind the triggers where the hand grips the stock. There are three basic types of grips; straight, semi-pistol and pistol grips.

ENGRAVING TERMS

BACKGROUND: When each side of each scroll represents a separate chisel cut, the area between the scrolls must be removed to distinguish them from one another. Backgrounding is often stippled or cut with cross-hatched lines.

BULINO: Also known as bank note engraving. An Italian term for the finest of fine-line engraving usually used to depict a portrait-like subject or scene. Some employs the use of a dot pattern rather that cut lines.

FULL COVERAGE: When engraving covers virtually every surface of the firearm. Half coverage, quarter coverage, etc. are terms used in factory catalogs to describe the amount of engraving. They are relative terms.

GRAVERS: The chisels engravers used to cut decorative lines in gun metal. They come in a variety of shapes and metal alloys. They are pushed by hand, tapped with a hammer (chasing), or used in a pneumatic air-driven tool.

NEGATIVE SPACE DESIGN: incorporates the use of two visual images. When closely viewed, the scroll embellishment appears to be the theme. When one steps back a few paces to view the work, another design, formed by the scroll masses and unengraved portions create a separate design that compliments the gun's shapes and contours. Often the negative space presents geometric forms, ribbons, circles or ovals.)

SMOKE PULL: A lift made from firearms engraving using the gun metal as a plate. The metal is coated with smoke or ink, transparent tape or paper is applied to make a print of the engraving. When well done, a smoke pulls gives a very accurate likeness of the engraving.

Selected Books

As compiled from my own library, this list contains the books I consider germane to the topic of double shotguns. As some readers may know, I've written a book review column for a number of different publications over the years and am an avid reader and researcher. The "one gun" or "one gunmaker" titles are obviously necessary to specific collectors. Others, particularly the older and historic titles, give good insight into the gunmaking process. Some of these titles are out of print and some are privately published and may only be obtained from the authors. Carol Barnes, of Gunnerman Books, P.O. Box 217, Owosso, MI 48867, (517) 729-7018, is my preferred source. She has helped me accumulate this library and has about the best list of double gun titles I am aware of.

GUN BOOKS

Adams, Cyril and Braden, Robert: *Lock, Stock, & Barrel*, Safari Press, 1996. A fine photo section with strong information about hammer guns.

Akehurst, Richard: *Game Guns And Rifles - From Percussion To Hammerless Ejector In Britain*, England, 1992. An excellent overview of the history of British gunmaking. Valuable lists of gunmaker serial numbers and dates of manufacture.

Austyn, Christopher: *Modern Sporting Guns*, Sportsman's Press England, 1994. Largely involves British best guns, good photos, auction prices and engraving.

Baer, Larry: *The Parker Gun An Immortal American Classic*, Gun Room Press, 1993. Information and perspectives may be slightly dated but a must have Parker reference.

Beaumont, Richard: *Purdey's - The Gun And The Family*, David & Charles, England, 1984. Much more about the family than the guns.

Bodio, Stephen: *Good Guns Again*, Wilderness, 1994. One man's opinions, many worth considering.

Boothroyd, Geoffrey: *Boothroyd On British Shotguns*, Sand Lake, 1993

> *Boothroyd's Revised Directory Of British Gunmakers 1850 To Present Day*, Sand Lake, 1997. Dates and addresses.
> Shotguns And Gunsmiths, A&C Black, London, 1986.
> *Sidelocks And Boxlocks - The Classic British Shotguns*, Sand Lake, 1991.
> *The Shotgun - History And Development*, A&C Black, London, 1986.

These titles all draw from Boothroyd's *Shooting Times* columns.

Boothroyd, Geoffery and Susan: *The British Over-And-Under Shotgun*, Sportsman's Press, London, 1996.

Brister, Robert: *Shotgunning - The Art And Science*, Winchester Press, 1977. Strong on ballistics.

Brophy, William: *L.C.Smith Shotguns*, Gun Room Press, 1995

Burrard, Major Gerald: *The Modern Shotgun*, Three volumes, originally published in 1931. Considered the classic reference on British double gun design.

Churchill, Robert: Churchill's Shotgun Book, Knopf, 1955. The classic of shooting instruction, and still good.

Crudgington, I.M. and Baker, D.J.: *The British Shotgun*, Two volumes, Ashford, England, 1989. Many patent drawings, explanations and photos of important and sometimes odd developments.

Greener, W.W., *The Gun And Its Development*, NRA, 1995. An incredible collection of double gun information, originally published in 1881. Reads like an English Herter's catalog.

Grozik, Richard: *Game Gun*, Countrysport Press, 1997. Probably the best text and photos about the process of building a British best gun.

Johnson, Peter: : *Parker - America's Finest*, Stackpole, 1985

Elliot, Robert and Cobb, Jim: *Lefever - Guns Of Lasting Fame*, Private Pub., 1986.

McIntosh, Michael: *A.H. Fox - The Finest Gun In The World*, Countrysport, 1994.

> *Best Guns*, Countrysport, 1995.
> *Shotguns And Shooting*, Countrysport, 1996.
> The Gun Review Book, Down East, 1997. All McIntosh is worth reading, these are excellent titles.

Muderlak, Ed: *Parker Guns - The Old Reliable*, Safari Press, 1997. A fine book with a different perspective than other Parker titles. Much opinion stated as such, wonderfully illustrated with period art.

Neal, W. Keith and Daehnhardt, Ranier: *Espingarda Perfeyta Or The Perfect Gun*, Sotheby Parke Bernet, London, 1974. Written by two gunmaker brothers and originally published in Portugal in 1718, a wonderful story of gunmaking at that time.

Nobili, Marco E.: *IL Grande Libro Delle Incisioni - Modern Engravings Real Boo*k, English Text, Il Volo, Italy, 1989. An intriguing collection of mostly Italian engraving including interviews with some advanced practitioners.

> *Fucili D'Autore - The Best Guns*, English Text, Il Volo, Italy, 1991. Perhaps the most complete text on double shotguns published in this century. The translation must be translated in places.

Schwing, Ned: *Winchester's Finest, The Model 21*, Krause Publications,1990.

> *The Browning Superposed - John M. Browning's Last Legacy*, Krause Publications, 1996. Schwing's books set the standard for reference material about some of the all-time great collectable guns.

Semmer, Charles G.: *Remington Double Shotguns*, Privately published, 1996. A good book with great photos of one of America's finest quality - and least known - double guns. Available from the author for $65 at: 7885 Cyd Dr., Denver, CO, 80221.

Smith, Ron: *Drawing And Understanding Scroll Designs - For Artists, Engravers And Collectors*, Privately published. A delightfully home-made book about engraving design from a long-time, full-time, top-of-the-line engraver. Available from the author for $22 at:5869 Straley, Ft. Worth, TX 76114.

Snyder, Walter Claude: *The Ithaca Gun Company - From The Beginning*, Private pub., 1991

Tate, Douglas: *Birmingham Gunmakers*, Safari Press, 1997. The only book on the subject. Has a variety of makers and reads like a well-told story.

Thomas, Gough (G.T. Garwood): *Gough Thomas's Gun Book*, Gunnerman, 1993.

> *Shotguns And Cartridges*, A & C Black, London, 1970. Gough Thomas knows good guns and doesn't suffer us with sidelock arrogance. A fine book.

Wieland, Terry: *Spanish Best*, Countrysport, 1994.

Wilson, R.L.: Steel Canvas - *The Art Of American Firearms*, Random House, 1995. A large, colorful collection of American-made and engraved firearms.

Yardley, Michael: *Gunfitting - The Quest ForPerfection*, Sportsman's Press, England, 1993. A fine text on this oftentimes vague subject.

> *Positive Shooting*, Safari, 1993. The modern view, and a good one.

Zutz, Don: *Shotgunning Trends and Transition*, Wolfe 1989. Excellent text from an expert shotgunner.

WINGSHOOTING BOOKS

For those of you that feel the best reason to own a double gun is to shoot and hunt with it, I am including a list of some of my favorite recently published wingshooting books. I see these titles as tomorrows classics.

Barsness, John: *Western Skies - Bird Hunting In The Rockies And On The Plains*, Lyons & Burford, 1994.

Bodio, Stephen: *A Rage For Falcons*, Nick Lyons Books, 1984.

De La Valdene, Guy: *Making Game*, Willow Creek, 1985.

> *For A Handful Of Feathers*, Atlantic Monthly, 1996.

Fergus, Jim: *A Hunter's Road*, Henry Holt, 1992.

Holt, John: *Kicking Up Trouble - Upland Bird Hunting In The West*, Wilderness, 1994.

Huggler, Tom: *A Fall Of Woodcock*, Countrysport, 1996.

Jones, Robert F.: *Dancers In The Sunset Sky - The Musings Of A Bird Hunter*, Lyons & Burford, 1996.

Lundrigan, Ted Nelson: *Hunting The Sun - A Passion For Grouse*, Countrysport, 1997.

O'Brien, Dan: *Equinox - Life, Love, And Birds Of Prey*, Lyons & Burford, 1997.

Proper, Datus C.: *Pheasants Of The Mind*, Wilderness, 1996.

Russell, Keith C. and friends: The Duck-Huntingest Gentlement, Dairypail Press, 1977.

Waterman, Charles: *Field Days*, Countrysport, 1995, *Gun Dogs And Bird Guns*, GSJ Press, 1986.

Waters, Tom F.: *Timberdoodle Tales - Adventures Of A Minnesota Woodcock Hunter*, Safari Press, 1993.

THE BEST RESOURCES FOR EVERY FIREARM ENTHUSIAST

Standard Catalog of Firearms
8th Edition
by Ned Schwing
The firearms enthusiast's best source for current values, technical specifications and history now boasts 1,200 pages with more than 4,000 photos. That's 100 more pages of text with 25,000 updated prices and 1,400 new photos when compared to the seventh edition! There are expanded sections for Savage, Sauer, Ithaca, Sturm and many others. The always popular "The Year in Review" is included for 1997, along with other informative articles by industry experts. Whether you enjoy identifying guns, checking current pricing, or are simply browsing for enjoyment, this book hits the mark. Gun enthusiasts will find they must have the current revision of this perennial standard of the firearms collectible field.

Softcover • 8-1/2 x 11 • 1,200 pages
4,000 b&w photos
GG08 • $29.95

Flayderman's Guide to Antique American Firearms & Their Values
7th Edition
by Norm Flayderman
This edition reflects the ever-changing collecting and buying patterns in the antique firearms market. There have been some dramatic price changes; a few areas have actually sky-rocketed. More than 3,600 models and variants are extensively described. Includes 2,800 individually priced firearms with full information on how to assess values based on demand, rarity and condition. More than 1,700 large scale photographs model descriptions for convenient identification. Histories of the makers are described with dates and locations of manufacture and quantities manufactured. A wealth of knowledge and keen insight compiled by the leading scholar and authority on American antique firearms. More than 400,000 copies of previous editions sold!

Softcover • 8-1/4 x 10-11/16 • 656 pages
1,700 b&w photos • **FLA7 • $32.95**

Handguns '99
11th Edition
Edited by Ray Ordorica
Top writers in the handgun industry give you a complete report on new handgun developments, testfire reports on the newest introductions and previews on what's ahead. There's solid information on ammunition and reloading, self-defense, ballistics, collecting, competition, customizing, military and law enforcement, hunting and accessories. Check out the most comprehensive catalog on the market for the handgunner, with more than 1,000 handguns currently manufactured in or imported to the U.S., including full specifications and retail prices. There's coverage of metallic sights and handgun scopes and mounts, a list of periodical publications and arms associations, the handgunner's library and a comprehensive directory of the trade.

Softcover • 8-1/4 x 10-11/16 • 352 pages
1,800+ b&w photos
H99 • $22.95

1999 Gun Digest, 53rd Edition
The World's Greatest Gun Book
by Edited by Ken Warner
The all-new 53rd edition continues the editorial excellence, quality, content and comprehensive cataloguing that firearms enthusiasts have come to know and expect. It's the most read and respected gun book in the world for the last half century. Also includes a complete catalog of all firearms currently manufactured in or imported to the U.S., including full specs and retail prices for more than 3,000 firearms. And there's lots more: ammunition tables, a complete catalog of metallic sights, scopes and mounts, chokes and brakes, the Shooter's Marketplace, a Directory of the Arms Trade and a special "Gundex" index that helps locate catalogued guns fast.

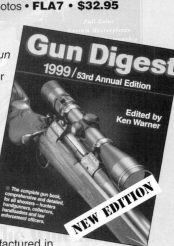

Softcover • 8-1/4 x 10-11/16
544 pages • 2,000+ b&w photos
GD99 • $24.95

If for any reason you are not completely satisfied with your purchase, simply return it within 14 days and receive a full refund, less shipping.

Credit Card Calls Toll-free **800-258-0929** Dept. FFB1

Monday-Friday, 7 a.m. - 8 p.m. • Saturday, 8 a.m. - 2 p.m., CST
web site: www.krause.com

FOR A FREE COPY OF OUR CATALOG
Please call
800-258-0929
Dept. FFB1

KRAUSE PUBLICATIONS • 700 E. State Street • Iola, WI 54990-0001